IN WONDERLAND

IN WONDERLAND

KNUT HAMSUN

Translated with
Introduction and Notes by
SVERRE LYNGSTAD

Brooklyn, New York

First English language translation
published by Ig Publishing in 2004
©1903 by Gyldendal Norsk Forlag
Originally published in Norwegian as *I Aeventyrland*
(Oslo: Gyldendal Norsk Forlag, 1903)
English language translation ©2004 by Sverre Lyngstad
Published by agreement with Gyldendal Norsk Forlag

Hamsun, Knut, 1859-1952.
[I Eventyrland. English.]
In Wonderland / Knut Hamsun: translated with introduction and notes
by Sverre Lyngstad. — 1st American pbk. ed. p. cm.
ISBN 0-9703125-5-5 (pbk.: alk. paper)
1. Caucasus--Description and travel.
2. Hamsun, Knut, 1859-1952 — Journeys — Caucasus. I. Lyngstad,
Sverre. II. Title.
DK509.H357 2003
914.7504'83--dc22
2003015756

10 9 8 7 6 5 4 3 2 1

INTRODUCTION
by Sverre Lyngstad

According to Hamsun's English biographer, Robert Ferguson, *In Wonderland* (1903) is "probably one of the most highly subjective travel books ever written." Its "main interest," Ferguson writes, is "not so much the overt theme of the book," which he sees as being Russia, as "the unusual personality of the writer."[1] Regardless of whether they are acquainted with Hamsun's creative work, readers of *In Wonderland* will find it easy to concur with this characterization.

It should be noted, however, that the "overt theme" of the book is not really Russia proper; the major portion of *In Wonderland* is devoted to the region of the Caucasus. In the opening paragraph Hamsun outlines his overall itinerary, not all of which forms *In Wonderland*: "I'll be traveling to Caucasia, the Orient, Persia, and Turkey on a government grant." A reader of the sequel, entitled "Under the Crescent Moon" and published in a collection of stories in 1905, will discover that Turkey became limited to Constantinople, the capital of the Ottoman Empire.

By the time Hamsun was able to undertake his journey to the East in the fall of 1899, many years had passed since the idea first came to him. It is mentioned already in the spring of 1890, with Constantinople as the destination[2]; a couple of years later he says how much he looks forward to "going to the Turk," as he oddly puts it. What "excites" him, he writes, is the "unknown, strange" character of the envisioned goal of the journey.[3] However, due to lack of money and the demands of literary work, the trip was repeatedly postponed. Thus, eight years after the plan was originally conceived, he writes to his German publisher, Albert Langen, with whom he usually corresponded in English: "I have at present no time to make the trip to Turkey, as I have new litterary [*sic*] works on hands [*sic*]."[4] Evidently, it was the grant to which he refers at the beginning of the book that finally enabled Hamsun to carry out his longstanding plan.

The first time Russia is mentioned as part of that plan is in November 1898, after Hamsun and his newly wedded wife, Bergljot, had arrived in Helsingfors (now Helsinki), where the couple lived for nearly a year before undertaking the journey described in *In Wonderland*.[5] The Hamsuns began their travels in Russia on September 8, 1899, and about three weeks later, on September 30, Hamsun writes from Constantinople: "We are here. We managed to slip through Russia's bedbugs, Caucasia's heat, and the endless nights and days of the Black Sea. . . ."[6]

One may wonder how Hamsun's fascination with the East originated. According to his most recent biographer, Ingar Sletten Kolloen, the interest can be traced back to his childhood in North Norway, during which the fishermen who brought Russian grain to be ground at his father's mill had the "most fantastic stories" to tell about the Russian empire, which extended far beyond Europe into Asia. As for the figure of "the Turk," Mr. Kolloen notes, Hamsun, with his well-known proclivity for "going against the tide," reacted negatively to the custom during his childhood and later used the Turk as a "bogeyman." Finally, my informant traces Hamsun's positive view of "Eastern fatalism" to his finding in it, "much of the almost equally fatalistic religion of his childhood."[7]

To judge by certain statements in his letters, the Orient's attraction for Hamsun may actually have been a disguised yearning for the simplicities of childhood, the time before he decided to become a writer. In a letter of 1894 from Paris, where he spent most of the period 1893-1895, he expresses a preference for a contemplative culture as against, of all things, literary pursuits. "Everything considered," he writes, "one should be silent, one shouldn't write. One becomes, little by little, curiously coarsened by this scribbling. The Turk, the Arab, is silent, he doesn't speak anymore; he has gotten over that, drinks his coffee, smokes his pipe and thinks. Thinks. Now and then he gives a faint smile." Then Hamsun goes on to dream about sending "literature and politics and art and nervousness to hell" and returning to a simple life.[8]

The antipode of Hamsun's dream of a simple life is his negative attitude to America, which appears as a leitmotiv in *In Wonderland*. The silence of the Orient, and of Old Russia as represented by orthodoxy, is opposed by the "roar" of America, known to Hamsun from his having lived there for a span of four and a half years during two periods in the 1880s. Already a couple of pages into the book, as Hamsun and his wife, who is usually referred to simply as "my traveling companion," arrive at the railroad station in St. Petersburg, we are presented with two irreconcilable worlds, epitomized by the "din of locomotives and rolling wheels," on the one hand, and by the "eternal lamps" burning before the icons, on the other. A description of Russians crossing themselves before these icons is followed by a one-sentence paragraph with the effect of a refrain: "But from outside comes the din of the locomotives and the wheels, the roar of America." In chapter 16, during the visit to Baku, America again figures as the representative of modern technology and industry: "The noise of machinery wasn't originally part of this place; America has desecrated it and brought its roar into the sanctuary. For here is the seat of the 'eternal fire' of antiquity. There is no place hereabouts where one can escape America."

It is to Hamsun's credit that neither his biased view of America, whose alleged lack of culture had been the subject of a previous book,[9] nor his praise of the East with its passivity and fatalism is unqualified. Thus, the symbolic as well as real locomotive, with its roar, is described in a wholly positive manner at the end of chapter 18. As the train moves around a curve, he observes "the shiny limbs of the machine in operation." Continuing, he writes: "I

8

IN WONDERLAND

have an impression of being lifted high up, that I'm flying—everything is marked by a proud grandeur. The screeching locomotive, invincible and roaring, passes between the cliffs like a god."

Conversely, while Hamsun's admiration for Eastern fatalism and a stoic attitude toward life is evident throughout *In Wonderland*, his rhetoric occasionally subverts it. At the end of chapter 13, a Muslim's total acceptance of his lot is contrasted with the westerner's tendency to gripe: "If he has enough to get by and fate hasn't deprived him of his health, he's content and grateful.... He doesn't write complaints to the newspapers." Characterizing the fatalism of the Orient, with its "simple absolute system," as an "ancient, tested philosophy," Hamsun concludes: "It's so simple and so tried, it's iron." Surprisingly, though, the account of the Hamsuns' visits to the Asiatic quarter of Tiflis, to which this passage belongs, is framed by the description of a fly-infested horse that comes to represent the Eastern attitude: "A horse stands in the broiling hot sun when we arrive; it is saddle-chafed and has big sores with countless flies in them. The horse doesn't pay attention to anything; nothing but skin and bones, its head hung low, it lets the flies just sit there. . . . It's a superior horse, a stoic horse." Several pages later, as they are about to leave the Asiatic quarter, the horse "still stood stoically in the sun. And the smell of its open wounds was attracting innumerable flies. . . ." Clearly, the superiority of this "stoic" horse and the attitude it is intended to symbolize are somewhat undermined, just as the "roar" of the locomotive is mitigated by the uplifting vision of the godlike machine.

These nuances are worth noting, in view of the prejudiced and reactionary attitudes displayed in certain passages of the book: Hamsun's blatant eulogy of autocracy and a cruel master morality in the anecdote about Nikolai I and the episode of the Circassian officer; his implicit glorification of war, expressed through the decadent phrase "blood on the flowers" put into the mouth of a Turkish officer; and the racial and other slurs on Jews, Armenian merchants, English tourists, and others. These attitudes exemplify the narrator's less attractive qualities. Although racial and national stereotyping are often laced with humor, no stylistic niceties can redeem the cruel, atavistic stamp of these passages.

Fortunately, the persona who betrays these troglodytic sentiments does not often rear its ugly head in the book. We may find the narrator's routine neglect and occasional ridicule of his wife to be rude, if not churlish,[10] yet, whatever faults he may have, they are more than compensated by his enthusiasm, the liveliness of his temperament, his joie de vivre and sense of adventure. These are qualities one finds in Hamsun's fiction as well, and in more ways than one *In Wonderland* can be read, to some extent, in the same manner as his novels.

Like so many Hamsun characters, the narrator is a wanderer, at home nowhere and everywhere. Describing his feelings on finding himself alone in a Moscow restaurant, surrounded only by strangers, he writes: "I feel at home here, being away from home and accordingly in my element." Indeed, the narrator's happiness appears most complete when he finds himself in a totally unfamiliar world, one to which he has no relation whatsoever. This happens as he roams the streets of Moscow, not knowing where he is and how to get back to his hotel. "It's a wonderful feeling," he writes, "I'm lost; nobody who hasn't experienced it knows how delicious it is. I have, on my own, taken advantage of my legal right to go astray." It is as though the narrator has broken free of conventional time and space, which anyway are of little interest to the wanderer figure, and is prepared to enter another dimension.

That does, indeed, occur in certain transporting experiences, during moments when the narrator ostensibly makes contact with a transcendent or otherworldly reality. An unforgettable example of such a moment is his startled reaction to the first sight of Mt. Kazbek, "its glaciers sparkling white in the sun. It is cheek by jowl with us, placid and tall . . . ; we feel as though a being from another world is looking at us." After he alights from the carriage, the experience becomes even more overwhelming: "At this moment I get caught up by a whirling sensation; lifted off the road, unhinged, I feel like I stand face to face with a god." In the recollection from childhood that follows, one in which a creature pops its head above the surface of the water as Knut is out rowing, the same other-worldly aspect is stressed: "It must've been a seal, but it was like a being from another world."[11]

One is tempted to use the word "sublime" in characteriz-ing the sentiment evoked in these passages; they call to mind a rec-ollected incident in *The Prelude* by William Wordsworth. As young William rowed on the lake one summer evening, "a huge peak, black and huge,/ As if with voluntary power instinct/ Uprcarcd its head." The most telling similarity to Hamsun's experience on see-ing Mt. Kazbek is seen in the boy's panicky reaction to the awe-some "spectacle," which in the aftermath gives him a "sense / Of unknown modes of being."[12] The mystical intuitions of unfamiliar realms of being articulated by both writers in these passages testi-fy to a romantic sensibility attuned to pantheism, while acknowl-edging the sheer terror of Otherness.

By contrast, human otherness, so prominent in *In Wonderland*, is treated in a wry, down-to-earth manner. The narra-tor's predicament, that of being a stranger in a strange land, is fraught with comic possibilities, which Hamsun thoroughly exploits to produce effects of droll and ironic humor. The noncom-munication between the travelers and the natives gives rise to a continuous sense of incongruity, an essentially comic quality; it certainly enables Hamsun to develop a slew of often bizarrely funny scenes and situations. There is, for example, the narrator's hunt for a tailor in Moscow, needed to fasten a loose button.[13] Because the persons involved can communicate only by signs and mimicry, this seemingly trivial quandary leads to a sequence of oddly ridiculous but at the same time warmly human moments, which may or may not have been correctly interpreted by the narrator. Due to the lack of a common language, the situations depicted have an unmistakable equivocal quality, and it is the presence of that quality, in addition to the quirky behavior of the narrator, who has nothing but dumb show to make his intentions clear, that sparks the reader's amusement. For example, the text suggests that the elderly woman, being offered money to help find a tailor, suspects a sexual motive, as evidenced by her "strange laugh"; yet, oddly enough, she plays along with the putative pursuer. This absurd little comedy is followed by a near-miracle of mutual understanding, without words, as the narrator develops an instant intimacy with the tailor's children, whose simple game he joins, and by the charade of negotiating the tailor's fee, with the end result that he "had to act princely again," a role he had already played vis-à-vis the old woman. The humor in these situations depends equally on non-communication and its suspension, real or imaginary, by way of a common humanity.

Other situations have an amusing air of parody or playacting about them. There is, for example, the narrator's imaginary romance with the favorite wife of the herdsman he meets on his ride into the mountains; a takeoff, with a difference, on the westerner's yearning for exotic passion, it is at the same time a spoof on women's liberation. In this incident the narrator also assumes the role of a bona fide explorer, a stance that combines self-mockery with deflation of the scientific pretensions of professional anthropologists. Finally, there are the many scenes in which the presumably more advanced Europeans are hoodwinked by the wily Orientals, thus reversing the expectations of the reader and enabling the narrator to indulge in an orgy of self-irony. In a work that, of sheer necessity, offers so many genre scenes depicting the quotidian life of both the travelers and the natives, these comedic devices add color, excitement, and delightful humor to Hamsun's account of his travels. Admittedly, they also occasionally entail bits of histrionic behavior on the part of the narrator.

Curiously, Hamsun's exploitation of strangeness for purposes of lighthearted comedy coexists with an attempt to assimilate the alien elements of his experience to the known and familiar. A great variety of sights and scenes—Mt. Kazbek, Tiflis, villages seen from a distance, farm activities like plowing and threshing—call up allusions to Norwegian and American practices, landscapes, and ways of life. The effect differs, depending on the specific nature of the unfamiliar experience the narrator wishes to convey. Mostly, the tendency is to denigrate the West, whether it happens to be represented by the New York Stock Exchange with its bull and bear markets by comparison with the simple life of the Caucasian natives, or European and American mountains as compared with Mt. Kazbek.

The principal effect of the device, however, belies its intent, since it usually functions like an epic simile, the tenor—that is, the point to be made—being muted in favor of the detailed elaboration of the vehicle, which assumes a life of its own and generates a digression. Thus, the account of the death of Kornei's horse and its aftermath contains an extensive recall of a pagan ritual from early Norwegian history, one in which the king, Håkon the Good, showed qualms about eating horseflesh, thus anticipating the predicament of the narrator of *In Wonderland* at the ensuing feast. Less impressive, though even more unexpected and digressive, is the narrator's attempt to convey how he feels at the first sight of Tiflis by describing his "sensation" when, as a young man, he was waiting to hear a lecture by the great Danish critic and literary historian Georg Brandes in Copenhagen. These digressions, which may owe something to Mark Twain, could be criticized as self-indulgence; they say very little, if anything, about the subject at hand but simply confirm one's impression that Hamsun's travel book is as much about himself as about the places and people that he visits.

Perhaps the book's subjectivity is most convincingly displayed by the obvious striving to invest it with some of the formal qualities characteristic of fictional narrative. For example, in several ways Hamsun attempts to give his account the coherence of a novel. Since the journey itself provides insufficient unity, being interrupted by essayistic sections and by obligatory passages of description, Hamsun uses motifs and themes of various kinds, two of which have already been noted, namely, the stranger in a strange land and the Orient versus the West, particularly America. More interesting from a formal perspective is Hamsun's interweaving of his travel description with developed episodes and relationships. One thinks of the story of the national guardsman and the beauty with the diamond rings; the perpetual altercations with Kornei, the milk-drinking coachman, one of the more memorable characters in the book; and most of all the recurrent appearances of the mysterious police officer, who is the source of much anxiety on the part of the narrator but also of suspense for the reader, as in a detective novel.[14] Beyond its unifying effect, the story as such is not without interest, embodying the ironic motif of being hoist with one's own petard: the hunter becomes the hunted.

Hamsun himself invites the reader's skepticism in regard to the truth value of his travel book. One recalls the unusual scene between husband and wife when he awakes one morning at five o'clock and finds her reading a book. Since it happens to be his travel diary, it leads to a somewhat tart exchange between them. The incident is virtually unique in giving voice to Hamsun's "traveling companion," in a manner that is both distinctive and memorable. Besides criticizing him for including "too many trifles," she tells him she believes neither in the reality of the police officer nor in her husband's ride into the mountains, which we can assume also includes his visit with the herdsman and the imagined romance with the latter's favorite wife.

It may be noted at this time that originally the book was subtitled "Experienced and Dreamed in the Caucasus"; for reasons unknown, the subtitle forms no part of the text of *In Wonderland* available in the collected edition of Hamsun's works, from which this translation was made. To sort out the elements that are "dreamed" from those that are "experienced," however, is probably impossible: fact and fiction, *Wahrheit* and *Dichtung*, are inextricably interwoven. And if Erik Krag, professor of Slavic literature at the University of Oslo, is right in saying that the "section that deals with Russian literature," about which Hamsun supposedly knew a lot, is the "weakest one in the whole book,"[15] the best parts may be those where Hamsun allows his imagination free rein. If the question is worth pursuing, readers of *In Wonderland* will have to decide for themselves what is fact and what is fiction in this hybrid piece of literature, and which of the two carries the deeper conviction of truth.

Port Jefferson, New York
April 2003

NOTES

1. *Enigma: The Life of Knut Hamsun* (New York: Farrar, Straus & Giroux, 1987), p. 184.

2. See letter to Gustav Philipsen of April/May 1890, *Knut Hamsuns Brev*, ed. Harald S. Næss, I (Oslo: Gyldendal Norsk Forlag, 1994): 158. This publication will henceforth be referred to as *Brev*. The translations are my own.

3. Letter to Caroline Neeraas of May 13, 1892, *Brev,* I: 253.

4. Letter of May 24, 1898, *Brev,* II (1995): 81.

5. Letter to Carl Birger Mörner of November 26, 1898, *Brev,* II: 97.

6. Letter to Alexander Slotte of September 1, 1899, *Brev,* II: 129, note 1; letter to Wentzel Hagelstam of September 30, 1899, *Brev,* II: 130.

7. E-mail message of April 4, 2003.

8. Letter to Elisa Philipsen of December 26, 1894, *Brev,* I: 441.

9. *Fra det moderne Amerikas Aandsliv* (København: Gustav Philipsen, 1889), translated by Barbara Gordon Morgridge as *The Cultural Life of Modern America* (Cambridge, Mass.: Harvard University Press, 1969).

10. One may wonder whether the relegation of Bergljot Hamsun to a virtual cipher in her husband's travel book is partly due to the couple's incompatibility. In any case, Hamsun's friends in Finland noticed that the relationship was "not a harmonious" one.—See editorial note (*Brev,* II: 127) to Hamsun's telegram of June 19, 1899, to Vienna, where his wife was visiting at the time.

11. Thomas Glahn, the central character in Hamsun's *Pan* (1894), uses similar language in describing his union with the moon goddess: ". . . I feel myself lifted out of my sphere, pressed to an invisible breast, my eyes are moist with tears, I tremble—God is somewhere near looking at me." (*Pan*, translated with an Introduction and Explanatory and Textual Notes by Sverre Lyngstad [New York: Penguin Putnam, 1998], pp. 85–86.)

A less intense example of this near-mystical moment occurs in Hamsun's *The Last Joy*, narrated in the first person by a writer very much like Knut Hamsun: "I feel a wave inside me and sense . . . that the place has just been deserted. . . . Right now I'm standing here alone with someone, and a bit later I see a back disappearing into the forest. It's God, I think. . . . I feel my whole face flooded with the sight." (*The Last Joy*, translated by Sverre Lyngstad [København & Los Angeles: Green Integer, 2003], p. 67.)

As with Glahn and the traveler in the Caucasus, the "insight into things," as the narrator puts it (ibid.), comes to him when face to face with nature.

12. William Wordsworth, *The Prelude: A Parallel Text*, ed. by J. C. Maxwell (New Haven & London: Yale University Press, 1981), p. 57.

13. Hamsun manages to get a good deal of mileage out of buttons. In *Hunger*, one of the most wrenching scenes is created around the narrator's attempt to pawn his buttons (*Hunger*, translated by Sverre Lyngstad [New York: Penguin Putnam, 1998], pp. 93–94), and Nagel, the central character in *Mysteries*, is reminded by Dagny Kielland, the young woman he is in love with, that he is "losing a button" (*Mysteries*, translated with an Introduction and Explanatory and Textual Notes by Sverre Lyngstad [New York: Penguin Putnam, 2001], p. 135).

14. It is tempting to speculate whether the apparent paranoia underlying this episode stems from a lecture that Hamsun gave in Helsingfors in May 1899, the proceeds of which went to a fund started by a leader of the Finnish resistance to Russian oppression, Finland being, until 1917, a Grand Duchy of the Russian Empire. Robert Ferguson reports that Hamsun was "slightly anxious that news of the lecture . . . might cause him problems at the border . . . ." (*Enigma*, p. 184).

15. Erik Krag, "Knut Hamsun og Russland," *Vinduet* 13 (1959): 110.

IN WONDERLAND

I

We find ourselves in St. Petersburg at the beginning of September.[1] I'll be traveling to Caucasia, the Orient, Persia, and Turkey on a government grant. We've come from Finland, where we lived for a year.

Two hundred years ago almost to the day, Peter the Great founded a city on nineteen marshy islands. Cut through everywhere by the Neva River, the city is strangely fragmented, broken up; and it is strangely mixed, abounding with splendid Western European style apartment houses, domed Byzantine buildings, and charming mud-built houses. The museums and art galleries have an air of massive grandeur, but the kiosks, sheds, and amazing human dwellings that occupy so much space also stand proudly in the sun. Although there has been talk of moving the city to a drier location, one might as well talk about moving all of Russia. There are things in St. Petersburg that will not budge: the Winter Palace, the Peter and Paul Fortress, the Hermitage, the Church of the Resurrection, the Isaac Cathedral. St. Petersburg moves as Russia moves, expanding, growing larger and larger. . . .

Our stay in St. Petersburg was a short one. The weather was raw and chilly, a mere ten degrees Celsius, and the gardens and parks were no longer in bloom. In need of a passport for the first time in my life, I drive up to the legation of the Dual Monarchy.[2] But I arrive at the wrong time: the office is closed. Standing in front of the legation reading a letter is a handsome young gentleman whose gold-knobbed cane has a coronet on it. As he doesn't look Russian, I tip my hat and address him in Norwegian. He answers in Swedish and informs me of the legation's office hours.

I show up at the proper time and once again encounter the young gentleman. He happens to be Captain Berling and is a military attaché. Later on his name often appeared in the papers, during his action against Colonel Björnstjärna.

Since I hadn't thought of getting my passport in time, the legation was put to a lot of trouble on my account. But Baron Falkenberg was very kind. He wrote out a large passport for me, with a coronet and ermine cloak, and then drove around to the Asiatic legations and got the letter decorated with the most wonderful curlicues, signs, and stamps. Without the Baron's help, we certainly wouldn't have been able to leave that day, and I'm most grateful for his friendliness.

What a small world we live in! Suddenly I meet an acquaintance of mine on the streets of St. Petersburg.

In the evening we arrive at the Nikolay Railroad Station ahead of time. Here I see for the first time the burning lamps in front of the icons. When the doors open in the back, a din of locomotives and rolling wheels reaches us from out there, but the eternal lamps burn before the icons day and night, day and night, in the midst of this din. They are like little altars two steps above the floor, shining in utter silence.

The Russians cross themselves before them when they come and go. They cross themselves, curtsy and bow, and once again cross themselves, and they do all this proficiently and with great dispatch. I'm told that the Russians never set out on a journey until this ceremony has been performed. Mothers push their children up to the saint, and old decorated officers doff their caps and, with many bows and signs of the cross, pray for a pleasant journey.

But from outside comes the din of the locomotives and the wheels, the roar of America.

Then some members of the National Guard turn up, wearing white caps with red trimming. The National Guard is composed of noblemen from all parts of Russia, men who during their stay in St. Petersburg have four horses in their stables and numerous footmen in their houses. Choosing this way of doing their military service, they avoid mingling with officers who are commoners. A young guardsman enters, followed by three identically dressed footmen carrying his luggage to the station. One of the footmen who has grown old in the service keeps pestering the young gentleman with his great concern and by using pet names when addressing him. The gentleman answers him every time and smiles forbearingly at the old man; he also spares him every trouble, while dispatching the two others in all directions. He takes only one of the footmen with him on his journey.

21

We notice a young beauty with a lot of diamond rings on her left hand. She has three or four rings on every finger; it looks odd, as the rings cover the whole joint. Obviously an aristocrat, she takes a loving farewell of two elderly ladies whose carriage is waiting outside. Our train is about to leave; the lady sets out on her journey accompanied by two servants.

We came away from the St. Petersburg station without a hitch. My wife left nothing behind except her coat.

We have the best and most charming company in the world on our journey: a Finnish engineer who is employed by Nobel's firm in Baku and has lived in Russia for many years, and his wife, a lady from Baku whose mother tongue is Russian.[3] Their little daughter is traveling with them.

Every compartment of the train is a sleeper. We are a great many passengers and my company are scattered about in the train. I myself get squeezed into a cramped compartment already occupied by three men, including a German who is quite drunk.

One can walk from one car to another in the train, but the corridor is so narrow that two persons can barely pass each other.

We are on our way into the vastness of Russia.

I awake at night, I'm sorry to say, and the drunken man's snoring keeps me from going to sleep again. I sit up in bed and cough in his direction, but he turns around somnolently without awakening and continues snoring. Getting up, I step closer to the sleeping man than strictly necessary to wake him up; his snoring suddenly stops and I go back to bed. Then he starts snoring again.

I lie awake for an infinitely long time, I can't tell how long, because I cannot without difficulty get at my watch under my pillow. Then I fall asleep.

And wake up. The train has stopped. It's no longer dark outside, and bothered by the heat in the compartment I pull the window a few inches down. At that moment a wonderful sound comes from out there. A soft feeling of happiness instantly glides through me at this sound, and I get dressed and rush out. There are starlings about, chattering. I cannot understand why there should be starlings at this time of year; have they gotten no farther south than here on their way back? Or are they starlings that nest in Russia and haven't gotten away yet?

There is a drizzle, but the weather is warm and agreeable. The train is moving again, the people are awakening and getting out of bed in the peasant houses we pass, I can see men standing on the doorstep in their shirtsleeves like at home. At seven o'clock I go into a station to get coffee; the waiters are in full evening dress, wearing white ties and white cotton gloves. I've learned to ask "How much?" but can't understand the answer very well; however, I don't let on and put down a coin that must be changed. When I get the change, I carefully check whether it's enough, though I know next to nothing about the money. Then I return twenty copecks to the tray for a tip, which I see the others doing, and board the train again. Sure, I think to myself, you're a real crackerjack at traveling in Russia! If I should meet some people from home now and they wanted a coffee, I would offer to show them how to go about it, and I would teach them to ask "How much?" and in general be helpful to them.

Brede Kristensen[4] acted like such a big shot with me when we were in Paris. He was going to teach me French. "And when you've learned French," he said, "it's fairly easy to learn Italian and Spanish," he said. That's three languages already, I thought. "And getting from there to Portuguese is by no means impossible," he went on. In short, he even held out the prospect of a little Coptic, to egg me on. But I never learned French, and so the other languages lapsed of their own accord. And though Brede Kristensen may not have worked half as hard as I, he's now a professor of Egyptology in Leyden. But in Russia, I think, he would be completely helpless; there he would need *me*.

My traveling companion hasn't yet risen. We are rolling over a flat landscape, cutting through scrub and rye fields. Here and there in the plains are hardwood forests, birch and alder as at home, and there are songbirds in the trees. In a gravel pit, men and women are working with pick and shovel. They are Slavs, I think to myself, but I can't see that they behave any differently from Germanic people. Dressed like us and no less diligent, they merely follow the train with their blue eyes before going back to work. We pass a tile works, with tiles laid out on the ground to dry in the sun. The workers toil just as tirelessly here, and I see no inspector with a knout in his hand.

The whole landscape is wide and open. To the left is a forest, and on a path leading into the forest walks a man. There is such a feeling of home about this picture; I've been away from home for so long that the sight gives me joy. The path is half overgrown, and the man walking there is carrying a sack on his back. Where is he heading so early in the morning? I think to myself; I suppose he has something to do at the other end of the forest. He shuffles on slowly and steadily, then I lose sight of him.

Again there is a wide plain, with a grazing herd. The herdsman leans on his long staff and looks at us as we pass; he's wearing a sheepskin coat though it's raining. He's an old man; I look him squarely in the face and wave to him from the platform, but he doesn't react. Perhaps he's as happy as the rest of us, needing just a bit of food, a few clothes and an icon; that right to vote in the village may not be the most precious thing in the world to him. I wonder if he'll later remember the traveler who waved to him from the train, just as I sit here remembering him.

After a fifteen-hour journey from St. Petersburg, my traveling companion finally gets out of bed. We are in Moscow.

II

I have so far visited four of the five continents. Naturally I haven't traveled very much in them, and I haven't been to Australia at all; still, I've set foot on a fairly large number of places around the globe and seen a bit. But I have never seen anything to match Moscow's Kremlin. I've seen beautiful cities, and I think that Prague and Budapest are beautiful; but Moscow is like a fairy tale. Incidentally, I heard Russians themselves call the city Moskvá. Whether it is correct or not.

At the Spassky Gate the cabman turns around on his seat, doffs his hat and gives us to understand that we should do the same. Tsar Alexis[5] ordered this ceremony. We bare our heads, noticing that everyone else, whether driving or walking, also passes through the gate bareheaded. The cabman drives up—we are in the Kremlin.

There are 450 churches and chapels in Moscow, and when the bells ring from all the belfries, the air trembles above the metropolis. From the Kremlin Heights you look out on a sea of splendor. I had never imagined that a city like this existed on earth: green, red, and gold domes and spires in every direction. The gold and the blue surpass my wildest dreams. We are standing at the Alexander Monument, holding on to the parapet and looking out; there is neither time nor occasion to say anything, but our eyes mist over.

On our right, in front of the arsenal, sits Tsarpushka, "The King of the Cannons."[6] It reminds me of the round body of a locomotive, it's so incredibly big. Its muzzle is exactly a meter wide across, and its balls weigh 2,000 kilos. I've read that it has been used, but I don't know its precise history; it is dated 1586. The Muscovites have often been at war and often defended their holy city. Beside a huge bell lying on the ground in another place, there are hundreds of captured cannons. The bell, Tsarkolokol,[7] is eight meters tall and can accommodate twenty people.

The Uspensky Cathedral stands on the elevation inside the Kremlin. The church is not very large, but it is the most bejeweled church in the world. Here the tsars are crowned. Gold, silver, gems everywhere, ornaments, mosaics from the floor to the uppermost vault, hundreds of icons, pictures of patriarchs, crucifixes, dark paintings. There is one place in the church that still has a bare spot, namely, where every new tsar puts up a huge precious stone that becomes the property of the church. There was a small bare spot awaiting the stones of new tsars. And around the walls were diamonds, emeralds, sapphires, rubies.

A church official is displaying some bric-à-brac. As solemn Muscovites are saying their prayers before the various altars and holy pictures, the official explains in a not overly muffled voice that this is a corner of Christ's coat, this curio under the glass cover a nail from his cross, this thing in the padlocked casket a patch of Virgin Mary's dress. We gladly give a mite both to the official and to the beggars at the door and leave, quite dazed by the adventure.

I do not feel that I'm exaggerating. There may be some errors in my recollections of the church, because I couldn't take notes on the spot, and I got confused and saw no way out among those unheard-of treasures; but I'm certain there are still many, many more things that I haven't mentioned and didn't even see. Every corner was aglow, but the light was dim in places, so many details were lost to me. The church is itself one great jewel. However, the excessive ornamentation wasn't always pleasing to the eye; in particular, I recall that the tsars' huge, extravagant stones on the wall seemed stupid and in poor taste. When later on I saw Persians with a single gem in their hat, that appeared more attractive.

We saw the Pushkin Monument, visited some more churches, a couple of palaces, the treasury, museums, the Tretyakov Gallery. And we climbed the 450 steps of the Ivan Veliky Tower[8] and took in the view of Moscow. This is where one gets an overall idea of Moscow's grandeur and uniqueness.

But how small the world is! Finding myself in the middle of Russia, one day I run into Captain Tawaststjärna in the street. . . .

The hour of departure has been set. It's no use begging for another day anymore, though there are so many things we haven't seen. Even Moltke[9] felt slightly bewildered in this city, writing that Moscow is a city "that one can picture in one's mind, but that one never gets to see in reality." And at that moment he had just stood in the Ivan Veliky Tower and seen the reality.

Standing in the entranceway of our hotel, I notice that a button in my green jacket is loose. It's the most important button, I think to myself, trying to set it straight only to make the situation worse. True enough, I had a sewing kit with me, but in which of our bags was it? That is the question. In short, I walk out into the city of Moscow to find a tailor.

I walk and walk. I have no idea what tailor is in Russian, but in Finnish it is räätäli, so in Finland I managed very well for a whole year, but here I don't know what it is. I walk through the streets for a quarter of an hour, looking into the windows for some-one who is sewing, but I'm out of luck.

In an entrance stands an elderly woman. I mean to walk past the woman and have nothing to do with her, but she says some-thing to me, curtsying and pointing at my dangling button. I nod: that's just it, the button is loose and I'm looking for a tailor. And I make signs to her about the tailor. Then the woman curtsies again and begins to walk ahead of me, pointing. After we've walked for several minutes, the woman stops at a gate. Here she points way up on the building and wants to leave me, curtsying and being quite satisfied with everything. I get out a silver coin and show it to the woman, trying to make her climb the stairs. She doesn't under-stand—or perhaps she misunderstands: she doesn't want to. I decide to lead the way myself and possibly coax her to come along; I understand it's impossible for me to find the tailor in this large building without her help. I show her the coin and beckon her to follow as I climb the stairs. Then she laughs a strange laugh but comes along anyway, though she shakes her head. The poor old thing!

Stopping at the first door, I point at the button in my jack-et and then at the door with a questioning look in my eyes. Then she gets the bright idea that I'm really looking for a tailor and stops laughing; she's satisfied with this turn of events also, takes the lead

27

and runs up the stairs ahead of me. She rushes all the way to the top and knocks on a door that has some strange letters on a piece of cardboard. A man opens the door. The woman hands me over with a laugh and a long speech; meanwhile the man stands inside the door, with the woman and me outside. When the man finally understands that I am in earnest, my mind firmly set on having a button fastened because I cannot get at my own sewing kit, he opens the door all the way. I pay the woman, who looks at the coin and curtsies, calling me general and *knyaz'*, prince. She drops another curtsy and walks down the stairs.

The tailor's room is furnished with a table, a couple of chairs, a sofa and an icon; there are also some religious paintings on the walls. Two children are playing on the floor. The tailor's wife was probably away; the father and the children were the only ones at home. I pat the children's heads, and they look at me with dim, dark eyes. While the tailor sews on the button, the children and I become friends; they talk to me and show me a broken cup they're playing with. I clap my hands, letting them know the cup is pretty. They bring me more things they've dug up, and in the end we start building a house on the floor.

When the button had been sewed on, I asked, "How much?"

The tailor answered something I didn't understand.

One thing I can say about the tailors I've known in the past is that, if you ask them how much they want for having sewn on a button, they answer, "Oh, it's nothing," or "It's up to you." This is a trick. If it's up to me, it will be an expensive button. After all, one must do one's humble best to act princely and be generous. The tailor could, in all honesty, simply ask for twenty-five øre and get it; if it's up to me it will be fifty. And this Russian tailor obviously knew the trick, saying something that sounded like it was up to me. How could I know the prices of the different things in Russia? That he hadn't thought of.

I pointed at myself and said, "*Inostranets*," foreigner.
He smiled, nodded and answered.
I repeated it.

He answered still more, but didn't mention the word copeck.

Then I had to act princely again. Many a time you try to travel like a lowly commoner to no avail.

Down in the street I decided to take the streetcar back to the hotel. After I've been riding awhile, the conductor comes and says something to me. He's presumably asking me how far I want to go, I thought, and gave the name of my hotel. Then the whole streetcar look at me and chime in, while the conductor points to the rear, ever so far, indicating that I'm heading in the exact opposite direction, the hotel is over there. So I have to jump off.

Walking down the street, I notice that a great many people go into a house and walk up the stairs to the second floor. There might be something worth seeing, so I follow suit. On the stairs a man talks to me. I smile and laugh and doff my hat. Then the man smiles too and walks beside me; he opens a door and lets me enter.

Inside is a large gathering; it's a tavern. My companion begins to introduce me, telling the bystanders something; I understand that he's explaining how he met me on the stairs. I greet everybody and take out my big passport. No one understands. I point at my name, there it is, and I am such and such. They don't understand a thing, but they pat me and decide I'm all right. Then one of them walks over to the counter and asks for music. And at once a band starts up. This is in your honor, I think to myself, and I get up and bow all around. As though by magic, I begin to feel very happy; I order wine and a great many of us start drinking. Heh-heh! It's rumored in the saloon that I'm visiting Moscow, and a man who knows French is called; but I thought it was going well in Russian, too, and besides I don't know much French, so the man is not wanted. But we also offer him a drink and give him a seat beside us.

Life here is very colorful, with many quaint costumes, elegant and simple all mixed up. Behind the counter stand an elderly woman and a young girl. A gentleman sees his chance and says something to the young girl, and it strikes me that it must be the first time something of the sort has been said to her. For a moment she doesn't get it, but then she turns red. Oh, if one could still blush like the first time! Nothing in life is like that first time. Later one blushes only with shame. . . .

When I left, two waiters rushed down the stairs and held the entrance door open for me, calling me Your Excellency.

Again I roam the streets, but I don't know where I am and what direction to take to my hotel. It's a wonderful feeling; I'm lost—nobody who hasn't experienced it knows how delicious it is. I have, on my own, taken advantage of my legal right to go astray. I come to a restaurant and decide to go in and get something to eat, doing exactly as I please in this respect too. But since it looks so grand and since, on top of it, a fair-haired waiter in tails comes toward me, I prefer a place I've just passed by and retrace my steps there. I find myself a seat.

This, too, is a large restaurant, but it doesn't look European; the guests are more strangely attired and the two waiters are wearing ordinary jackets. In the background, the room recedes into a garden with trees.

I feel contented and free. It's as though I've gone into hiding and there's no urgency to be back for a long while. I've learned to say *shchi*. Not many have, but I've done it. And I can write it without using any outlandish characters. Shchi is vegetable soup. But it's no ordinary vegetable soup, which is quite impossible, but a delicious Russian dish full of different kinds of meat, eggs, cream, and greens. So I order shchi and am served. But the waiter wants to be of further use to me and also brings various other things. Along with this, I order caviar of my own accord, whether it is the right thing to do or not. I also order *pivo,* beer.

A long-haired priest suddenly stands in the middle of the open door, making the sign of the cross and blessing us, and when this has been done he walks on down the street. It makes me happy to have found this place. Some distance away a number of good old people are chatting and eating, and their faces aren't ugly and ravaged like those of old people generally, but open and strong, and they have all their thick hair. Slavs, I think to myself as I look at them, the people of the future, conquerors of the world after the Teutons! Only in such a people can a literature like that of Russia well forth, endless and heaven-defying, flowing in eight thick, warm streams from its eight creative giants. The rest of us must content ourselves for a long time with trying to sight them and draw nearer to them. But they prefer to let other writers take care of the literature that the theater dishes out to people.

Customers come and go. A group of entering Germans settle down close to my table, engaging in *Bier* talk and barking *verdammt* and *famos* in a loud voice.[10] By the food and drink they are served, I figure they intend to sit there a long time, so I signal the waiter to move my spread to the back of the room, toward the garden and the trees; but he doesn't understand. Then it happens that one of the Germans graciously asks me what I want, and I'm obliged to make use of him. I get moved, but forget to thank the German and have to retrace my steps through the whole length of the room to do so.

The waiter brings me some meat. I find it almost impossible to eat any more after that filling shchi, but the waiter does the right thing: he assumes that a man must be able not only to eat a lot, but also to keep it going for a long while; that is healthy folks' view of the matter. I feel like smoking and having a coffee, and I get both cigarettes and coffee without making faces more than once.

At one of the tables sit a group that look like a family: father, mother, two sons, and a daughter. The young girl has a dark, mysterious look in her eyes, heavy and deep, a world. Her hands are large and long. Observing her, I try to find a word that might encompass her whole appearance and nature: the word is tenderness. When she sits quietly or leans sideways or glances at someone, she is tender in everything. The look in her eyes is as kind and warm as that of a young filly with a foal. I've read that the Slavs are supposed to have prominent cheekbones, and so do these people, and the large cheekbones gave their faces a horse-like appearance. But they were interesting to watch. Then the head of the family pays up and the group leave.

I'm left with a full table, and the waiter doesn't take anything away. It's good that way too; for if I should eventually wish to partake of a bit of meat, I won't be prevented from doing so. In fact, I'm beginning to look at the food. Who has decreed that coffee and tobacco are no good in the middle of a meal? In short, here

I can make any decision I please. I dine excellently on the meat.

I feel at home here, being away from home and accordingly in my element. It's the most pleasant restaurant I've ever visited. Suddenly I get up and walk over to the icon, bow down and make the sign of the cross, just as I've seen others do. Neither the waiter nor any of the guests takes notice, and I experience no feeling of embarrassment when I return to my place. My joy at being in this vast country that I've read so much about becomes my only emotion; it manifests itself in an inward unruliness that I don't care to rein in at the moment. Thus, I begin to hum without intending to offend anyone, just to please myself. I'm looking at the butter on the table, noting that it has been handled with the fingers; there are a couple of clear imprints on it. What does it matter? I think to myself, in Caucasia it will certainly be worse, butter is a sensitive piece of merchandise. I see my chance and poke the butter several times with my fork, making it unrecognizable. Then I catch myself thinking that this is motivated by a false theatrical psychology, and I don't give in to any further impulses.

I could have remained in the restaurant much longer, but the German comes and drives me away. He's going to a booth in the garden and on his way there he accosts me, offering to help me again if necessary. He's extraordinarily amiable, and I owe a great debt of gratitude to this man; but he breaks me down so, leveling me with the ground. As soon as he's gone, I pay up and utter a word I learned already in Finland: "*Izvozchik.*" And the waiter provides His Excellency with a cab.

To the cabman I said, "*Vokzal.*" But there are five railroad stations in Moscow and the cabman asks, "Which one?" I pretend to think it over. As this takes time, the cabman starts guessing, and when he gets to the Ryazan Vokzal I jump at it and tell him that's it. And the cabman drives me there, crossing himself at every church we pass and at every gate with an icon on it.

I had a vague idea that the Ryazan Vokzal was indeed the destination I wanted, and it proved to be correct. Having arrived there, I found my way to the hotel without difficulty.

III

It got too late for us to leave that day, so we left the following day. If only I could see Moscow once more!

At the station we were surprised to see again the lady with the many diamonds on her fingers. She was taking the same train. This strange coincidence would be explained in a fashion far into the land of the Don Cossacks. The young member of the National Guard is also there, he has joined the lady; they talk together and look at one another with enraptured eyes. He has the cross of St. George on his breast. I notice that his cigar case, which is of gold, has a coat of arms with a coronet. I cannot fathom how these two people have become inseparable, even to having their own small compartment that is off limits to strangers. They must be man and wife, newlyweds, who have stayed overnight in Moscow for the fun of it. But on the railroad station in St. Petersburg they seemed not to know one another. And their servants didn't arrive at the station together.

We are passing Moscow's summer cottage section. The houses are numerous, modern Swiss, boring. But after three hours' travel from Moscow we find ourselves in the endless rye and wheat fields, Russia's black earth.

The fall plowing has begun. They plow in single file, two or three horses walking one after the other, each with its small wooden plow, and behind them comes a horse with a harrow. I remember how we used to plow in America, with ten plows for days and weeks, on the boundless prairies in the Red River Valley. And we sat on the plow like in a chair, there were wheels under it, and we sang as we drove.

Here and there in the plain people move about, men and women working the land; the women wear red blouses, but the men are in their white and gray homespun shirtsleeves, except for a few clad in sheepskin coats. All along there are villages of thatched huts.

Through our fellow travelers, the engineering family, it is rumored farther back in the car that the two of us plan to cross the

Caucasus but cannot speak the language. The engineering family will go by way of Derbent and with steamship across the Caspian Sea to Baku, while we will be crossing the mountains to Tiflis. An officer stands nearby when the conductor stamps our tickets; hearing that we're going to Vladikavkaz, he leaves and brings back another officer who, addressing me, says he will be glad to assist us over the mountains. He's going the same way, he says, but will first make a side trip to Pyatigorsk, a city with sulphur springs and baths and high life. He'll be away for one week, during which we can just wait for him in Vladikavkaz. I thank the officer. He's a stout, somewhat older man, but with strangely dandified manners; he speaks many languages loudly and boldly, but faultily. His face is unpleasant, Jewish.

The engineer, who knows this country inside out, suggests that we bribe the conductor with a couple of rubles so that we, too, can have our own compartment. We bribed him and were moved. Later it occurs to the engineer that we have to bribe him once more, to get him to take our tickets. Otherwise we would be awakened at each change of conductor during the night. So we bribed him once again, according to our means. Everything was taken care of in a trice. The system of taking bribes is an easy and practical system. You stop the conductor on his hurried official tour through the train and drop a word about wanting your own compartment. Your word is not taken amiss. The conductor leaves but returns shortly, when the compartment is ready. He shoulders most of the luggage himself and leads the way, while we follow behind him in single file; presently we find ourselves in a small room that is ours alone. This is the moment when we simply put our couple of rubles into the conductor's hand. We all look at him, and he returns our looks and thanks us, and both parties are satisfied. True, one must also come to terms with all subsequent conductors, but they can, without embarrassment, be offered a far smaller bribe, a sort of friendly gift.

Night is falling, it's getting darker and darker. The compartment is lighted by two candles in gas lamps, but the light is very poor and there is nothing we can do but go to bed.

Now and then, through my sleep, I can hear the whistle of the locomotive. It's not an ordinary whistle, as on the locomotives in other parts of the world, but sounds like a steamship whistle. Here, on Russia's wide expanses, the railroad is after all the only ship.

Well into the night, I wake up from the heat in the compartment. I try to sit up and open the vent in the ceiling, but cannot reach it. Then I fall back and go to sleep again.

~

A bright morning, Sunday, it's six o'clock. We've stopped outside the station in the city of Voronezh. This is where Aleksey Vasilyevich Koltsov was born, on these fields he went about and wrote.[11] It's said that he never learned to write his language faultlessly, but he certainly was a poet and had written a volume of lyrics by the time he was sixteen. His father, a mere cattle dealer, wasn't entitled to have serfs, though he could afford to and both bought and mortgaged serfs. Among them was Dunyasha, the young girl the poet Koltsov loved and was loved by. He's said to have written some very beautiful poems to her. He wrote them as he was herding his father's cattle out on the meadows; there were many of them, ardent and full of longing. But once when he was sent away to buy cattle, his father sold Dunyasha to a landowner way down by the Don River. When the young Koltsov returned home and found out about it, he became deathly ill, but recovered. He went on to write better poems than ever before and never forgot his Dunyasha. Then he was "discovered" by the nobleman Stankevich[12] and came to Moscow and St. Petersburg, where he became debauched, took to drink, and died at the age of thirty.

Because of his love.

His monument stands in Voronezh. . . .

The national guardsman and the lady with the diamond rings have opened their door on account of the heat. I can see them inside their compartment, already up and all set, but their faces are sad. A slight disagreement, I think to myself. But a moment later I don't think so anymore, they whisper to one another in French and behave tenderly before our very eyes. When the officer tries to go out, the lady suddenly detains him for a moment, pulling his head back and kissing him. And they smile at each other as if they were the only ones in the whole train. Their relationship couldn't be better. You could tell they were newlyweds.

It turns out that the candle in our compartment has been dripping paraffin wax on my jacket all night. Now that I discover it, it's already too late; my appearance has been considerably spoiled and I scratch at the wax with both a knife and my fingernails. I would have felt comforted if the wax had ruined others as well, but of course, that rogue of an engineer had not hung his jacket near the other lamp. I get hold of a member of the train crew and demand in several languages that something must be done about me, and the man nods his emphatic agreement. Then I let him go. Naturally I assume he'll be back in a moment and do what has to be done; I can see him in my mind's eye bringing various fluids, warm flatirons, woolen rags, blotting paper, embers and a brush. For I'm extremely multicolored.

A Circassian officer stands beside me, dressed as follows: he's wearing patent leather jackboots over his white trousers and a flowing brown burnous with a leather belt. A long dagger stuck in his belt rests slantwise against his belly, the haft chased and gilded. Across his chest sit the tops of eighteen round metal doodahs, some sort of thimbles on a garnet ground. They are imitation cartridges. On his head he has an astrakhan hat.

Some Armenian Jews walk past. They are merchants, wealthy people who seem untroubled by earthly afflictions. They are dressed in caftans of black satin and wear silver- and gold-studded belts. A couple of the Jews are very handsome, but a young boy they've taken along has a flabby body and the face of a gelding. It makes an absolutely revolting impression to see his traveling companions treat him like a woman. These trading Jews are constantly traveling between Russia and Caucasia. They bring merchandise from the big cities into the mountains, and from there they carry the fabrics and rugs of the mountain people back to the big cities.

The train starts, moving in a vast curve. After twenty minutes, the great city of Voronezh with its thousands of buildings, domes, and spires still sits alongside us. Then we pass large areas with watermelons and sunflowers, all mixed up in the same fields. The melons lie on the ground like big yellow snowballs, with the sunflowers swaying above them like a flame-colored forest along the plain. The sunflowers are cultivated in south and central Russia for the sake of the oil. The petals are made into preserves and become a delicacy of high rank. But you also see people everywhere chewing sunflower seeds and blowing out the husks. They are their clean and enjoyable chewing tobacco. The conductor is genially munching as he checks our tickets, the coachman on the box and the clerks behind the counter also munch on them, and the mail carriers in the cities go from door to door with their letters chewing sunflower seeds and blowing out the husks.

On the horizon we see a large dark spot just off the ground. It looks like a balloon out there on the plain, motionless and unable to rise any higher. We are told that it is the crown of a large tree we are seeing. It's called "the Tree" for miles around.

We are in the Don area.

Innumerable straw- and haystacks sit like honeycombs in the plain; here and there stands a windmill, dead and still, and the grazing herds of cattle are barely moving. Now and then I try to count the animals, to make a quick estimate, using the following method: first, I count fifty of them fairly accurately and check how much space they occupy on the plain, then I close one eye, sight off a similar space and put it together with the first, which adds up to one hundred animals. From now on I count only with spaces of one hundred animals, estimating roughly how much to add or subtract where the animals are tightly bunched or scattered. In this way I discover that there are herds of up to and over one thousand steers, cows, and calves. Two or three herdsmen with long staffs in their hands guard the cattle; wearing sheepskin coats in the strong sun, they probably loaf around a lot, although they have no dogs. I cannot help thinking of the bustling activity on the vast pastures in Texas, where the herdsmen are on horseback and suddenly have to use their revolvers on the neighbor's herdsmen when they try to steal cattle. I haven't experienced this myself, though; I did try to get a job as a cowboy a couple of times but was turned down for various reasons. Apropos of nearsightedness, I can see farther now than I did ten years ago. But then there is the catch that at night, in lamplight, it's gradually becoming difficult to see close up. Next, I suppose, one must go over to convexity. Whereupon one must go over to lorgnettes and the hymnal.

The Kolodyeshnaya station. Here is a gathering of gaudily dressed women, wearing so much red and blue that, from the train, they resemble a field of swaying poppies moving about. They are selling fruit and we get ready to buy grapes. I want to buy an incredible amount of grapes to be well supplied, but the engineer advises me against it. It's the grape harvest season right now, and there will be better grapes later, as we approach Caucasia. The women understand that the engineer is hampering me in my dealings with them, but they don't bear any ill will toward him on that account; they talk amiably with this man who knows their language and tell him all sorts of things. They are strong and healthy peasant women; their faces are brown, with black hair and upturned noses. Their eyes are brown. They have red-and-blue kerchiefs on their heads and necks, because today is Sunday, and red-and-blue skirts. Most of them are wearing sheepskin sarafans with the wool on the inside, but some have fur-edged cloth sarafans. But however much fur they wear, it doesn't keep them from walking barefoot. Their feet are beautiful.

The steppe is beginning, but there are still clusters of willows or lime trees near the villages. Flocks of geese nibble grass on the steppe; I count up to around four hundred in one large flock. Those nearest by turn toward the train and snap at us as we pass. Everything is peaceful and quiet because it's Sunday. The windmills are at rest, now and then we hear the peal of bells. We often see groups of walkers, most likely churchgoers chatting about their things, just like people do back home on their way to church. When we pass the villages, the children wave to us and the chickens run for dear life to take cover.

I say hello to the officer who was willing to be our traveling companion across the Caucasus, but he replies condescendingly, as if to a stranger. Then he suddenly recognizes me and gives me both his hands. . . . Didn't he know me? He knew me instantly, of course. . . . Had I slept well? Miserable transportation in Russia. . . . All right then, just a week in Vladikavkaz, then he would come. He couldn't do without Pyatigorsk, there were ladies!

I cannot stand his Jewish snoot, and he himself helps me to escape. When I move away from him and remain silent, he notices it immediately and reciprocates by talking to others and overlooking me, thank God!

Tea is brewing in every compartment and people are smoking everywhere; several ladies also smoke. Piping-hot water is fetched at the stations, and the passengers have brought samovars themselves. From now on the tea drinking is kept up until late in the evening.

It's eleven o'clock and the sun is making the compartment feel uncomfortable. We have opened the vent in the ceiling and lowered our window to mid-position. But then there is the dust!

At twelve o'clock we are at a small station called Podrognoye. Here, on the sandy road, we see outriders, soldiers, and an empty carriage and four with flower garlands on it, followed by a mounted Cossack escort. Flanking all this, a general and a young officer, both in uniform, go on foot. The carriage, the escort and the soldiers line up at the station the moment the train stops.

Then I hear sobs and French exclamations from the compartment of the newlyweds; the lady with the diamond rings comes out, tearstained, distracted. She turns around in the door and embraces the national guardsman, lets go of him and suddenly rushes out of the train. The man remains behind, he too moved and distracted; he throws himself against the windowpane and looks out.

When the lady stepped on the ground, there was a presentation of arms. She throws herself upon the general's breast, and joyful greetings and words of welcome in French are heard; then she abandons the general and throws herself upon the young officer, and these three people embrace and kiss one another in a state of the highest excitement. Were they a father, daughter, and brother? The brother used such strange exclamations. "Now, don't cry anymore!" the gentlemen say, soothing and stroking her. But the lady cries all the same, smiling only now and then. She tells them she was ill in Moscow and didn't feel like sending a telegram until the moment she had recovered and could travel. The young man calls her his beloved and is delighted by her heroic illness and silence and excellence in every way. The engineer learns from a member of the escort that it is Prince ***, his daughter, and the daughter's fiancé; the young couple are to be married today. The bride recovered and returned home just at the last moment, God bless her!

Then the lady climbs into the garlanded carriage, and her father and her fiancé mount their saddled horses and ride behind her, bending forward and talking to her all the time. But when the carriage, along with the horsemen and the escort, has reached the sandy road, the lady waves her hand to the rear of the carriage—not as though she is waving, but as though she's merely shaking her handkerchief before using it.

Then our locomotive gives a whistle and we glide away from the station.

But the national guardsman stays with his face glued to the windowpane as long as he can make out the flower-decked carriage. Then he closes the door to his compartment and remains in solitude in the hot room for several hours.

The door to our compartment opens onto the corridor. Here an Armenian has settled down. He has prepared a bed out of pillows. Under him he has an embroidered yellow silk mattress, and on top of him a red-and-brown silk coverlet. He lies full-length in these costly fineries, in a cloud of dust beneath a lowered window. He has pulled off his boots; his cotton stockings are full of holes, making his toes stick out. His head rests on two pillows, the cases of which are very dirty but made of pierced work; through the openings one can see the actual pillows, which are of silk with gold thread.

New people arrive and settle down in the corridor by the Armenian. They are Caucasian Tatars. Their women are veiled, dressed in solid-colored red cotton fabrics, and sit still and dumb on their pillows. The men are tall, dark-complexioned people with a gray cloak over their burnous and with a multicolored silk sash around their waist. In the sash they carry a sheathed dagger. They have long silver chains on their pocket watches.

Our locomotive is now stoked with crude oil from Baku, and the smell of this fuel is much more unpleasant than the reek of coal in the great heat.

We suddenly stop at a tiny little station out on the steppe. We are to meet the train from Vladikavkaz. While waiting, we get out and stretch. The sun is hot and it's calm, and a large crowd of passengers buzz around one another, chatting and singing. And there, once again, is the national guardsman. He's no longer grieving, those solitary hours in his closed compartment have set him up again; perhaps he has had a fortifying sleep during these hours, God knows. He's now walking with a cigarette-smoking young lady. Hatless, she lets the blazing sun shine on her rich hair. They are speaking French, and neither is ever at a loss for an answer. They go into peals of laughter. But the prince's daughter, the lady with the diamond rings, may right now be standing at the altar with someone else.

A man jumps off the train with a bundle in his hand. His face is yellowish brown, and he has glistening inky-black hair and beard. He's a Persian. Finding a little spot for himself, he unties his bundle and spreads two pieces of cloth on the ground. Then he takes off his shoes. My first thought tells me he is someone preparing to do tricks with knives and balls, but in that I'm mistaken; the Persian is about to do his devotions. He takes some pebbles out of the breast of his caftan and places them on top of the cloths, then turns toward the sun and begins his ceremony. First, he stands bolt upright. From now on he doesn't see a single individual in the whole crowd of bystanders, keeping his eyes upon the two pebbles and being absent in prayer. Then he throws himself on his knees and bends the upper part of his body to the ground several times; at the same time he makes the pebbles change places on the cloth, moving the one which was farthest away closer and to the left.

41

Standing up, he holds out his palms before him and moves his lips. At this moment the train from Vladikavkaz roars past and our own locomotive signals, but the Persian doesn't let himself be disturbed. The train won't depart until he's finished, and if it does, that too was Allah's will. He again throws himself on the ground and makes the pebbles change places; indeed, he mixes them up so recklessly that I can no longer keep track of them. Now he's alone out there, all the passengers have boarded the train. Hurry up, man! I think to myself. But the Persian still takes the time to do some bows and to stretch his arms well out before him. The train starts moving, the Persian stands for a final moment bolt upright facing the sun—then he gathers his cloths, pebbles and shoes and boards the train. And there wasn't a trace of haste in his movements. Some of the spectators on the platform murmur a kind of bravo to him, but the imperturbable Mohammedan doesn't take notice of a single word spoken by those "infidel dogs" and stalks to his seat in the train.

At a station where we stop to take in water, I finally catch sight of the conductor who was supposed to remove the wax from my jacket. He's standing on the ground a few cars down. I say hello to him and smile so as not to frighten him away, because I intend to catch him, and when I've reached him I smile a little more broadly and act amiable. He nods and smiles in return, and when he sees the wax like a white trail down my jacket, he spreads both hands and says something, whereupon he rushes into his cabinet in the train. There he runs to pick up the fluids and the warm flatiron, I think to myself. I didn't understand what he said, but it probably was that he would be back in a moment, milord! And I waited. The locomotive drank, whistled and started to move—then I couldn't wait any longer.

I have several times met the officer from yesterday, our future traveling companion over the mountains. He doesn't know me at all anymore, I've offended him. Thank God. At a station where we had supper he sat right beside me. He put his thick wallet well into the light. It was hardly because he wanted to tempt me to steal the wallet, but to show me that it had a coronet in silver on it. But God only knows whether the coronet was of silver and whether he is entitled to have a coronet. When I paid he didn't say a word and didn't interfere, but a gentleman on my other side pointed out to me that I'd received too little change. He corrects the waiter's mistake and I receive my money immediately. I get up and bow gratefully to the gentleman.

We have decided not to have the officer for our traveling companion and to avoid him in Vladikavkaz.

At nine in the evening it's completely pitch-dark. There are lights in the villages out on the steppe; otherwise, we don't see anything. Now and then we pass a single little light, coming from a solitary thatched hut belonging to frightfully poor people, no doubt.

It's a balmy dark evening, sultry and dark. I'm standing by an open window in the corridor holding the door to the platform ajar, but it's still so warm that I have to keep the handkerchief in my hand and wipe my face all the time. Sounds of singing are heard from the Armenian Jews farther back in the car; a very fat old Jew and the fat gelding are doing a kind of antiphony. The nuisance goes on forever, for two hours; now and then they both laugh at what they've sung and then begin their monotonous song afresh. The gelding's voice is more like that of a bird than of a human being.

During the night we pass the big city of Rostov, where one can see practically nothing because of the darkness. Many of the passengers get off here.

On the platform I happened to see a group of Kirghiz. How they had strayed to this place from the steppes of the Orient, I have no idea; but I heard that they were called Kirghiz. To my eyes they didn't look very different from Tatars. A nomadic people, they drive their sheep and cows before them from place to place and let them crop the steppe. Sheep are their monetary standard, they have no other: for their wives, they pay four sheep, but for a cow, eight sheep. For a horse they give four cows, and for a rifle three horses. I've read this someplace. I look at the dark-yellow, slightly slant-eyed people and nod to them; they nod back and smile. I give them some nickel coins, and they're delighted and thank me. We are two Europeans looking at them, and the second European can talk a little with them. By our notions they're anything but handsome, but their eyes have a childlike look in them, and their hands are exceedingly small and sort of helpless. The men are dressed in sheepskins and green-and-red jackboots; their weapons are dagger and lance. The women wear colorful cotton dresses; one of the women has a straw hat edged with fox fur. They wear no jewelry and seem to be very poor. The European beside me gives them a ruble, and when they accept it they thank us once more and tuck it away in a kerchief.

~

A beautiful clear morning in the steppe; the tall grass, roasted brown, whistles softly in the wind. There is an immensely wide expanse wherever you look.

There are three kinds of steppes: grass steppes, sandy steppes, and salt steppes; but here there are only grass steppes. The grass is good for cattle-feed only in early spring; by July it has already turned stiff and wooden and can no longer be eaten. Then fall draws near, like now, with heavy rain at times and a less scorching sun; then a fine, soft green grass and lots of beautiful flowers quickly sprout afresh under the dry, whistling steppe grass, and insects and animals and birds wake up and come alive again. From far out on the steppe come the different trills and calls of the birds of passage, and the butterflies tumble once more up and down, back and forth in the air. But if you don't pay close attention, you'll see nothing but the tall parched yellow grass for miles around; at this season, therefore, the steppe does not resemble an ocean—it's akin to a yellow desert.

Of all the inhabitants of the steppe, the Cossacks have probably produced the most intensely felt and most beautifully sung poetry. Never have such beautiful and loving words been said about their steppes by the Kalmucks, the Kirghiz, or the Tatars as by the Cossacks about theirs. And yet the steppe is fairly uniform for all these peoples in the vast Russian lands. But the Cossacks are different from the other inhabitants of the steppe. First, they are the aborigines, while the others are immigrants, some of them remnants of the "Golden," others of the "Blue" Horde. Furthermore,

44

they are warriors, while the others are herdsmen and tillers of the soil. They have never been slaves under a khan, a Polish "pan" or a boyar;[13] the others have. "Cossack" is supposed to mean "free man," I've read somewhere.

The Cossacks inhabit their own land. They own a large amount of extremely fertile soil. They are exempt from taxes to the empire, but have to pay for their own equipment in wartime. In peacetime they, too, till the soil, produce corn and wheat and wine and hunt in the steppe, but in wartime they make up an adventurously brave contingent of the brave Russian army.

We are now traveling through the land of the Cossacks. . . .

Out here, far from all stations and all cities, we meet a telega with a Cossack escort carrying an officer with a red band around his cap. He's heading into the steppe on a slant from us. Maybe he is on his way to town, maybe there is a stanitsa, a Cossack village, someplace or other in the steppe, though we can't see any of it because the globe is a ball. After a while we pass a Tatar aul. Its tents are like haystacks. The Tatars are found everywhere in southern Russia, also here in the land of the Cossacks. They are chiefly herdsmen; diligent and highly gifted people, they all, without exception, can read and write, whereas not all Cossacks can, according to what I've read.

One of the Armenian Jews says something to me, of which I understand the name Petrovsk. "*Nyet,*" I reply in good Russian, "*nyet, Vladikavkaz, Tiflis.*" He nods and understands every word. That means I can begin to carry on a conversation in Russian; now somebody back home should have heard me! Thinking that the Jew might want to look at the officer in the telega out on the steppe, I hand him my field glasses. He shakes his head and doesn't accept them. On the other hand, he unhooks his silver watch from its long silver chain, holds it out to me and says, "*Vosem'desyat rubl'!*" I check my list of numbers and see that he's asking eighty rubles for it. I take a look at the watch for the fun of it; it's large and thick and resembles the old-fashioned spindle watches. I listen to it: it has stopped. Then I take my own gold watch from my pocket, meaning to crush the Jew by the sight of it. But he shows no sign of consternation, as if he'd heard that I have this watch simply to be able to pawn it in a pinch. What would I get on his watch? I think to myself. Ten kroner, perhaps. But on my own I had managed to get forty. There was no comparison. "*Nyet!*" I say firmly, rejecting his watch. But the Jew holds it out and lingers over it, cocking his head. In short, I take it into my hand once more and show him how old and poor it is, and I put it up to my ear and don't hear a sound. "*Stayu!*" I say tersely, because I do not want to talk with him. Then the Jew smiles and takes the watch back. He gives me to understand he's going to do something. He opens the watchcase and lets me look inside. The interior of the watch, while interesting, being pierced and chased, is not overly remarkable. But the Jew asks me to keep an eye on what is going to come. He also opens the chased cover and lets me look again. There is an extremely obscene picture inside. The picture appears to tickle him, he laughs and cocks his head as he looks at it. And all the time he urges me to keep a close eye on it. Then he inserts a key and gives a half turn—the watch is going. But it's not only the watch that goes, the picture goes too, the picture is moving.

I immediately realize that the watch has greater cash value than mine. There were doubtless those who would value it very highly and be willing to pay a great deal for it.

Then the Jew looks at me and says, "*Pyat' tysyacha!*" "Five thousand!" I scream, appalled, understanding nothing. But the Jew closes the watch, sticks it in his pocket and walks away. The old beast! Ten thousand kroner for an indecent watch. If he had met a less determined person, the deal would have come off. Did you notice how he barely could afford to wind the watch, giving the key a mere half turn to go easy on the precious mechanism! . . .

It's only nine o'clock, but the sun is just as hot as it was at eleven yesterday, so we keep in the shade. Here in the steppe we see some familiar flowers, hollyhocks, buttercups, bluebells. Otherwise the landscape is like yesterday, with plains, only plains, fields of rye, corn, herds of cattle; now and then there are hay- and strawstacks, now and then even a village surrounded by clumps of willow. Steppe dwellers, too, must have a few trees; near the larger stanitsas, with a church, there are even acacias. People and horses are at work in the fields everywhere, and far away an eagle sails slowly back and forth above a flock of sheep.

Suddenly we are moving very slowly, and with the practice I have from my stint as a conductor in America, I could jump off the train, grab the last car and jump on again. We are on a stretch of the track that is being repaired, that's why we are moving so slowly. It's mealtime, and the workmen are inside their tent to stay out of the sun, but both male and female heads protrude from the tent opening. A dog sitting outside barks at us.

Tikhoretskaya station. The engineer, our traveling companion, had his money stolen here last year. He was standing at the buffet with a bottle of pivo; the moment the glass touched his lips he felt a tug, but he emptied the glass. When he checked his breast pocket, his wallet was gone. The thief had disappeared. However, he was too greedy; eager to steal more while he was at it, he extended his activity to the train. But there he was caught just as he tried to get away with an officer's bag. Gendarmes were sent for, the thief was frisked, and the engineer got his wallet back on the spot. It probably wouldn't have gone so quickly with someone else, but the engineer brought it off.

We arrive at the Kavkazskaya station, where we are given fifteen minutes for breakfast. This is where Caucasia begins. We see large fields of corn and broad plains of sunflowers; and now we also see large vineyards. On the left sits a princely residence. With my field glasses I can see the castle with its wings and domes, the roof is luminous with an intense green. The castle is surrounded by many other buildings with red and gold roofs. Behind it lies a forest, the park most likely. Everything rises up here on the steppe, with its black earth. In the quivering sunshine, things seem to be slightly raised from the ground and to float outward, toward the horizon, farther out. Soria Moria. . . .

The closer we get to the mountains, the fewer people there are in the train. The Armenian with the silk mattresses has found himself another seat, one in the sun, so I take his, which is in the shade. But first I brush it thoroughly to be on the safe side. The good Armenian had been lying rather unquietly in his finery.

Hours go by.

At Armavir, which is a town as well as a station, we again buy pears and grapes. The grapes are the most delicious I've ever tasted, and I feel a bit ashamed that I had previously eaten such things as European grapes with pleasure. By comparison with these, French, German, Hungarian, and Greek grapes are like woodland berries. These melt in your mouth. And the skin melts along with the flesh in mouthfuls of juice. They *have* no skin, they are practically without a pellicle. That's how Caucasian grapes are. As for color, they are like grapes from other countries, brown, green, and purple, but they may be a bit larger.

On the platform of this station there is, among others, a young Circassian officer. He is wearing patent leather top boots with gold buckles on the outer side of the leg. His brown cloth cherkeska, reaching almost to his ankles, is held together around his waist by a gilded belt, from which a gold-studded dagger is slung obliquely over his belly. On his chest sit the heads of eight gilded cartridge shells. By his side he has a long narrow saber, which trails on the ground; the haft is inlaid with turquoise. He's wearing a shirt or slip of white raw silk; the cherkeska is open above the waist, and the white raw-silk breast looks like silver in the sun. He has glistening black hair and sports a perfectly snow-white hat of long-haired Tibetan fur, the wool of which overlaps his forehead a bit. His attire makes a dandified impression, but not his face. I'm told that, while his uniform is prescribed, what in others is made of linen, he has in silk, and what in others is of brass, he has in gold. He's the son of a prince. Everybody bows to him at the station, and he returns every bow; some he even speaks to, then listens calmly to long answers. It looks as though he asks them what their lives are like and how they are doing, and what the wife's life is like and whether the children are in good health. In any case, he doesn't seem to say anything unpleasant, because they all thank him and look contented. Two muzhiks, peasants in blouses and with leather belts around their waists, walk up to him and greet him; they doff their caps and put them under their arms, bow and say something. The young officer also listens to them and gives them an answer they seem satisfied with. But then they start again, and trying to explain something they get in each other's way. The officer interrupts them curtly and the muzhiks don their caps. They were probably ordered to on account of the heat.

Afterward, they continue talking, but then the officer laughs and shakes his head in refusal, saying, "*Nyet, nyet!*" whereupon he goes away. But the muzhiks follow him. Suddenly the officer turns around, points at them and says, "*Stoyat'!*" And the muzhiks stop. But they're still whining and continue talking. Others laugh at their whimpering and try to make them see reason, but they refuse to give in. I can still hear their whiny voices after the train has started.

I stop to think about this officer and the muzhiks. He was probably their master, perhaps he owned the town we were in; perhaps he also owned that Soria Moria castle we saw this morning and the ever so many miles of black earth we have passed since. "Stop!" he'd said to the muzhiks, and they stopped. When Nikolay I[14] was pursued in the streets of St. Petersburg by a threatening mob one day, he simply turned around, pointed at them and shouted in his large voice: "On your knees!" And the mob fell to their knees.

One obeys a man who *knows* how to command. People were delighted to obey Napoleon. It's a pleasure to obey. And Russians still know how to.

Waliszewski relates in his work about Peter the Great: When Bergholz was in Moscow in 1722 he witnessed a triple execution in which the convicts were broken on the wheel.[15] The oldest of the criminals died after a six-hour torment, the two others survived him. When one of these, in great agony, managed to raise his broken arm a bit to wipe his face, he noticed he had spilled a few drops of blood on the wheel he lay on. Then he used his mutilated arm once more and wiped the blood off as best he could. With such people one can go far. If it is a matter of overcoming natural instincts, ideas, and prejudices, one will scarcely get far with mildness. That's when the command, the tsar's word, accomplishes a miracle. The knout. "Stop!" the officer had said. And the muzhiks stopped. . . .

A gentleman says something to me as I stand there. I don't understand the words, but as he simultaneously points at my jacket I understand he's talking about the wax. I explain to him with good old Norwegian words that I'm waiting for a man to come with all sorts of fluids and a flatiron to remove the wax. But then his face assumes a pitying expression, as if he doesn't have much confidence that the man will ever come. Without further ado, he begins to rub my jacket with his sleeve. He's wearing a pince-nez and the pince-nez falls off his nose, but he doesn't take notice and goes on rubbing. Shortly the wax begins to disappear. To my surprise, I see I'm dealing with an expert and that the white streak on my jacket is completely gone, at last. I wonder what to give the man, my card, a cigar, or a ruble. I decide on the card as the most elegant; but when I look for my cards I can't find them, they must be someplace or other in my luggage. So I restrict myself to thanking the gentleman; I use all my languages and thank him, and the man smiles and nods for all he's worth in return. Then, as though we have become friends for life, he starts a conversation with me in Russian. I don't understand everything, that's an impossibility, but that he's talking about wax I understand by his mentioning the word "stearin" several times. So I'm clear about the gist of what he's saying, but cannot answer him—he doesn't seem to understand any of my languages. He summons several others and makes them also get involved in the matter; in the end I'm surrounded by ten people. I can't stand there without opening my mouth, so I begin to speak Norwegian again, and I don't talk the least. It goes better than expected, they nod and agree when I've said something in a loud voice and drowned them out. Among my listeners is also the conductor who promised several times to remove the wax, and when I show him my jacket with no longer a spot on it, he says something and nods, expressing his satisfaction along with the others.

But my traveling companion sticks her head out of the door to the compartment and cannot figure out what sort of Norwegians I've gotten hold of. Soon they burst into loud, rude laughter in there, making my listeners prick up their ears, whereupon they fall silent and leave, one after another.

At a small stanitsa where we stop, they are threshing grain on the hard-packed earth of the steppe. Masses of sheaves of wheat are spread out on the ground. Then they drive around on the sheaves with horses and oxen until the spikes have been trampled to pieces. This is the threshing. I'm no longer surprised that there are pebbles and sand in Russian grain. I recall from my childhood in Nordland that those who took part in the Finnmark fisheries brought home cereals from Arkhangelsk and that my father's little mill struggled hard with this merchandise. It even happened that I saw the mill emit sparks when grinding Russian food grain. And it struck me as odd. I hadn't yet seen a great variety of threshing methods. Now I have. Including the method used in the wheat fields of the American prairies, where the huge threshers were steam-operated and where chaff and dirt and straw drifted over the prairie like clouds of smoke. But the most amusing method was the one we could observe here, where young Cossack girls were threshing with oxen. Holding a long whip in both hands, they shouted encouragement to the animals. When they cracked their whip, it described a beautiful figure in the air. And, of course, the Cossack girls themselves weren't thick and fat or fully dressed, quite the contrary.

The plain is more undulating now, it's no longer so even; far, far out to the left we can even make out a continuous ridge against the sky, the beginning of the Caucasus mountains. This region is very fertile, towns are becoming more frequent on the steppe, and villages dot the ridge. There are large vineyards and orchards, but still no forests, only small groves of acacias around the towns. The heat is increasing; we occupy the compartment by turns and dress in the thinnest underclothes we have.

The telegraph poles that have accompanied us all along have sometimes more, sometimes fewer wires; here they have nine.

The heat is getting worse and worse, surprising me by its intensity; I have, after all, been much farther south in the world before. True, we are far east, but on the same latitude as Serbia, northern Italy and southern France. Nor is it so calm that it feels close; we have all the windows and doors open on both sides of the car, and the gale-like wind forces us to hold on to our hats. But the wind is hot, we can barely breathe in it. Our faces look like dark peonies, and the ladies get swollen and acquire amusingly big noses, making them a laughingstock to everybody. They obviously washed this morning, the ladies did. But that sort of vanity revenges itself on a long railroad journey; one should only wipe oneself gently with a dry rag.

When we meet the petroleum and kerosene trains from Baku, the smell of these oil transports further befouls the hot air.

Pyatigorsk is out there on our left; we stop at a small station and drop off spa visitors. Here the Jewish officer also leaves the train, thank God; he doesn't know me at all anymore. We will certainly make sure to get away from Vladikavkaz before he manages to catch up with us there!

Pyatigorsk, the "five mountains," has health resorts and baths. The mountains stand all apart with their peaks. There are hot springs, up to forty degrees Celsius, and there are springs so sulphurous that, if you steep a cluster of grapes into the water for a few hours, the sulphur becomes crystalized on it, forming stiff branches and grapes of sulphur. These curiosities are offered for sale at the stations.

In the distance we see snow-capped mountains, which nearly merge into the white clouds in the sky. It's like a fairy tale to see these mighty mountain ranges rise from the steppe and sit there shining in the sun.

By seven in the evening, the heat has abated. The Caucasian mountains are on our left all along, and as we get closer to them it becomes cooler and cooler. We start closing the doors in the train. After another couple of hours it gets cold and we even close the windows. Then the wax stain on my jacket comes back. The cold makes it visible again. So my expert was a cheat after all, someone who throws dust in one's eyes.

The sun dipped under the horizon long ago and the mountains have turned pale green, looking in their remoteness and majesty like a world apart. There are peaks and saddles and towers and minarets, all snow. Though we are foreigners, we can understand what Pushkin, Lermontov, and Tolstoy have written about their first sight of this mysterious splendor.

The darkness falls quickly. We are approaching the Beslan station, where the engineer and his family are to catch another train and travel directly to Baku. From now on we will go on by ourselves. There is a moon, a half-moon only, but a multitude of stars have also come out. The massifs loom beside us all along. After a couple of hours it clouds over, the moon and the stars are gone, and pitch-darkness reigns. In the midst of this darkness we see two large bonfires on the steppe; they are limekilns out in the open. Now and then the sparks fly high in the air, figures move about near the fire, dogs bark.

It's quite dark at the station; a lantern here and there gives only a sparing light, and we can barely see well enough to bid our fellow travelers farewell. Long after the train to Petrovsk and Derbent has departed with the engineer and his family, we are still wandering about on the Beslan station in the dark. What are we standing here for? Ah, if one only knew! But whom could we ask? And who would answer us? Walking about on the station for over two hours, we get more and more accustomed to the dark and in the end see quite well. A drunken peasant has taken a tumble by a wall. He's asleep or unconscious and shows no sign of life. A gentleman in uniform and with a band on his cap orders the peasant to be taken away, and two railroad employees pull him by the arms along the platform and bring him under cover. He had no suspenders, and his stomach was exposed between his trousers and his vest, making us realize that he didn't have a shirt either. And he was dragged off like an animal, like a corpse. But even if we could have helped him a little, there was no longer any time to do so. A train roars by and our track is finally clear. As we hurry into our compartment at the sound of the whistle, we have a sensation of rolling out into the night.

In one and a half hours we are in Vladikavkaz. It's now half past eleven. We are three hours late.

IV

Vladikavkaz.

"*Nosilshchik!*" we call several times. Our pronunciation of the word is finally understood; a porter comes up. He brings our luggage over to an *izvozchik,* who is a cabman. And the *izvozchik* drives us to the inn.

It's one o'clock in the night, but the inn is still illuminated. Two doormen in gilt-edged caps appear in front of the entrance.

"Do you speak French?"

"*Nyet.*"

"German?"

"*Nyet.*"

"English?"

"*Nyet.* Only Russian, Tatar, Georgian, Armenian, and Persian."

Only.

We get out anyway, pay the cabman and take ourselves and our luggage up to No. 3. There is only one bed. Using sign language, we ask for an additional bed and receive an affirmative nod. It's late, we are hungry and must get some food right away, before the cook goes to bed. My traveling companion drops a word about having a good wash first. Knowing my duty, I pound the table a bit, insisting on food first and fripperies and vanity afterward. And I impose my will by force.

Downstairs in the dining room we are served roasted mutton, pirogi and shchi. The waiter knows Russian; he also knows "beer" and "meat" in English, but we know the same in Russian, so it is of no use to us. But we have fun and all goes well. Except that the food is unusually expensive.

After the meal we go out. It's now two o'clock, but on the other side of the street we can still see many open fruit and tobacco shops. We walk over and buy some grapes.

When we get back, there is an extra bed in the room all right, but it hasn't been made. We ring the bell. A maid appears. She's barefoot and is also otherwise very lightly clad, because of

54

the heat. We give her to understand that something has to be done about the other bed, and she nods and leaves. She didn't say a word, so we couldn't decide what language she spoke, but her looks suggested she might know Tatar. While waiting, we go out and buy fruit again, two bagfuls, to be well provided. It's a warm night and we linger outside, walking about.

It's pitch-dark, but there are hanging lamps at each of the open sheds where fruit and tobacco and warm pirogi are sold. A Lezghian or Kist,[16] or whatever he may be, stands in every shed strongly armed and sells peaceful grapes and cigarettes; he has a saber, a dagger, and a pistol in his belt. Lots of people are walking back and forth among the acacia trees; a few shop a little, but most of them walk about humming or dreaming in silence. Some have stopped under the trees and just stand there. The closer one gets to the Orient, the less people speak. The ancient peoples have put behind them the stage of chatter and cackle; they smile and keep silent. Maybe it's best that way. The Koran has shaped a view of life that cannot be debated or kicked around at meetings; its meaning is unambiguous: happiness is to endure life, afterward things will be better. Fatalism.

In front of one of the sheds a man is strumming on the strings of his balalaika, vaguely, simply, a music from a fossil life. Thank goodness that he sits there strumming all the time, we think. He gives us all a modicum of sweet pleasure that way, and since he doesn't stop, he must also take pleasure in it himself. How strange the people are in this strange land! They have time to play and the ability to keep their mouths shut. God bless such countries for being there, in the midst of our world! And they couldn't have better neighbors than the Slavs, for the Slavs have a quivering string in their own breasts. When the Greeks warred with the Arabs around the year 500, they once captured a detachment of their enemies. Among the captives were three Slavs. These Slavs were carrying guslis or psalteries, string instruments, in their hands. Those were their weapons.

The musician begins to sing softly to his strumming. We don't understand a word, but the rocking husky intensity of his humming makes an impression on us. We are reminded of Drachmann's *Sakuntala,*[17] a mere trifle, nothing at all—just a stream of gold. Occasionally a Russian officer who is garrisoned here passes by. A Christian, he has to walk past all this Mohammedanism. But he does so without reluctance, because he is a Slav. He may be coming from his club and is going home and to bed. But the Lezghian does not go home, he continues to make music in the night. We Europeans have come a long way, we look forward to lying down, and our bed is full of blankets. We have even taken to longing for the winter after a few weeks of summer; snow, the stiffness of death, makes us feel good. Nobody is depressed at summer being past, nobody is miserable and grieves over it. It seems so wrong, and quite incomprehensible. "The worst judgment on life is that nobody mourns its death." And when we have once again attained our heart's desire and got our winter back, we don't go despondently into hibernation, which would be quite natural, but we work, strive, and struggle in the snow. And during the long evenings, when not a soul can stir outdoors for fear of frost, we light the fire and read. Read novels and newspapers. But the ancient peoples do not read, they are out in the night strumming songs. There the man sits under the acacia tree, we see and hear him play—that's the kind of country we're in. When a barbarian emperor was Europeanized, he began to use the Caucasus for—a place of exile. And preferably he exiled poets.

The night wears on, yet people do not go to bed; that's the way it is here. As long as the night is warm and full of stars, life is more precious to them than sleep. The Koran has left all sorts of things unprohibited; people are free to feast on grapes and to sing under the stars. The weapons they carry in their belts here do mean something: they mean war and glory, victory and drums. But the balalaika also means something—love and an undulating steppe and a soughing among the acacia leaves. When the last war broke out between the Greeks and the Turks, a Turkish officer declared who were bound to lose as a matter of course. And he went on to say: "Oh, blood will flow in streams and there will be blood on the flowers, thus will the Greeks fall!" I once read this someplace, and it struck me by its language and its remarkable conception. Blood on the flowers! Ye Prussian officers, when did ye speak thus? . . .

When we get back to the inn, the beds are indeed made in some fashion, but we lack wash water, towels, and matches. And the beds aren't really made, they simply have each a couple of sheets spread askew on top of them. My travel companion begins to stretch and smooth the sheets, not, to be sure, for any great benefit she might herself reap from it, but to teach the maid an excellent skill, that is, for the love of it. The two of them lend each other a hand, and since they imitate one another's speech, I hear the greatest oddities. We suggest they give us blankets for the beds, for there are only sheets—the maid leaves and comes back with a blanket. We ask for an additional blanket, one for each bed, that is, and the maid brings another blanket. How about some water? The maid doesn't understand a word. We explain for all we're worth, and finally it dawns on her that it's water we want. But here *we* were the stupid ones. The maid just puts her naked foot on a pedal on the washstand and the water spurts into the basin in a jet. That's how the washstands are made here; in Russia they always wash in running water, and we ought to have remembered that from Moscow. "You foreigners wash yourselves in your own dirt," the Russians say. Last of all, there was the matter of towels—could we have some towels? The maid leaves and returns with one towel. Could we have one more? The maid brings one more. Matches I have in my pocket, so now we nod good night to the maid and lock her out to be rid of her.

The long railroad journey has shaken up the multifarious contents of our heads, so that many loose things are dancing about in there—we are still on the move. I myself feel, besides, a little extra fatigue, uneasiness, fever. That will have to be cured with a tiny little drink, I say to myself. And so I seize the opportunity to pour myself some cognac in a beer glass.

After an hour's sleep I'm awakened by the intense heat in the room, and I now understand that I should never have asked for the blankets. I fall asleep again, this time covered only with a sheet. Around five o'clock I wake up from being cold, and I realize that I shouldn't have thrown off the blanket. In short, I had caught the beginnings of the Caucasian fever and had to spend a restless night.

Alas, I had to spend many such nights.

V

In the morning we inquire about transportation across the mountains; we communicate through a German- and French-speaking gentleman we were lucky enough to meet in the hotel. There are no post horses or coaches to be had; an arriving group of sixty-four Frenchmen has telegraphically engaged all conveyances. There we were. We are referred to the posting station apropos of the matter; there we meet an official who speaks German. He explains to us that all the government horses will be busy for the next six days. Six days in Vladikavkaz! In the mountains we could have taken it easy for a while if necessary, but not here, on the flat, in a steppe town. And besides, if we stayed here for six days, that officer from Pyatigorsk would catch up with us and could scarcely be avoided.

The posting official suggests that we hire a private coach and four. It will cost a little more, but still. Further, he advises us to find a Molokan,[18] a milk drinker, for our coachman. These people are religious sectarians and never taste alcohol in any form.

The posting official's two suggestions sound reasonable, with one exception. The suggestion about the four horses didn't sound reasonable. With regard to the question if we were persons of rank, I denied nothing, as he didn't expressly ask me about it, but whether out of caprice or necessity, we wished to travel like ordinary commoners, and this I give him to understand. He then explained that four horses were necessary on the steep road, if we were two persons and had luggage; he had traveled over the mountains himself in a coach and four. That was different; then both his suggestions were reasonable. This man seemed never to have been unreasonably extravagant; on the contrary, he looked as though that one-time journey with the four horses had cost him his last penny; that was the impression he made, a shabby, emaciated civil servant with unkempt hair and a long thin nose. I thank him sincerely for his kindness to us and want to leave. Then my traveling companion suggests I give the man a couple of rubles. I haggle it down to one and hand him the silver coin in a discreet manner. Thanks, but we owed him nothing, it didn't cost anything. To be sure, but we wished to show our gratitude. Then the man accepted the coin and put it away on his desk. Whereupon he began to busy himself with his papers again. But my traveling companion said, "There you can see for yourself, he would've been much happier if he got two rubles."

From the hotel we send for a Molokan with a coach and four; the French- and German-speaking gentleman is again of assistance to us. This helpful gentleman is a civilian, dressed in the usual European manner—modern, elegant—but he gives the impression of being a military person; we size him up as a colonel. He's somewhat gray.

The Molokan arrives.

"Are you a Molokan?" I wanted to know. Incidentally, it was the first time in my life that I inquired about a coachman's religious views before hiring him.

Yes, he was a Molokan.

The coachman asks fifty-seven rubles for driving us over the mountains to Tiflis. But naturally, he won't provide us with a Cossack escort for the same money.

A Cossack escort? What did we need that for? Didn't he dare drive without one?

For his part, the coachman asks if *we* dared drive without.

We look at one another.

Then our interpreter, the colonel, decides the issue, saying that we don't need any escort; we belong to those who place their fate in God's hand. What would robbers or murderers want with us? We didn't have a copeck on this earth, we were missionaries bound for Persia and China, and there was nothing but Bibles in our luggage. So we needed no escort.

The Molokan, on his part, refused to be outdone. What did we want with a seven-man Cossack escort in front and behind? In short, there was no danger, he'd traveled the road before and was familiar with it.

We are agreed. We give the coachman ten rubles in advance and accept his *izvozchik*'s badge with a number on it as a pledge. On the way he shall have five rubles to live on for himself and the horses, and when we arrive in Tiflis we'll pay the remainder with forty-two rubles. The journey will take three days and nights. It shall start tomorrow morning at five o'clock.

But at the door the Molokan turns around to tell us in no uncertain terms that if we begin to kick over the traces up in the mountains and make excursions to auls and different tribes in the adjacent mountains, then he wants a compensation of fifteen rubles a day. We get it haggled down to twelve and are agreed.

Everything is in order.

We go out to take a look at the town. Vladikavkaz, the "Lord of the Caucasus," has 45,000 inhabitants, is half-European, and has a theater, parks, and tree-lined boulevards. There isn't much of interest to the sightseer, except for artisans who do their work sitting out in the street as in southern Europe, but with the difference that these artisans are handsome men like all Caucasians, tanned beauties of the Arab type. We go up to a bench where three men are doing metalwork. They chisel and chase mounts for daggers and sabers, ornaments for belts, women's jewelry. I buy a cane that one of the artists is just finishing; it's damascened with metal and inlaid with four green stones. It's very inexpensive—eight rubles; its design is Byzantine. I have calculated that almost 9,000 pins and metal splints have been engraved into the knob of the cane.

The man wasn't eager to sell his merchandise. Though he got up when we came over to his table, he just remained standing without uttering a word. I looked closely at all his canes and took my time; when I asked the price, he gave his short little answer in Russian and then fell silent. When I paid him he didn't thank me in Russian, but said a word in another language and nodded. He remained standing throughout, and only after leaving did we see him sit down again.

We are going to buy some lap robes. It will probably be cold in the mountains, and we have barely any outerwear with us. We soon find a shop with lap robes; though the colonel is also a stranger in town, it's quite easy for him to nose out the right place.

Boring European lap robes of many kinds are laid out for us, and we reject them all. On the other hand, we get hold of some soft, shaggy wool blankets, which are the nicest things we've seen. "How much do they cost?"

A blue-eyed man in a black silk jacket stands behind the counter; he looks at the price tag and replies, "Eighteen rubles."

"For two, that is," the colonel says to us by way of explanation. "Eighteen rubles for both blankets."

But the blue-eyed man understands German, may in fact be a German, and answers, "No, eighteen rubles apiece."

The colonel had understood this from the beginning, of course, but nonetheless pretends to be surprised. He picks up his pince-nez, puts it on his nose, looks at the blankets, then looks up at the shopkeeper and cannot get over it; he doesn't say a word. The shopkeeper returns the colonel's look, and they both stand like that for a while.

The shopkeeper has to give way first: "Certainly, eighteen rubles apiece," he says. And he opens the blankets wide and begins to explain the color, the kind of wool, the quality. These were no ordinary blankets, surely we realized that. . . .

But the colonel pokes at the blankets in silence and prepares to leave. We follow suit. Then the colonel turns around and says, "Let me ask you something—how much do you want for the blankets?"

The shopkeeper replies, "Thirty-six rubles," and begins to explain the blankets afresh.

Then the colonel says to us in French that it's probably not possible to get them any cheaper.

"No, it's impossible to sell them cheaper," says the damn German, who may even be a Frenchman.

The colonel spars with him still awhile, but to no use: the blankets are packed and I am about to pay. While I count out my paper rubles, the moment I get to thirty-four the colonel suddenly calls out, "Stop!" And he hands the shopkeeper the money, saying he won't get another copeck. The shopkeeper squirms and doesn't accept the money.

"Then take the blankets back, keep them," says the colonel. But at the same time he puts the big parcel under my arm and points to the door. Whereupon he tossed the bills on the counter and followed us into the street.

~

An almost sleepless night on account of the Caucasian fever and Caucasian bedbugs.

I awake at half-past three and get up. It's dark, but the fruit and tobacco shops on the other side of the street are illuminated as usual. I hear a bell ringing somewhere in the house. So it's not too early to ring the bell, I think to myself and pull the cord. Nobody comes. I ring once more and lean out of the open window, looking down and waiting. No one comes. I ring again.

We rang six times to get our shoes and a bit of breakfast.

We notice from our windows that, true enough, our Molokan pulls up in front of our hotel at half-past four. He talks to the doorman for a moment and drives off again. We go down and get hold of the doorman, but we cannot talk with him in any language and don't understand a word of what he tells us. It's now five o'clock.

The Molokan again rolls up to the hotel entrance, but when I begin to put our luggage onto the carriage, it is gently taken off again and brought back into the hotel. We cannot understand this oddity, nor do we understand what the doorman is talking with the coachman about. But we conclude that the hotel is holding on to the luggage because we haven't yet paid our bill. Then I stretch to my full height and, acting the big shot, recite in Norwegian a big speech, a fat speech, words of affluence. Forgetting that we are missionaries, I take out my wallet and, tapping it, use the word "million," which is almost the same in Russian, so they will be a bit impressed with us. When this doesn't help I speak much louder and yell for the bill—"Let me just have that trifling bill!"

But when the hotel staff realize that they are unable to explain anything, in their distress they go and wake up our interpreter from yesterday. The colonel. He comes down, somewhat lightly clad, bowing and begging pardon for his toilette. And now it comes to light that it is the police who are preventing our departure. There is a horse epidemic in the area, our animals must be checked, and the police sent a summons to our coachman late yesterday evening.

There we were again.

When, then, could we leave?

Sometime in the afternoon.

But then we wouldn't be able to reach our agreed-upon mountain station before nightfall.

The colonel racks his brain and negotiates a goodly while with the doorman and the driver. It was decided that we would drive to the residence of the chief of police and appeal to him personally. I'll have my passport and my card sent in to him, and a waiter from the hotel will come with us and try to sway him with his guarantee for the horses.

Then it becomes necessary to find my card. As we ransack our bags it becomes evident to everybody, I'm afraid, that they do not contain Bibles. But we don't find my cards. Where were they, then? I had a boxful of them; I always do, since they are never needed. They must be tucked away among the articles we left in Helsingfors.[19] Instead of my own, I find by chance the card of Sibelius, the musician; of Albert Edelfelt, Wentzel Hagelstam, and Mrs. Mascha Hagelstam.[20] The colonel selects Wentzel Hagelstam's card, saying that it will be all right. We are afraid that the name on the card goes too poorly with the name on the passport, but the colonel replies that no comparisons will be made so early in the morning.

Then we set off.

But the chief of police isn't up.

We drive back to the hotel. Once more the colonel has to come forward. He telephones the chief of police in bed and gets him to authorize a travel permit that can be picked up at the police station.

Then everything was in order.

We load our luggage onto the carriage and pay the hotel bill. The room itself was inexpensive, five rubles, but on the bill was entered the use of two pillows, one ruble; two towels, fifty copecks; together with other oddities. But we pay without objection, thank our wonderful colonel for the last time and roll away from the inn. It was now half past six.

At the posting station I present Hagelstam's card. The friendly official from yesterday takes it, looks at the name and takes out the chief of police's written permit. Then we have done with Vladikavkaz. "Have a pleasant journey!" says the posting official.

VI

It was a cool morning, with clouds over the mountains and yet no sun. Driving through an avenue of Lombardy poplars, we meet numerous fruit wagons heading for the city, and we buy a few bags of grapes for next to nothing. Then we drive along the Terek River and come to a watering hole. It occurs to us that this spot has a perfectly Norwegian character, and we alight from the carriage and linger a bit longer than necessary. The clouds are easing up and the mountains become more and more visible to us, but not the peaks. We come to a bar where they ask for toll, and as we have to wait a long time before we get the receipt for our two rubles, we again alight and talk to the horses and the coachman. Our Molokan's name is Kornei Grigorevich, a Russian of fifty in a pale-blue coachman's caftan and with long, dark hair and beard. He asks if we're French, but when we explain where we are from he understands nothing and looks hopelessly at us. If we'd been French, he would have known at once that we were from France; the name of France has just penetrated Caucasia, subsequent to the tsar's and Felix Faure's alliance in Kronstadt.[21] Kornei Grigorevich even mentions the alliance and chuckles at his knowledge.

Then comes the receipt, the bar goes up, and we roll through.

There is no rise in the road worth mentioning. We are going through a deep valley that seems impassably narrow, with huge mountains on both sides; we can barely hear the faint roar of the Terek down there in the depths. The Terek is not high at this time of year, but it is very swift, because it comes from all the way up by Mt. Kazbek and has such a long drop. We drive through some limestone mountains, where the road is cut into the side of the cliff; it has a roof and lacks only the one wall toward the Terek to be a tunnel. There is an awful lot of lime dust; the dust is stationary and muddies the air, and it coats one's eyeglasses and binoculars. The mountainside we look out on is covered with a leafy scrub, juniper and small conifers almost all the way up.

After a couple of hours the mist withdraws from the

mountaintops; the sun is shining. It gets warmer and warmer. Kornei unbuckles his leather belt, pulls off his caftan, folds it neatly, stickler for order that he is, and sits down on it. We open our umbrellas against the sun.

We arrive at the first station in the mountains, Balta, which we pass. I knew from all the accounts I had read that here, at Balta, the mountains begin. As if we hadn't had mountains before! With the landscape changing, we can see the snow-capped peaks in the distance through a vast chasm whose sides touch the sky, but both on the right and the left side of us the cliffs are green; there are no trees, no bushes, only grass roots. And above the peaks the eagles are circling. We have already seen many eagles today.

After passing these naked cliffs, we come to others that are overgrown with shrubby plants. This is a peculiarity of Caucasia. While one cliff is green to the very top, clean, without a single bush, the adjacent cliff is covered with a most lush vegetation. There are no forests, but thickets, at times tall thickets of broadleaf trees. At different altitudes one finds oaks, chestnuts, beeches, a few spruces, but mostly birch trees. Our beloved Nordic birch doesn't give up, but goes all the way to the top, while the other trees get cold and stop.

From now on the road rises steeply, with short intervals we ride at a walking pace. We pass the Lars station, which is surrounded by mountains that rise to over one thousand meters. The road runs zigzag now, every view is blocked, we cannot see anything either forward or backward; we see only Kornei's back and head. Here and there men lie sleeping at the edge of the road; they must be laborers, hired to sand and repair the road, goofing off. They are dressed in the Circassian manner, but have unhooked their weapons from their belts. It turns out that all the men along the road over the mountains are in Circassian attire, without being Circassian; even the Tatars, indeed the Russians, dress that way. But there are no Circassians here—most of them emigrated to Turkey when the Russians defeated them; those who are left live in Ciscaucasia, around the Kuban river, and one tribe, the Kabardians, lives north of Vladikavkaz. This people, which at one time was most intransigent and even refused to join Shamil's army[22] in order to fight the Russians the more forcefully on their own, now lives closer to Russia than any other Caucasian people that previously lived in the mountains. The Slavs defeated it, and it became a neighbor.

The road is so blocked that it looks as if it will permit us only to make our way foot by foot. Then it opens a bit, and we cross the Terek on an iron bridge. Here, at the bottom, it is very cramped, and the river is turbulent, the water yellowish-gray with lime; it's like soup. Near the bridge stands an occasional burned dandelion. We get out and wipe the lime dust from a few of them, trying to help them breathe again; we also fetch water for them from the Terek in Kornei's zinc bucket. Kornei himself just watches us and begins to grow impatient. As a rule we didn't indulge in such silliness, but this time a dispute had arisen in the carriage about whether these miserable dandelion plants were alive or dead, and it was this question we wanted to clear up. Kornei finally simmers down and gives up on us; he too gets out, sits down on the roadside and looks on. Perhaps he imagines that it is a kind of religious ritual we are going through in front of the dandelions, since we are missionaries.

But the plants were not dead. When we had the bright idea of snipping one of them, it proved to have plenty of sap inside.

Kornei drove on with us.

We fold our umbrellas, because now the sun is completely shut out. We pass a group of carriers sleeping on both sides of the road. There are six of them, and all have weapons in their belts. They have probably chosen this resting place because it is in the shade. They have unhitched their horses, tied them up and given them corn; but one horse hasn't got anything or has eaten up, so we stop and give it a little from the other horses. Meanwhile the men wake up, and they lie there on their elbows watching us and talking among themselves. When they see what we are doing, they nod and laugh; getting up to join us, they too started offering the unfairly treated horse more corn. When we drove off they lay down again.

We are coming to Fort Daryal with its round wings and

with cannons and sentries outside. I've read that Pliny[23] described the Daryal Pass and the powerful Cumania fortress that was situated here and hindered countless peoples from breaking through. A few soldiers could stop a whole army at this narrow hole.

The rise of the road increases, the mountains close in more and more tightly, and it seems as though there is no longer any hope; only a bit of sky is visible directly above our heads. It has a disheartening effect on us; we are overwhelmed and keep silent. Suddenly, at a sharp turn in the road, a huge chasm opens up on our right, and quite close to us we see the ice-covered peak of Mt. Kazbek with its glaciers sparkling white in the sun. It is cheek by jowl with us, placid and tall, mute. A mysterious feeling courses through us—the cliff stands there as if conjured up by the other cliffs. We feel as though a being from another world is looking at us.

I scramble out of the carriage, get behind the folding top and hold on there to see. At this moment I get caught up by a whirling sensation; lifted off the road, unhinged, I feel like I stand face to face with a god. It's still as death; all I hear is the soughing of the wind up there around the peak; the clouds drift across it halfway up but do not get to the summit. I've been in the mountains before—I've been on the Hardanger Plateau and in the Jotunheimen Range[24] and up in the Bavarian Alps a bit, and in Colorado and many other places—but I've never before felt so completely without a foothold on the earth; but here I stand holding on. Then the peak is wrapped in a cloud that hides it. The vision is gone. The mountain goes on soughing up there in the sky.

Then I hear someone call from the carriage and I scramble back on.

I remember a mysterious night from my childhood in Nordland, a calm, sunny summer night. I came rowing in a boat, except that I wasn't doing so the usual way, but backward, so that I was facing the bow. The seabirds were silent, and not a living thing was to be seen on shore. Then a head pops out of the smooth surface, with the water pouring off it. It must've been a seal, but it was like a being from another world; it lay there fastening its wide-open eyes on me, pondering. The look in its eyes was like that of a human being. . . .

We again cross the Terek by an iron bridge. Here the road opens up nicely, so we can see half a verst ahead. We ascend sharply. The road now runs roughly along the middle of the mountainside, and there is a constant traffic of people, horses, oxen, donkeys, and horsemen with rifles over their shoulders. As for human dwellings, we see none.

Near the road stand a large flock of sheep, tended by four herdsmen with long staffs. The herdsmen have enormous fur caps on their heads, but are otherwise lightly clad and rather ragged. The sheep are all white; the whole flock stand stock-still on the rocky slope, looking like stones among the other stones. Maybe they stand like that to simulate a scree, on account of the eagles.

A while later we see the Kazbek station ahead of us, a regular little town. Round about, rugged cliffs rise majestically, but up along the sides it's green, with little cocks of mown hay to the very summit. Sheep graze in the mountains all the way up; we can see them against the sky on the highest one, like white dots moving about. On the pinnacle of one of the mountains sits a monastery with tall, snow-covered towers. Down by the station, the houses are surrounded by lots of small fields; some men are bathing their horses in the Terek.

We drive into the station.

At our arrival we are encircled by enterprising children who offer for sale rock crystals and precious stones in many colors. We have traveled forty-three versts without stopping and will take a three-hour rest. Kornei unhitches the horses. When I ask him if our luggage can remain in the carriage during the rest period, he seems to make an uncertain gesture, so I find that the safest thing is to bring the smallest articles inside.

Here we are served dinner, excellent roasted lamb and excellent soup, and afterward we even get some delicate pirogi. But the cleanliness is very moderate. The waiter, dressed in a brown caftan and gorgeously armed, does his best to please the princely pair; he is even able to set out a silver-plated centerpiece. On the other hand, the glass stoppers for the oil and vinegar bottles being gone, the good waiter has had to replace them with new stoppers from old newspapers. But his stately demeanor when he set the gorgeous thing out on the table muffled all criticism.

Pointing at the window, he displays the glacier, which is right now hidden by mist, incidentally. "Kazbek!" he says. To this we nod, knowing it already, but when we ask him about the monastery that we see up there in the snow, what he answers merely gives us to understand that it is a Russian monastery. None of the Caucasian peoples count themselves as Russian. And there are even now, after so much time has passed since the conquest, naively bellicose Caucasians who say that the Russians will be allowed to remain in their country only if they show good behavior, otherwise not.

Kornei has said we'll rest up until four o'clock. We understand a few of his words, and he's also quite good at communicating by signs. When we hold out our watches to him, he understands the dial without difficulty; usually he picks up a twig or straw from the ground and points at the exact hour he wants to drum into us, while repeating the number again and again.

Suddenly there is a rumble of thunder. Shortly afterward big drops of rain begin to fall, but the sun is shining. I run out to bring in the rest of our luggage, but a man in a blue canvas shirt that reaches to his knees looks up at the sky and assures me that the rain will soon stop; he also points at himself and gives me to understand that he will take care of the luggage. Walking into the stable, he comes back with his caftan, which he spreads over the suitcase that is most exposed.

The rain turns violent, changing to hail. The hails are very large and rebound briskly when they hit the ground. I'm reminded of the heavy hailstorms on the American prairies in the midst of the summer heat. Then we sometimes had to throw our jackets or whatever we could find over the horses' backs and crawl in under the wagons so as not to be wounded by the hails. And the horses, who were familiar with the phenomenon from the time they were colts,

71

just hung their heads to save their eyes and endured the raps.

I run to the stable for shelter. In there stand a cow with a calf, a camel colt, and other animals; all seem to be comfortable, with the exception of a fat-tailed sheep lying in a stall. The sheep is sick and bloated; it groans loudly and closes its eyes. It has presumably been left there for slaughter. I go to my bag for some cognac and pour it into a beer glass; looking about me and finding myself alone, I pour several big mouthfuls into the sheep. I struggle for a long time with this, since the beast is stubborn, but when I finally get hold of its tongue, it swallows very well. The tongue was blue.

After the drink, the sheep snorts, shakes its head, and then lies still. I hope it will go into a sweat.

The hail shower is over and the sun scorches undisturbed, as before. I leave the stable and nose about; a hot steam rises from the earth. We now find ourselves 1,727 meters above sea level, and over the forty-three versts we have put behind us since early this morning, we have ascended nearly one thousand meters. Hereabouts, around Kazbek, the Ossetians are supposed to live, a people whose descent and name nobody can figure out; this people calls itself Iron. Since I wanted to do something for science while on this journey, it seemed reasonable to undertake some investigations among the Ossetians. I could simply climb up the cliffs for a few hours, get to the Ossetians and figure them out. Having read many books about Caucasia in the course of time, I had fairly good qualifications for doing so. Here is the cradle of humankind, here Prometheus was chained to his rock, here, at Baku, is the eternal fire; a great many Jews settled here after the Babylonian captivity, and nearby stands Mt. Ararat, which is in Armenia, true enough, but visible from here as well. I simply ought to have plenty of time at my disposal and not just a couple of measly hours. I've read that the Ossetians supposedly have a lot of tools that are unknown among other tribes in the Caucasus—fire tongs and kneading troughs, butter casks and beer mugs, rakes and much else; this has surprised all previous investigators and put them in an awkward position. But if only I could get over to them, I would ask them pointblank where the hell they had these tools from, whether they had bought them or were born with them. Unexpected things could possibly come to light. I might even have to invent an entirely new theory of the great migrations, refute my predecessors in the field, Erckert and Brosset and Opfert and Nestor and Bodenstedt and Reclus,[25] and arrive at my own independent results. Perhaps it wouldn't be without importance to myself either—they would hoist the flag for me when I came home; I would be requested to give lectures in the Geographical Society and be awarded a fat St. Olav's Medal.[26] I could already see it all in my mind's eye.

Then, as I stand beneath a cliff some distance away, Kornei comes up to me and announces that we'll be on our way.

On our way? That's not the agreement. And I take out my watch and show Kornei where he had pointed with the straw, letting him know that it is a whole hour too early. But Kornei doesn't allow himself to be turned around; picking up a straw, he points to the hour hand and decides that where it is right now is the time to be on our way. We stand there with each a straw and with the watch between us, negotiating under the cliff; in the end I must give in and follow him.

My first thought concerned the sheep in the stable, and I drag out our departure for its sake. I feared it was done for; by the time we left, it had rolled on its side and didn't seem to have much life left in it.

As we leave the station, we bump into an enormous flock of sheep in the middle of the road. It halts our horses, packs itself tightly around us and stops us in our tracks. The four herdsmen have long staffs, daggers across their bellies, and rifles over their shoulders, besides dogs. The dogs are yellowish-gray; they are not very dog-like, mostly resembling polar bears.

Then we're finally free and roll off.

The road runs through some flat country—it even begins to slope downward; we travel many versts this way and move fast. Then the road rises again, rises worse than ever, and from now on we ride at a walking pace for a long while. We pass a Georgian muzhik village with a church; in general, it's more built-up here and the nearest mountains aren't so steep. The floor of the valley is wider and greener, and God himself has erected the finest walls around the tilled patches and the villages. There are also cows and bullocks, small but solid and chunky, and flocks of sheep with thousands of animals. Some women are mowing barley in a field.

More Georgian villages. Such a village is often only a single continuous complex of dwellings, one above the other up the mountain. They aren't separated by streets or roads, but rather by stairs; they sit like shelves on top of and beside one another, dug into the mountainside. The houses have no windows and no other opening than the doorway, besides a hole in the roof above the fireplace. The roof is flat, either of turf or stone slabs. Here live the women, reclining on their pillows; they also dance and play games up there, and weather permitting, the family doesn't leave the roof night or day. These Georgian villages all look as if they have been hit by a storm, as if all the houses have had the upper half blown away.

Village after village. At each village we are surrounded by child beggars. The little creatures beg with an aggressiveness the like of which we found only when entering Turkey on our way back. Again we observe women mowing grain in a field. The older ones stoop shyly toward the ground and go on with their work, but a young girl stands straight up, looks at us and laughs. She's dressed in a blue sarafan and has tied a red kerchief around her hair; she has sparkling white teeth and dark eyes. When she no longer feels like watching us, she stops laughing, tosses her head nonchalantly and turns away. A brief exclamation escapes us travelers: that toss of the head was matchless.

Village after village. The road zigzags because of the rise, and Kornei, who wants to spare his horses, drives them gently and often waters them. At one watering hole we are overtaken by a foreign carriage that Kornei quietly lets slip past, causing the dust to become unbearable for us who are behind. We order him to stop a while, to allow time for the dust to drift away; on the whole, we do not appreciate his somnolent way of driving. Kornei, on the other hand, seems to think it's going very well now; he's humming.

Evening is upon us. It's getting dusky, and it's noticeably

colder. We throw the blankets around our shoulders. I notice that the spot of wax on my jacket is congealing again and turning white, it's like a thermometer up here on the heights; we are at an altitude of 2,000 meters. We are still winding our way between the mountains. Kornei waters the horses yet once more, though it is so cold. All fields cease; we have nearly reached the timberline.

Then we rumble across another iron bridge and arrive at the Kobi station, where we will spend the night. Shortly before we get there, Kornei suddenly jumps down from the box and starts pulling on the tail of one of his horses. At the outset we didn't understand this odd behavior, but in a little while we noticed that the horse's belly was very bloated and that the animal could barely walk.

VII

A good place; interesting, too.

We ask for lodging, but all separate rooms are occupied. However, that doesn't mean we'll be without a roof over our heads; my traveling companion is shown into a large common room for women and I into one for men. There are leather-covered benches along the walls, and I am to sleep on one of them. That's fine. We request some food and are served, without any waiting, an excellent filet, shchi and fruit. My fever has worsened again, so I'm exhorted to abstain from certain foods and drinks; but my satisfaction at having found this place in the mountains and its being so pleasant make me forget about the fever, and I order the following wrong diet: filet, shchi, fruit, beer, and afterward, coffee.

While we are eating, Kornei comes into the hallway and insists on talking with us. We can hear him very well out there; besides, we can see him every time someone walks through the door. But the waiter is on our side and won't have us summoned, to avoid disturbing us during our meal. Then Kornei sees his chance and slips into the dining room to us.

What does he want?

Kornei explains that we are leaving from here at six in the morning. Why? It goes against our agreement—we've already agreed on five o'clock in order to reach Ananuri tomorrow evening. He then gives an extremely complicated answer, but we understand that he's asking us to come outside with him.

We follow him.

We put on neither hats nor outdoor things, thinking we're just going outside, but Kornei takes us far up the road. The moon is only slightly more than half, but it shines brightly, and besides, a multitude of stars have come out. At the edge of the road we see a dark point; Kornei leads the way to that dark point. A dead horse! It's one of Kornei's horses that has died. He has watered it to death. It lies there with a belly so swollen, it looks like a balloon. "It's a hundred rubles!" Kornei says. He is inconsolable; walking us back to the interrupted meal, he constantly repeats it's a hundred rubles.

Well, those hundred rubles have been lost; no one will give them back to Kornei, so there's no need to go on talking about it. And in order to dismiss him, I say something like this to Kornei: "Good night! We'll be off tomorrow morning at five."

"No, at six," Kornei replies.

We cannot reach an agreement. Kornei tries to say something, from which we understand that a hundred rubles have been lost and tomorrow he'll have only three horses.

The logic of this isn't clear to us. With only three horses, there is even more reason to begin our journey at five if we are to reach Ananuri. And after much negotiation, with straws and watches and loudly spoken Russian times of day, Kornei finally nods and complies. Good night.

After supper we go to look at the dead horse again. Why has it been dragged so far away from the station? Could there be a bit of Caucasian Christianity behind it? Here, as in many other countries, one of the first things the Christians learned was, of course, to give horseflesh a wide berth. Anyway, there that huge pagan carcass was lying on the highway, far off, remote from people; they didn't seem interested in saving even the skin. And in this respect the Caucasians were right. Unless, everything considered, their Christianity was only so-so. True, there are still ruins of churches from the time of Queen Tamara (1184–1212)[27] about the Caucasus, and there are also more recent churches; but a great many Caucasians have remained Mohammedans, more or less, to this very day. In the Baku region there were even fire worshipers barely a generation ago; indeed, in south Caucasia, toward Armenia, there are supposedly still devil worshipers. When the Kists of central Caucasia were defeated by Russia and had to swear allegiance to the tsar, they made it an express condition to be allowed to swear by their own god, Galgerd. . . .

The moon and the stars are out. The horse is still lying there, swollen and pagan and gross, with two dogs guarding it. Then a man comes with a farrier's pincers in his hand. A young man, he rolls the balloon around, makes jokes about the dead body, and says whoa to it to make it lie still. He might not have done that with a Christian body. He salvages the shoes of the fallen horse; shortly afterward Kornei comes, and they also prepare for saving the skin. Why not?

The two men slit the skin along the belly and the legs and begin flaying. Kornei is quiet and doesn't say a word, but the young man complains he cannot see very well, glancing up at the sky and grumbling, as if to say: he has forgotten to clean his lamp tonight, all right! Then he goes to get a lantern and returns, bringing several people with him, young and old; it's as though the smell they have picked up of a slaughtered animal has made them eager to follow him.

We are all looking on.

Suddenly more men unsheathe their knives and begin to skin. They seem to act out of sheer desire; feeling the naked flesh with their hands, they warm themselves on it and laugh with subdued excitement. Is their inner pagan awakening in them?

The skin is stripped off the animal in a trice, and another horse comes with a cart to pull the cadaver away. At that moment a lusty young man sticks the point of his knife into the animal's belly and opens it. They all let out a muffled exclamation as a modest expression of how good it makes them feel, and soon many of them run their hands around the intestines, speaking extremely loud, as if they were trying to outshout one another. Kornei himself doesn't take part in this—he's too good a Christian for that; he has even tossed the pagan skin on the ground, wanting no truck with it. But he does watch the butchering, and a low fire seems to be kindled in his eyes as well.

A man comes up from the station. We cannot believe our own eyes: it's the innkeeper. Does he want to be part of it, too? He stops the mutilation of the dead body and seeks Kornei's permission to take portions of the carcass, some limbs. Kornei turns away, refusing him. The innkeeper slips some money into his hand, and Kornei also turns away when he accepts the money. Then the innkeeper points out the parts he wants, and several men take pleasure in dismembering the carcass. With the help of two men, the innkeeper takes the tenderloin and the legs away. Filet, I think to myself, filet and shchi for future travelers! If the innkeeper and his household are of the right sort, they may also taste the meat themselves tonight. For it's horseflesh.

Kornei is busy getting the remainder of the horse taken away in the cart, but the butchers are still having fun with the leftovers; there are still some tasty pieces left and everyone takes his portion and carries it off, the shoulders, the liver, the lungs. And Kornei turns away and permits it. The part that was left and at long last hauled away in the cart was still big enough—namely, the bloated intestines.

I couldn't help recalling Håkon I during the sacrificial feast at Lade.[28] The king struggled to avoid the horseflesh, but the people insisted he eat it. However, the king had been given a Christian education in England and refused to taste horseflesh. Then the yeomen requested that he drink the soup, but he refused to do that as well, turning away. Finally, they demanded only that he eat the fat, but no, the king stuck to his conviction. Then the yeomen threatened to go against him, and Earl Sigurd had to come forth and arbitrate. "Simply take the pot handle in your mouth," he told the king. But the handle was greasy with the steam from the pot, and the king placed a linen cloth over the pot handle before taking it in his mouth. Then he went ahead and closed his mouth over it. However, neither side was satisfied, the saga reports.

And so a fresh quarrel broke out during the Christmas celebration at Mære the following winter. The yeomen had come there in large numbers, and now as before they demanded that the king sacrifice to the heathen gods. But he refused. When he was to drink the commemorative toasts, he made the sign of the cross over them. "What is he doing?" asked Kåre of Gryting. "He's making the sign of Thor's hammer," Earl Sigurd, that rascal, replied. But the yeomen were suspicious and demanded that the king drink the toast without making the sign of Thor's hammer. The king turned away for a long while, but gave in and drank the toasts without making the sign of the cross over them. Then the horseflesh was put forth again, and the king was urged to eat. But he turned away. When the yeomen threatened to use force, Earl Sigurd asked him to give in.

But the king was an English Christian—he couldn't be moved; he ate only a few pieces of horse liver.

Alas, Kornei Grigorevich, you have many predecessors and will no doubt have many successors. That's the way it will be. . . .

We return to the station and get ready to go to bed. Good night. But I have only an old issue of the Swedish paper *The New Press* to read; it's my only reading and I've now read this issue so many times that I can no longer find anything of interest in it. It reports on "the court-martial in Rennes," on "the conspiracy against the republic," on "the rumors of war from Transvaal," on "the disturbances in Bohemia," and on "the plague in Oporto"—I couldn't bring myself to lie down and read about these things any-more. Alas, I would yet go to bed with this reading many a time and find solace even in its most humble "market prices." It was only on our way back home, on the plains of Serbia, that I sent the old paper sailing through the window of our railroad compartment. . . .

I walk out into the night again and wander about on the station. I enter the backyard. It's a large open square with horses on all sides. In the soft light from the moon and the stars, men dressed in caftans come and go, leading horses to the stable or taking them out for departure. Now and then the door to the main building opens and some unintelligible word or name is shouted into the backyard, to be answered by another unintelligible word from one of the stables. A camel lies chewing cud in the middle of the yard; a man teases it in passing and pokes it with a stick, making the camel cry and raise its head the height of a man without moving. I can hear the horses snort and munch corn in the stables.

I feel strangely at ease among these people and animals in the starry night. It's as though I've found a place where I can be happy also here, very far from home. I stop a man here and there and offer him a cigarette to make friends with him and avoid being banished from the square, and when I give him a light I shine the flame on him at the same time and take a look at his appearance. They are all lean, handsome figures, rather similar to one another, swarthy, Arabic. What's more, they are like steel springs, and it is a pleasure to observe their posture and their walk.

Everything would now be fine if Kornei hadn't lost his horse, those hundred rubles.

While I wander from one stable to another, listening and looking, Kornei also appears again. "Hundred rubles!" he says, shaking his head sadly. Stop it, Kornei, I think to myself. But Kornei doesn't stop; he trails after me. Then he again mentions six o'clock as our time of departure tomorrow. I take to speculating why in the world Kornei wants to annoy me with this late hour, and I come to the conclusion that he's trying to extort money, a bribe, from me for leaving at five o'clock. Since we are not real missionaries, we may possibly be wealthy people to whom a hundred rubles do not matter. It's not impossible that this is his reasoning, I think to myself.

I seize Kornei firmly by his arm, pull him over to a man with a storm lantern in his hand, and point to the number five on my watch. Then I say in a loud voice in Russian, whether it's correct or not, "*Pyat' chasa,*" five o'clock. At the same time I put my forefinger within an inch of Kornei's forehead. Kornei nods apathetically and has understood me. But it looks as though he absolutely refuses to rest content with my decision. I have to leave the yard to be rid of him.

Kornei will of course show up only at six o'clock anyway, despite our contract and my resolute demeanor. We must be prepared for that. The question is whether we can reach Ananuri with three horses.

In any case, I guess I have to go in and get to bed.

In the large common room a man is already asleep. By the other wall an officer in uniform is making a bed for himself; he has brought sheets and white pillowcases of his own. He looks arrogant and I don't dare talk to him. Down by the door a soldier lies on the bare floor. He isn't yet asleep. He's presumably the officer's batman.

I go out again and stroll up the road where the horse used to be. At some distance I hear elated talk by several people and I follow the sound. Then I see that a fire has been lighted beneath a crag and I go there.

I come upon seven men around a bonfire. It looked great. They have cooked the horseflesh and are now eating it; their hands and faces are greasy, and every mouth is chewing and chattering. As soon as I get there they invite me to have a taste as well, and a man holds out a piece of meat in his fingers and says something, smiling; the others also smile and nod to me for encouragement. I accept the meat, but shake my head and say, "*U menya likhorad-ka,*" I have a fever. I had found this in my Russian phrase book. But they don't understand Russian very well and consult with one another on what I've said, and when it dawns on them they all start talking with great animation. From what I can understand, they explain to me that horseflesh is the best medicine in the world for fever, and now others also offer me pieces of meat. Then I begin to eat, and it tastes very good. "*Sol'?*" I ask. One man understands and hands me salt in a little rag; but it's not clean and I have to shut my eyes when I help myself to it. The men themselves eat without salt, hurriedly and without moderation, their eyes looking quite insane. They act like drunks, I think to myself, though horseflesh cannot possibly intoxicate them like that. I sit down among them to observe them and find out.

They start drinking the broth. They use a ladle that is passed from man to man; the ladle is dripping wet with grease along the handle. When they have drunk the broth and quenched their thirst, they again eat meat and continue doing so. I'm quite through with my meal, which incidentally has done me a lot of good and suppressed my fever, and I say thank you, that I've had all I want, when they keep repeating their invitations.

They behave more and more strangely, handling the meat with unnecessary gestures. Pressing the pieces of meat against their cheeks, they slide them over to their mouths, as if caressing them blissfully in advance, all the while closing their eyes and laughing. Some cram the meat against their nostrils, holding it there to get the full fragrance of it. They were all shiny with grease up to their eyes but felt quite proper and comfortable, although a stranger was watching. When they were full, they rolled on the ground, letting out an assortment of sounds and taking notice of nobody but themselves. . . .

Then I see Kornei coming, get up, say good-bye and leave. Good old Kornei was beginning to be tiresome.

I again walk down the road, but when I get to the station I don't feel like going to bed, now that I was strong and free of fever. I take a stroll past the buildings and turn off toward the cliffs. At the foot I see a pair of horses and carts. There are drifts of stars in the sky, a faint roar rises from the Terek, and the mountains stand dark and mute round about. Moved by their awesome majesty, I lay my head all the way back and glimpse their tops against the sky. I also look at the stars, recognizing a few, but they are in the wrong place for me. The Pleiades are directly above my head.

It must be evening in Norway now, I think to myself, and the sun will be setting in the ocean in many places. Then the sun is red when it sets; at home, in Nordland, it's even redder than elsewhere many times. Well, enough of that. . . .

Never have I seen such bright starlight as here, up in the Caucasian mountains. And the moon, though only half, shines like a full moon. This strong light from a night sky without sun is new to me, it interests me and prevents me from being homesick. I sit down on the ground and look up, and since, unlike many others, I'm one of those who haven't yet fixed things up with God, I sit lost in thought about God and his creation for a while. The world I had come to was one of magical depths, an ancient place of exile that was the most wonderful country in the world. I let myself go more and more, oblivious of sleep. The mountains begin to seem fantastic, looking as if they had come from somewhere else and had stopped directly opposite me. Like people who have spent much time alone, I talked overmuch to myself, cuddling up and trembling with delight while talking aloud. I felt like lying down to sleep right there. As I lean back, my body is quickened with a lively joy because it is all so good. But it's getting nippy now, and my top side starts feeling cold, so I get up and walk over to the horses.

The two horses standing there are unharnessed and unhitched, but they are tied up, each to its cart. Both have feedbags, now empty of corn, over their muzzles. I remove the bags and give the horses a longer tether so they can nibble a bit on the green mountainside. Afterward I pat them and leave.

Then the horses stop nibbling, lift their heads and follow me with their eyes. When I pat them once more, they want to follow me when I leave. It turns out they feel lonesome and want to be with people.

I cannot consider that, but after walking away a few steps I feel that a ride would be a good idea and turn back. I choose the best-looking horse, though that too looks skinny and inelegant, and untie and mount it. Then I ride slantways uphill and into the mountains.

The stillness is unbroken, the only sound that of the horse's hooves. The station has been out of sight for a long time, cliffs and valleys have hidden it, but I know the way back.

There is no trail, but the horse runs fast over the hard knolls; when it trots, its sharp back cuts into me, since I have no saddle. But it likes to gallop too, and then I feel fine.

Here the mountain is no longer bare; there are leafy coppices and brackens here and there. After riding through these for a while, we hit a trail. It cuts straight across our path. I stop, look up and down, and don't quite know which direction to take. As I halt to deliberate I see a man coming down the trail from the heights; my horse sees him too and pricks up its ears. Frightened, I dismount; I look up at the man and at the horse, listening. I can hear my watch ticking in my pocket.

When the man has come sufficiently close, I nod how-de-do to him and I'm your friend. To this he makes no answer, he just comes closer. He's wearing a gray burnous and an enormous fur cap that I've seen herdsmen use. So he must be a herdsman—his ragged burnous would go with someone like that; but he has a splendid belt and both a dagger and a pistol by his side. He walks indifferently past me. I follow him with my eyes, and when he has gone a few steps I stop him. I offer him a cigarette. He turns around and, surprised, accepts the cigarette, and when he has lighted it he says something, a couple of quick words. I shake my head and answer that I don't understand. He says something again, but since

I cannot talk with him he soon goes away.

I feel the greatest satisfaction at this meeting having gone so well and calm down. I pat the horse, tie it up to a bunch of brackens slightly off the trail and let it graze, then sit down beside it. No, the herdsman hadn't meant any harm, of course not, and why should he! What's more, he was probably afraid of me. He thanked me sincerely for the cigarette. And suppose that this man had wanted to murder me in my deep solitude and abandonment. Well, so what? I would have jumped him and clamped my paws around his throat. And when I'd nearly strangled him I would have paused for a moment and given him an opportunity to rue his life. Whereupon I would have finished him off.

I'm rather cold, but that doesn't prevent me from feeling good. Those people who sleep in beds and use the hours of the night for nothing but nursing their rottenness, weren't they just insufferable? I have myself lain in European beds, with blankets in them, for more than a generation, and that I've been able to endure it is a godsend. But I've been a giant.

The spot where I'm lying is like a morass of rocks; I could imagine myself living here, among the moon and the stars and maybe some sky-born creatures who would come to me. I don't know where I could find water, but I would call the place the Spring, because there is such depth upward, although a spring means anything but lack of water.

I get on my horse and decide to follow the trail downhill. The horse is rested and would like to trot again, but since I am on the point of sliding forward onto its neck, I rein it in. At a turn I suddenly look down into an inhabited valley. Here I dismount to consider. The dwellings in front of me are Georgian—a few small huts set into the mountainside. I'm uncertain what to do, being afraid to go there. They might take my horse away.

Deciding to hide the horse, I quickly lead it back and tie it up away from the trail. Then I walk a bit farther down to explore; being responsible for the horse, I had to find out whether it would be safe. My first thought was to leave the horse where it was and go down the valley by myself, but then I thought, if something happens, it's nice to have a horse at hand. I mounted and rode down.

However, when I was getting close to the huts I stopped to think it over once more. Maybe I shouldn't pursue my venture any further. But by now it was too late; the dogs had seen me and burst out barking. Shortly afterward I see a man standing bolt upright on the roof of his house looking at me. I had no choice but to ride down to him. But I would have preferred to be at the station.

Already the dogs were unpleasant to look at, large and yellow, like polar bears; they pulled their heads back when they barked and raised their hackles. I have a small hope that the man on the roof is the herdsman I recently gave a cigarette to and became friends with, but when he climbed down I saw at once it was someone else. His feet are without stockings and boots and are wrapped in pitiful rags; he, too, is wearing a huge sheepskin cap but is otherwise thinly clad.

"*Dobryi vecher!*"[29] I say some distance away. He doesn't understand my Russian and says nothing. He maintains a hard, sinister silence as he gazes at me. Then I remember the Mohammedan greeting I've read that Caucasian tribes use, and I recite the Arabic "*Salam aleikum!*" This is immediately understood, whether I had come across a linguistic genius or Arabic was his native tongue. He replies, "*Va aleikum sala-am!*" and bows. He now prefers to speak in the same style, but I, of course, don't understand a single word and cannot decide which of the half-hundred languages of the Caucasus he speaks. In order not to stand there speechless, I use a half dozen Russian words that I know, but they make no impression on him.

A couple of half-naked children also come down from the roof, looking thunderstruck. They live so far away from people, these little ones, that they haven't yet learned the art of begging and just stand there, quiet and frightened. They are dark-complexioned and ugly, with round brown eyes and a wide mouth.

I hand the man a cigarette to make him well-disposed toward me, and since he accepts it and also lets me light it, my manly courage is restored. It occurs to me that perhaps I could accomplish something for science on this trip all the same; I could figure out the dwelling of this Tatar herdsman. I begin by examining the structure's exterior, and since Russian is of no use I simply switch to Norwegian, which I know better, and ask the man if I can take a look at his house. He doesn't appear to refuse my request, only turns a little aside and goes about a bit of private business. In order not to debase the tone of our intercourse further, I bow where it is called for and speak politely all along, as if he understands me; here and there I even smile, after he says something that in my opinion is a joke. I leave it to the children to hold the horse and slip a couple of copper coins into their hands.

The house is dug into the mountain, but in front, on both sides of the door opening, are stone walls caulked with lime. The roof, which protrudes far out, rests on stone pillars in front; these pillars are even carved slightly. There's no door in the opening.

Enough of that.

When I look up to examine the roof, I see two human beings up there looking at me; then they withdraw farther back on the roof and cover their faces with kerchiefs. The harem, I think to myself, the shepherd's harem! Oh, these Orientals—how awfully hard it must be for them to forbear! I would like to examine the roof and its inhabitants, but the man doesn't seem inclined to encourage me in that; on the contrary, he acts as if my visit were over. Then I take out my diary and note down what I've already seen, to show him that my purpose is purely scientific, and since it is my duty to see the inside of his dwelling, I position myself in the door opening and entice the man to follow me by means of another cigarette. He accepts the cigarette and lets me step in.

It's dark in there, but the man lights a lamp. It jars on me that it is a stupid European kerosene lamp that he lights; but then I remember that the "eternal fire" of the ancients was petroleum, and that if kerosene was to be burned anywhere in the world, it would be here in Caucasia. The fireplace doesn't sit in the middle of the floor, but considerably to one side; it's built of large stones. Scattered here and there on the floor are all kinds of dishes of wood, clay, and iron, and as far as I can see it's neither rococo nor Louis XVI I here have before me; the absence of a strict style immediately brings to mind a certain fire station back home, in Kristiania, in all its touted glory. There are hangings on the walls. That's the influence of the harem, I think to myself, the gentle female hand. I pick up the lamp and shine it on the hangings: charming Caucasian tapestries, old and new, close-weave woolen fabrics with multicolored figures in them. The pattern is Persian.

Enough of that.

I would like to sit down, but there is no chair; seeing some piles of dry fern stalks on the floor, I sit down on one of them with a crash. Suddenly I notice that something is moving in a corner, and a human voice is heard. I again pick up the lamp and light up the corner: an old shriveled woman lies groping in the dark; she's blind. The herdsman, who so far hasn't shown a trace of sentimentality, now suddenly becomes tender and devoted, rushing up to soothe the old one and tuck her in again. She's his mother, I figure. And I remembered what I'd read, that the Caucasians don't give a damn about what their wives want but go obediently by their mothers. That's their custom. The old one won't be soothed; she wants to know what's happening around her, and the son repeats and repeats his explanation. She's so old and sharp-nosed and hollow-cheeked, and her eyes are of foam, coated with white films, and recognize no one. When you tie up horses and cows too close to the wall, they become nearsighted, and I think to myself: the Caucasian woman has a similar lot, being tied up too close to the wall. And so she goes blind.

The old woman seems to give an order, a command, which the son obeys by lighting a fire of fern stalks on the hearth. It was a gorgeous fire. Then he starts roasting mutton ribs in an iron pan, dropping bits of meat in the fire as an offering, according to ancient pagan custom. The meat is good and fat—it greases the pan by itself; it emits a rather acrid smell, but when the man offers me some I accept it and eat. It tastes unfamiliar, but I'm given more pieces and also eat them. It's no doubt the old one in the corner I have to thank for this hospitality, and upon my emphatic gestures and signs she, too, is offered some meat.

After this good meal I again have to start thinking of my

investigations, and I long to get started with the roof. There the two women lay frozen stiff while the rest of us were having a feast, and I felt hurt that the man had a heart for his mother but completely forgot about his wives. I wanted to rehabilitate them and shower them indiscriminately with copper coins, if only I could get at them. I figured that one of them was the herdsman's favorite wife and that she really was an enchanting creature. A man like the herdsman didn't deserve her, and I was going to let him know it. If I tried real hard, I should be able to cut him out. Besides the personal satisfaction it might bring me, it wouldn't hurt if I had another little gallant adventure in my diary.

For that matter, it could also be of lifelong importance to the favorite wife herself. It would awaken her. It could give the impetus for an entire little women's movement in Caucasia. I wouldn't treat her harshly and offend her—a woman is a woman after all; to begin with, I thought, I'd better write something for her. She would come to respect a man who could make such quaint shapes on paper. Then there was the content of what I would write, and precisely in this regard my superiority would win hands down. If she had an autograph book, I would write something in it, then she could browse in it when she liked to. I would refer to the sad life she was leading, but simultaneously I would console her with—her children. This was where my superiority would win hands down. I would write the following:

> Love begins like a resurrection,
> becomes a benediction and then an imprecation,
> ending as the imprecation's benediction—
> if I'm understood using this description.

That is what I would write. It's very nicely intertwined, a figure eight. She would completely agree with the first two lines, but she wouldn't understand the third. The children a benediction? For a young wife? And she would sigh, causing her bodice to burst at the small comfort I offered her. But this comfort I add out of cunning. She simply has to understand the hopeless situation in which she finds herself with this shepherd. And sure enough, then it dawns on her.

That's this evening.

Tomorrow evening we'll meet, as agreed, on the other side of the Terek, where there must be several nice places. There is a lovely moon- and starlight, and that makes us feel emotional.

"Those first two lines you have learned from Allah himself," she says, "they are so true."

"And what about the third?" I ask to test her.

"Uh, the third one isn't meant for a young woman," she replies.

I knew beforehand that this was true. Everything has gone according to plan.

"So now I've cut out your husband, haven't I?" I say, wanting to take advantage of it.

But she doesn't agree about that, nor does she agree when I try to take advantage of the situation. I'm not altogether to her taste—I have no belt around my middle and no shining weapons in my belt, nor are my eyes deliciously dark.

Then I begin to disparage the shepherd and to make cruel fun of his cap. "Do you think I ever saw such a monstrosity on my travels around the world?" I ask. "Never." That took care of the cap. "And what kind of boots is he wearing? Rags, my dear lady, rags!" Whereas I could show her what over- and undergarments civilized people use, if my tact didn't require me to be buttoned up.

Nevertheless, I show her my vest buckle, which she takes for hat trim. I press my arm tightly against my wallet while we're busy with this, in order not to tempt this child of nature. She is also surprised at my mother-of-pearl buttons. She hasn't even seen cloth buttons before. But when she discovers the fittings on my suspenders she declares herself conquered and insists, with a slight exaggeration, that it's far more ingenious than her husband's belt. I promise her a pair of suspenders. Suddenly she says, the little devil, "That third line is for a young woman, after all! Now I understand it!"

Then I can't help nodding with satisfaction, my whole plan having proven so wonderfully right. And I remove my suspenders on the spot and present them to her.

In short, she is getting awakened. On the very same starry night she promises me she will start a women's movement in Caucasia. "And the last line I added for the rhyme," I say finally, "it's better that way if you should wish to sing it." I imagine that my verse could become a national anthem in these parts. . . .

This was my plan. But how will the herdsman react to it? Blood revenge is rampant in Caucasia; old Shamil abolished it in Daghestan and Chechnya, but didn't overcome it elsewhere. The herdsman certainly looked sinister enough, and already at this point I take the precaution of offering him another cigarette. "Please!" I said, bowing. He took the cigarette and lighted it. His composure makes me suspicious; when Tiberius[30] was courteous he was the most dangerous. Perhaps you're one of those who sneak up on a person, I think apropos of the herdsman; you act as if nothing were the matter but watch for your chance. That's exactly what you look like!

One had better stay close to the horse.

I say good-bye and step out of the cave onto open ground. The herdsman follows. Frightened, I don't cast as much as a glance up at the roof; I only saw with half-closed eyes that the favorite wife was leaning on her elbow up there, looking imploringly at me. When I approached the horse to mount it, the herdsman called to me, pointing to the adjacent cave, where he wanted me to go. *A trap!* I think to myself, but I have to act nonchalant to keep his viciousness and bloodthirst in check. Far from giving up, he trudged over to the house and beckoned to me, so I was obliged to follow.

The house looks like the previous one. Here the herdsman let me examine the roof without objection. It was flat, made of stone slabs resting on wooden rafters; it was anything but water-tight. The door opening here is considerably darker than the other one; it probably led deep into the mountain, so deep that no sigh nor scream could penetrate to the outside world from there. The murderer enters this door opening and beckons to me.

I began to debate with myself. It might be a scientific door

91

opening of the first rank, and an inner voice bade me do my duty and examine it. However, I maintained that my certain death was of no use to science. Duty—what was that? Being eager to serve. Quite so, but even a dog is eager to serve: however tired it may be, it will always retrieve. And a human being should be a little more highly developed than an animal, right?

I argued pro and con, and considering the difficult circumstances I couldn't blame myself for my state of indecision. For that matter, I've often been put off by a sly and mechanical certainty; a little weakness, a bit of vacillation that was nothing but tact, really made it more agreeable for people to live with one another.

Then the herdsman laughs and tries even harder to make me enter, and his favorite wife over on the roof now seems to mock me as she lies there leaning on her elbow. She was in cahoots with the scoundrel, was she? That caused me to make up my mind. I would show her! I clenched my teeth and stepped into the cave. That is, my scientific interest won out.

It was dark in there, but the herdsman lights a kind of lamp here too. It's made of iron and has a woolen thread for a wick; the light is poor, but it's good enough for a stabbing.

I'm on the point of rushing at the man to forestall him when the herdsman uncovers two small animals in a nest of ferns on the floor. They are two bear cubs. I stare at the animals and at the man and feel more courageous. He says something, of which I can make out the word "rubl'"; he picks up one of the bear cubs and holds it out to me, wanting to sell it.

All at once I have the upper hand. That poor stunted Tatar has nothing but peaceful commercial intentions. I act superior, crinkling my nose at his having in reality invited me to a cowshed; there are even some fat goats standing by the wall, and the man begins to milk the goats and give the milk to the cubs.

"How many rubl'?" I ask, holding up five fingers.

The man shakes his head.

I hold up ten fingers, but he shakes his head again. Out of curiosity concerning Caucasian bear prices, I would have liked to know the man's asking price, and I was sorry I didn't know more Arabic than "*Salam aleikum.*" The man unsheathes his dagger and scratches some marks in the earthen floor. He scratches twenty marks before he stops. That means there will be no deal. He crosses out five marks. Then I exclaim, "Fifteen marks for a bear chick? Never!"

Whereupon I left the cowshed.

My mission was finished. I could report home that I was bringing copious scientific results, adding that I would need at least four years to work them up. With a composure and confidence I hadn't felt so far on this whole expedition, I went up to my horse and patted it and was its master. Then that accursed old herdsman stretched out his hand. I put up with him and gave him a last cigarette. He stretched out his hand once more, and I nodded to him to let him know that I was still favorably disposed toward him and tossed a copper coin into his hand. Then I swung myself onto my steed.

Once mounted, I sent the women on the roof a wonderfully supportive glance, to the effect that they should wake up in Caucasia, wake up and sing my verse and get out of their sorry plight.

Then I rode off. . . .

I rode straight down the mountain and eventually found the main road to the station. It was now well into the night, almost morning; but since it's just the moment of transition when the stars disappear and daylight hasn't yet broken through, it's getting darker. I meet up with the highway and ride along it, ride hard to reach the station before it gets light. I suddenly call to mind that horse theft is the most dishonorable act in this country, and I instantly feel anxious. What would happen to me now?

But it went very well. I took care not to ride the horse too hard, so it wouldn't be in a sweat; and, you know, these remarkable Caucasian horses are made of iron and endure everything, nothing bothers them—with the exception of too cold water.

The day was breaking. When I sighted the station I dismounted and led the horse straight up to the cart instead of following the road any further. And this saved me. I would otherwise have run into two burnous-clad men who came down the road, chatting. They looked up at me as I was tying the horse to the cart in the old way, but they probably thought that the stranger was simply patting the animal. Which was certainly true.

I walk down to the station. Here and there near the houses tall figures walk about, shouting some word or name and being answered from nearby or far away. By a stone wall at some distance from the houses, I find a man who is playing an instrument. These Caucasians are simply incredible, they never go to bed! The man is alone, sitting on the ground with his back up against the wall and playing as best he can. And it's still dark, you know, it's half past four, and besides it's cold. Perhaps the man is mad, I think to myself. But his music makes good sense, although it's poor and monotonous. He produces a whistling sound, like that of a shawm.

Feeling it takes too long before Kornei comes, I go into the backyard and call out his name at random. And Kornei does indeed reply; he wasn't far away. "*Totchas!*" right away, he answers, coming. I show him the number five on my watch and look at him. Kornei nods and explains that he's making himself ready.

But Kornei didn't even come at six o'clock. My traveling companion and I eat breakfast and get all set, but Kornei doesn't come. Then I felt a slight resentment against Kornei.

Not until half past six did he pull up in front of the entrance door.

VIII

It's a cool morning. There is hoarfrost on the ground and, unlike yesterday, the road doesn't give off dust. Kornei is not the same as yesterday either; he sits silent on the box and doesn't hum. The three horses jog along, but in a little while, when the climb increases again, they move at a walking pace for ever so long.

The Terek Valley is at an end; the river curves into the mountains and away from our route. There is no vegetation anymore. Up from us sits a naked knoll, and at a place where we can see the road going zigzag all the way to the top, we get off and take a shortcut uphill, while the carriage makes one turn after another until it has reached us. From up here we again get a glimpse of the ice-covered Kazbek peak, which points up at the sky in the morning sun.

We again drive up the mountainside. Here and there the road is roofed over on account of avalanches and landslides. It's as though we are driving through tunnels with iron roofs over us. In many places the road has collapsed and repairs are going on; inspectors and engineers point and give orders to crowds of workmen. Of other people we again see herdsmen with huge flocks of sheep.

At another naked knoll Kornei stops the horse and leads us to a cross and a spring. He takes water into his hand and shows it to us; the water is boiling. Like him, we drink from the spring. The water is ice-cold but it boils, throwing off beads of foam; our hands turn white in the water, which tastes like club soda.

We keep going higher and higher; the hoarfrost persists and we have to wrap ourselves in our blankets again because of the cold. We'll soon be at the highest point on our journey; my altimeter indicates almost 3,000 meters. A stone statue with an inscription gives the height in feet. Here Kornei unhitches one of the horses and ties it up to the back of the carriage. For from now on the horses won't have to pull anymore, but only make themselves heavy and hold back.

We start downhill right away. Up here there is no

plateau—the road is laid along the mountain ridge as the only passable place. The tall mountains round about are green and bare, and here too there are little haycocks to the very top.

The horses trot evenly downhill, at times slipping a step or two because they cannot hold back the carriage; but they do not fall. From Russian novels one receives the impression that in Russia they drive at an unheard-of speed. Pictures of Russian couriers also often show the horses in a fabulous chase, and even so the coachman's whip points skyward. So we had formed the idea that we probably couldn't avoid racing across the Caucasus with a four-in-hand, coming down on the other side like a pair of lunatics. We were surprised by the fact that the speed was very reasonable. Either Kornei Grigorevich was particularly careful with his horses, which he no doubt was, or the Russian poets and painters had exaggerated, which they no doubt had. Of all the drivers we saw from the train through Russia, there wasn't a single one who drove conspicuously fast. If, on the other hand, you are interested in riding at breakneck speed, I know no better country for you than Finland. In Finnish cities I've experienced the utmost in that respect. The small Finnish horses, which resemble our West Norwegian breed, rush like the wind through the streets, and rounding the corners I've more than once floated on one wheel. The Finns feed their horses well and drive them hard; when I pleaded for the horse at times, I was called a "horse weeper," with a smile. I have only once in my life reported a man to the police, and that man was a Finnish cabman. . . .

The fever, a wakeful night, and the cold up here make me drowsy; I doze now and then and feel fine. At long intervals we meet carts hitched to two or four buffalo; as we drive slowly past them, the even rhythm of our carriage is broken and I wake up. We also pass a few flint-stone houses up here on the heights, herdsmen's dwellings where the women sit on the roof in attractive blue sarafans working with yarn for rugs or clothes. When we pass they look at us briefly, talking among themselves, but when we look back a moment later, they have resumed their work. Half-naked children run after us for long stretches and can be driven back only with a copper coin.

The road is becoming rougher than ever, and the iron roofs over it more frequent. During the spring thaw I bet there are quite interesting avalanches hurtling along these roofs. On our left we see nothing but a bit of wall and beyond that the precipice. I've never seen such precipices before; I have to get down from the carriage occasionally and go on foot, keeping close to the rock wall. But the depths lure you, they lure you on. Looking down there now and then, I make out through my field glasses tiny little patches of fields at the bottom. When I sit in the carriage I hold on very firmly.

The sun beams at us, the spot of wax on my jacket has vanished completely, and we remove the blankets. Downhill it goes, always downhill; the chasms become even more terrifying; we wind our way in zigzag down through the gorges. The road is often collapsed, and burnous-clad men are repairing it. Kornei is not particularly attentive—he lets the horses stumble rather more than necessary, because he likes to gape into the depths sitting there on his high seat. We pass the Gudaur station in this manner.

Here there are many properly built stone houses, even one with two stories. The surroundings are bare, hard as rock, but it looks clean and pleasant here; some people stand in the doorways watching us as we pass the station. The idea occurs to me that it's Sunday today, though it's only Friday; these people standing in the doorways looked so free and contented. Maybe they follow Mohammedan custom, so that today really is their holy day.

We continue downhill in long zigzags, in and out between the rock walls. The telegraph wires that accompany us are some-times fastened to the rock, but sometimes they run underground because of the avalanches. I no longer go on foot; it's just too slow, delaying the whole expedition—but I'd much rather be on foot, for the sake of my nerves. A mail coach, with an armed seven-men Cossack escort, is approaching from the opposite direction; the driver blows his horn and we give way and stop while it passes. Then it's downhill once more.

Kornei sits with slack reins looking somnolently into the endless depths; if one of the horses slips, another must back it up. I don't dare take hold of Kornei and shake him, because then he would have his attention distracted even further from the horses. I have to let matters take their course. Here the road, built above the naked rock wall, rests on iron logs; it is hanging in the air. However, we didn't see this until we had wound our way down the mountain in several hairpin turns; then we put our heads back and looked up at the route we had traveled. The sight made us tremble.

In one of the worst places, where even the small miserable wall on the outer edge of the road had collapsed, two little boys of six or eight pop up and begin to dance and turn somersaults for us. The little depraved creatures no doubt had a permanent begging station here when the traffic was busy. I was deeply annoyed that they popped up so suddenly, even making the horses shy toward the rock wall, so I tried to chase them away with my excellent stick from Vladikavkaz; but it was no use. They continued their dance and, what's more, had the daredevil cheek to turn a little somersault on the shoulder at a point where the wall had disappeared into the abyss. There was nothing for it but to get out one's pennies and pay them. They looked at us with the most audacious, wide-open eyes and pretended not to have the faintest idea of the reason for His Excellency's furious mien. When they had picked up the money from the road, they again crept outside the wall on the edge of the precipice, where they must have had a small foothold to stand on. And if another carriage happened to come by in the course of the day, they would again flip their little bodies onto the road and dance their perilous dance.

Along the inner edge of the road where the sun shines, coltsfoots and shaggy thistles grow; eventually we come across dandelions and a blue carnation that is extraordinarily attractive; farther down we encounter red clover. Our descent goes on hour after hour, though the horses trot all along. After nearly three hours we finally reach a somewhat flatter road; we are at the Mleti station and will take a rest. Mleti is situated 1,500 meters above sea level, so in the last three hours we have come down 1,500 meters from the top of the mountain. Here the sun is hot, and in addition to the blankets we have discarded as much clothing as possible.

Kornei wants to rest for four hours. Astounded, I yell and

shake my head at him for a long while. Kornei then points at the sun and gives us to understand that the heat will get worse, but in the course of four hours it will abate somewhat; nevertheless we will reach the Ananuri station before evening. We think it over and examine our contour map: it's still forty versts to Ananuri, but thirty-five versts of the road slope sharply downhill, so it will go very fast. We let Kornei have his four hours and wave to him that, all right, we're agreed.

~

Here in Mleti the telegraph wires are fourfold. Outside our window there are rowan trees loaded with berries, and a short distance from the station there is a hazel copse; but otherwise there is no vegetation. It's the haying season, and a needlessly large crowd of laborers are carting hay from the fields. Mleti is a big place, maybe the biggest of all in the mountains, but the uncleanliness is very bad, here as elsewhere. After we felt obliged to clean our knives and forks on our napkins, it turned out that the napkins themselves had to be discarded, forcing us to use our handkerchiefs. But here, too, the food was tasty; we simply had to avoid thinking of how it might have been handled in the kitchen.

While we were dining, a gentleman suddenly stepped into the room and stood there looking at us. We return his look in amazement: it was our fellow traveler from the train, the officer who was supposed to have accompanied us over the mountains but got off and went to Pyatigorsk. He gave a start when he recognized us, turned upon his heel and went out the door without saying a word. No carriage had reached the station since our arrival, so the officer got here before we did, and this was incomprehensible to us. He had interrupted his stay in Pyatigorsk ahead of time and had used the days we stopped in Vladikavkaz to slip past us—was that it? And why had he made all this fuss about avoiding us? After all, we hadn't wanted his companionship. And why had he stopped in Mleti?

When I was smoking by myself on the veranda after dinner, the officer came through the door and straight up to me. He tipped his hat and said in English that I was no doubt surprised to see him here. I replied that I really hadn't considered where the officer rightly ought to be at the moment. Then he just looked at me and didn't ask me any further questions.

"You didn't stay long in Pyatigorsk," I said to be polite.

"No," he replied, "I finished my business there earlier than expected."

Sitting down while he was on his feet, I got up, but after standing for a few moments I turned my back on him and went in.

The officer followed.

In the corridor was a flight of stairs up to the second floor; the officer stopped at the stairs and invited me to come up with him.

At first I wanted to go on into the dining room, to show I felt offended by this stranger, but then the thought flashes upon me that I am in Russia, after all, and that many Russians are a bit different from other people.

"What do you want?" I asked.

"Be so kind as to follow me to my room," he replied politely. "I want to tell you something."

After thinking it over for a moment, I followed him, although I disliked his face.

When we entered his room he closed the door and the window, in spite of the heat.

"Please sit down," he said. "Of course, you're surprised to find me here. The fact is, I finished my business in Pyatigorsk sooner than expected."

"You already told me that," I said.

"I was looking for a man but didn't find him."

"What man? Why should he be a concern of mine?"

"Right. In any case, let me tell you at once that I intend to speak politely."

Laughing, I asked, "You do? Thanks."

"You must've noticed that I started when I caught sight of you on entering the dining room downstairs a little while ago. That start was an act."

"An act? Really."

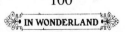

"I knew you were sitting there."

"Well, so what?"

"And when I left the train and went to Pyatigorsk I didn't thereby let you out of my sight."

Growing impatient, I said, "Listen, my good man, what do you want with me?"

"I'm traveling on official business," he said. "My travel actually concerns someone else, but that doesn't mean that I neglect my business with you. Where do you come from?"

"From Finland."

He picked up a document, looked at it and said, "That's correct."

"Correct?" I exclaimed. "What's correct?" I was really beginning to imagine the possibility that it was a police officer I was dealing with, and therefore I replied that I came from Finland, which was the truth.

"We Russians aren't hard people, you know," he went on. "I'm reluctant to make trouble for you on your journey."

"On the contrary, it's a pleasure to talk to you," I replied.

I quickly considered what he might want with me if he were a police officer. Naturally, he made a ridiculous mistake when thinking he had a quarrel with me. I came from Finland, where I'd lived for a year, had done nothing wrong, had never attempted to do anything wrong. I had given a lecture at the University of Helsingfors, but it was on a literary subject, and a couple of articles that I'd written for Finnish papers had also been about literary topics. I was of no importance whatsoever in a political context.

"You're going to the Orient?" the officer asked.

"Yes. But would you, please, tell me what you want from me."

"What I want?" he replied. "I would prefer to let you go about your travels. We Russians aren't hard people, you know. But I have my orders."

"You do?" I said, laughing. "And what is the nature of your orders?"

"Permit me to ask you a question," the officer replied.

"Weren't all post horses engaged when you got to Vladikavkaz?"

"Yes. A company of Frenchmen had hired all the horses for a week."

Then the officer smiled and said, "I was the one who had hired them."

"You?"

"By telegram from Pyatigorsk."

"Well. And so what?"

"I wanted to have your departure postponed for a day, so that I could get to the mountains ahead of you."

This sounded unbelievable, but it was said by a grown-up man sitting right there.

"Perhaps you could tell me what you really want with me," I said.

The officer replied, "I'm going to arrest you."

"Why? For what?"

"Well, all that you'll know later. I'm not an examining magistrate. I only have my orders."

"And your orders are to arrest me?"

"Yes."

I sat awhile thinking it over.

"I don't believe you," I said, rising.

The officer walked up to the window, leaving me free to use the door if I wanted to. This made an impression on me.

"In any case, you're making an egregious mistake," I said. "You're mistaking me for someone else. Here's my passport."

And I showed him my passport.

He looked at the passport, read in it, closed it again and returned it to me.

"I know all this already," he said. "I knew that your passport was in order."

"Then you will admit that you've got the wrong person, won't you?"

"The wrong person?" he replied with a hint of impatience. He took some photographs from his pocket, all of the same size, unmounted. He selected one of them and handed it to me.

I could scarcely believe my eyes: it was a photograph of myself. It took some time before I recovered from my surprise—I forgot to look at the photographer's name, forgot to look at the clothes I was photographed in; anyhow, I didn't recognize the picture, had never seen it before, but it was a profile of me.

After the picture had been returned to him and put back in his wallet, my suspicion was awakened and I said, "That picture couldn't, by any chance, have been taken in the train to Vladikavkaz, could it? I don't remember seeing it before. Let me take another look at it."

He hesitated. "Wasn't it your picture?" he asked.

"Please let me see it again," I said. "It was a snapshot—I thought I recognized the clothes, the very same I'm wearing now."

He made his decision and quickly handed me the picture once more, saying, "Of course they are the same clothes you're wearing now. I photographed you in the train. That's what I always do when I shadow someone. So you see, I haven't got the wrong person."

Since he took it that way, it again sounded reasonable, and once more I felt rather strangely affected for a moment. If this man arrested me, our whole itinerary would be screwed up; moreover, God only knows what endless troubles I might get into in this country, where I couldn't hold my own. Rather crestfallen, I said, "Under other circumstances it would've been a pleasure to let myself be arrested, for the sake of giving some variety to my travels, but right now it's rather inconvenient. I'm not alone."

"I'm very sorry about that," he replied. "I wish I could spare both you and your companion."

I thought the situation over in earnest. "Where, then, will you take me?" I asked.

"I'm going to take you back to Vladikavkaz," he replied.

"Will you arrest both of us?" I then asked.

"No, only you," he replied.

Back over the mountains again! I had nothing against the trip per se, but our travel to the Orient would be delayed or perhaps come to nothing.

"Couldn't you take me to Tiflis instead?" I asked. "Tiflis is on our way, and in Baku there is a consul we can turn to; he will clear up this little misunderstanding in no time."

The officer deliberated. "To do my part in getting you out of trouble as soon as possible, I'll take you to Tiflis," he replied.

"I'm very grateful to you," I said.

We both sized up the situation. Then he bowed and said, "You may go anywhere you like until we depart."

My suspicion wouldn't quite leave me and I asked, "Why did you say at first that you would take me to Vladikavkaz?"

"*First* to Vladikavkaz," he replied, once again betraying some impatience. "I would first bring you to Vladikavkaz. That would also have been most convenient for you. Because actually you will be going to St. Petersburg."

"Ah."

"And if I take you to Tiflis, it's simply to comply with your personal wish. But it's against my orders."

"Let me see your papers," I said abruptly.

Smiling, he took from his pocket a large stamped document, which he presented to me. The language and the characters were Russian, so I didn't understand any of it. But the officer pointed here and there in the document, explaining that *there* was his name, *there* it said that he was a police officer, and *there* it said finally that, wherever he went, the police should assist him.

Not daring to go any further, I retreated and fell silent.

"Then perhaps you'll permit me to go down and inform my companion that our journey has been interrupted," I said.

"I'm considering it," he replied after a moment. "And I'm mostly considering it for the sake of your companion. Well, don't misunderstand me, also for your sake. It will be very unpleasant for you both."

"Just let's get to Tiflis and we'll be home free."

"I'm reluctant to deprive you of your high hopes," he replied, "but I must warn you that getting home free may take a long time."

"But I've done absolutely nothing wrong!" I cried.

"Of course not. I believe you. But to prove that will require much time and a great deal of unpleasant work. Take my word for it."

And in regard to this I believed him. I felt uneasy again and stared at the floor, absorbed in thought.

"There may possibly be a way out," he said. "I'm merely mentioning it."

"There is a way out?"

"There *may* be a way out. With a little mutual good will."

"How?"

"We Russians aren't hard people, you know," he said. "We occasionally come to terms with one another."

I stared at the man. "Can I come to terms with you?" I asked.

He shrugged his shoulders and, spreading out his arms in a Jewish gesture, said, "There is a way out. The suggestion of a way."

Then I instantly felt safe and burst out laughing. I patted his shoulder and said, "You are magnificent, a real gem! How can I reward you for the last half hour's entertainment?"

He stood there calmly, on his dignity, letting me pat him on the shoulder.

"I've witnessed many such exclamations," he said. "I readily permit them. They provide relief, after all."

"But now you must pardon my leaving," I said. "And you will also pardon me for continuing my journey to Tiflis in our own carriage and without you."

"I have no objection to that," he replied. "But at every single station where you stop, be prepared to find me taking a rest too. You'll arrive in Ananuri this evening; so will I."

"Welcome!" I said and left.

He wouldn't come, of course. He was not a police officer, he was a poor swindler who was trying to blackmail me. He had probably been to Pyatigorsk and gambled away his pennies, and now he found himself in the Caucasus and couldn't get any further; he was stuck.

I would put him completely out of my mind and not say a word about the man to my traveling companion.

We left Mleti.

IX

We are traveling along another river, the Aragvi. It's just as large and beautiful as the Terek and accompanies us all the way. The mountains are the same as on the other side, three to four thousand meters high, some bare and green from the very floor of the valley up to the clouds, others shaggy, overgrown to the top with dense, very dense, leafy scrub. Among the measly flora along the road, we see cranesbill, mustard, and yellow hollyhocks completely coated with lime dust. The human dwellings are also the same as on the other side, and here and there we pass herdsmen, flocks of cattle, and road workers. It is very dusty and the sun is scorching; Kornei's back is covered with flies.

We come to a two-story stone house with corbiestep gables, German style, familiarly Teutonic. A black-and-white painted bar extends across the road; here the Russian authorities collect toll. When Kornei presents his receipt, showing that the toll was paid in Vladikavkaz, the bar goes up and we drive through.

After a long downward ride in the mountains we come to the Pasanauri station, which we leave at once. Here there are several private-looking stone villas, snow-white with limewash; a Russian chapel in the most variegated colors, brown, blue, and red, rises above everything. We have again descended about four hundred meters, the vegetation is becoming richer, and the valley is very hot. The population consists of Georgians and lives in the same kinds of shelf-like houses we have seen before, one above the other up the mountainside.

At an immense gap in the mountain range, we see on our left, far, far off by itself, another valley where there are villages and huts like here and small yellow fields up the rocky slopes. There, too, people live, we think to ourselves, and they may be just as happy as we are; they too have their joys and griefs, their work and their rest. And in youth they have their loves and in old age their patch of field and their sheep.

There is nothing, nothing in the world like being away from everything! I go on thinking. That I can remember from my childhood, when I was tending the cattle back home. In good weather I would lie on my back in the heather and write with my index finger across the sky and have a glorious time of it. I let the cattle wander at their sweet will for hours on end, and when I had to find them again I simply got up on a knoll or climbed a tall tree and listened, my mouth open. Up there I could hear very well where the sound of the bells came from, and as soon as I heard it I found the cattle. The billygoats would now and then get a quid of tobacco that I'd stolen for them, and the cows got salt. And I taught the rams how to play at butting with me.

It was a wonderful life. And whatever one might think, it was no worse in rainy weather. Then I would sit beneath a bush or a crag and be well protected. I would sit there and sing, or I would write something or other on white birch bark, or carve something with my sheath knife. I knew every spot in the pasture, and when I had to catch up with the cattle I simply moved on to another crag I knew of and continued to have a good time. No one who hasn't been brought up that way from youth upward can have any idea of the delicate, mysterious pleasure one can feel being out in the wild in rainy weather and sitting in a hideout. I have since attempted to write about it, but without success. I wanted to try shaping it up a bit in order to be understood, but then I lost it.

I wore pattens, or clogs, when tending cattle, and in rainy weather I naturally got my feet wet in the soggy pasture. But though I was soaked, the pleasure I felt having that good, warm wood under my soles tops any ten pleasures I've had in later years. It was probably because I didn't know any better at the time. And yet I discriminated every bit as well as I do now between what felt good and what was painful. During the mushroom season in late summer the cattle ran like crazy after mushrooms. The cows especially went wild, but since the cows wore the bells, they pulled the entire herd along with them in their frenzy. Then the herder had to be on his feet almost all day and got little rest. My puny body was sore and aching from the ceaseless running around day after day, and the only amusement I had was to look for mushrooms and give them to the cows I was most fond of. Mushrooms made the cows give lots of milk. Anyway, it wasn't much fun to be a herder at that time of year. Oh no.

I think about all this as I roll forward in a carriage on a wide road in the Caucasus. I feel so strange, as though I could put down roots here and be blissfully shut off from the world. It would be a different matter if I had sufficient culture to take advantage of my present life, but I don't. . . . I take a last look into the valley on my left, where the small yellow tilled patches, the flocks of sheep, and the little huts are, and it strikes me as being wonderfully attractive and peaceful. Up in the mountains, large eagles are sailing above the flocks. The village has a festive air. Today, no doubt, the herdsmen have polished their shiny belts and are now showing off in front of their favorite girls.

I doze and think and drop off. After a couple of hours we begin to come across chestnut trees; we're still going down, and the horses are trotting.

A caravan of empty carts is coming toward us, drawn by buffalo; the drivers lie sprawling on the bottom of their carts, asleep. We swerve aside and slip past. But one ox has got the yoke between its horns, wrenching its neck crooked, and it has to walk sideways. My traveling companion requests permission to get off and straighten the yoke, but when we explain to Kornei what it is about, he doesn't stop but continues to drive, not understanding a word. Anyway, we are now well past the caravan, it's too late to do anything, and Kornei puts the horses to the trot again. And the buffalo will go on like that for miles and miles, mute, staring, with a twisted neck. The mood in the carriage immediately worsens, which is not surprising. But time, the hours, smooths out everything: after a while I hit upon the solace that there are people who suffer, too. The sooner such an ox is worked to death under the yoke, the better. That is its hope. It's like when people are in agony and remind themselves that they still have the alternative of making life as short as they please. Nietzsche is right: this alternative has comforted many a human being at night. . . .

The hours go by, time passes. The wonderland is beautiful once more.

At a watering hole good old Kornei Grigorevich again allows a strange carriage to pass us. It's a Russian family. They are driving faster than we are. We saw these people at Kobi, but since we started such a long time ahead of them this morning, they shouldn't have been able to overtake us. Now we'll be riding in the dust they raise and we won't be able to breathe.

I punch Kornei's shoulder, giving him to understand what he has done. He looks at me horror-struck for a moment and stops the horses. But he doesn't seem to understand anything and wants to drive on. Then I jump off and hold the horses; all in all, I act quite high-and-mighty toward Kornei, whose surprise at the strange sickness I must have caught becomes greater and greater. He sees the dust hovering above the roadway where the carriage has gone, it burns his eyes as well as ours, being lime dust, and it covers the carriage with a white coating; but Kornei doesn't grasp that we cannot drive in it. I have to hold the horses for five minutes before we can go on. It begins to dawn on me why commands, a tsar's word, are necessary in this great nation. In certain matters these people are so stupid. They can waddle out on the steppe and tend sheep and stand out in the field doing a few tricks with a spade, but when it comes to abstract things their brains are stupid. I promise myself to have it out with Kornei in Tiflis.

The moon is already quite bright; it's five o'clock, the sun and the moon light up the landscape at the same time, and it's very warm. This world is like no other world I know, and again I come to think I could wish to remain here for life. We have now descended far enough for vineyards to start again, there are nuts in the woods, and the sun and moon try to outshine each other. One is helpless before this splendor, and if one lived here one could watch it every day and beat one's breast with wonder. The people that lives here has endured struggles that threatened to destroy it, but it overcame everything; strong and sound and flourishing, it is today a people of ten millions. The Caucasian native doesn't know the difference between a bull and bear market on the New York stock exchange; his life is not a race—he has time to live and can shake his food from the trees or butcher his sheep to live on. But the

110

Europeans and the Yankees are greater people, aren't they? God knows. God and no one else knows, it's that doubtful. Some are great because the surroundings are small, because the century is small, despite everything. I'm thinking of great names in my own field only, and there are a large number in a long row, members of the proletariat of geniuses. I would exchange a score of them for the horse from Marengo.[31] The value of values is mutable: the nimbus of the theater *there* corresponds to a shiny belt *here*, and time takes them both, exchanging them for other values. Oh Caucasia, Caucasia! It's not for nothing that the greatest literary giants the world knows, the great Russians, have visited you and drawn from your springs. . . .

It's six o'clock. We are now two thousand meters lower than we were at the highest point of the Daryal pass. The sun has set, only the moon is shining, and it's warm and quite still. Suddenly the road starts rising again and we ride at a walking pace. The mountains are becoming smaller, turning into long ridges with the sky sailing above them. It's quickly getting dark. We are at the Ananuri station.

On this warm evening there are many people out in the yard and on the veranda. We get off and go in. A man who seems to be the innkeeper says something to us and bars our way. He doesn't speak Russian, but presumably one of the Caucasian languages. We put our things down without bothering about the innkeeper. Suddenly a burnous-clad man addresses us in the most fast-spoken French, explaining that there isn't a single vacancy at the station.

So what was to be done?

He calls down to a little man in an enormous burnous on the road. His name is Grigor. As soon as Grigor hears what it is about, he nods, indicating that we can have lodgings, and points further on.

We fetch our things, climb into the carriage and drive on. Grigor runs alongside. He must be around fifty, but he runs like a boy, although he's wearing that enormous caftan and is carrying many weapons.

Grigor takes us to a strange two-story stone house that rests on stone pillars. I'd never seen the like before. The house also had the quaintest holes, shelters, and hiding places. We were shown into a room upstairs. Could we have this room for ourselves? Yes. Our luggage is brought in. Could we have steak, potatoes, bread, and beer? Grigor nods and flutters down the stairs in his burnous.

We go out and look around: quite low dark mountains, moonlight; directly south, the towers and domes of a monastery whose copper roof is luminous in the moonlight. Viewed against the dark background, these shining domes possess a singular beauty. Down in the road are people and horses; a mail coach driver rushes past, blowing his trumpet.

When we get back, Grigor comes to tell us that he has been to the station but without being able to find any beefsteaks. On the other hand, if we would like something else—? And Grigor pulls a live chicken from the breast of his burnous. We nod that chicken is excellent, too. And Grigor flutters down again.

After a while Grigor has beheaded the chicken. From our window we see a light in the courtyard: it's Grigor lighting a fire and about to play cook. The fireplace is in the open, with sunflower stalks, which here are like small trees and burn superbly, being used for fuel. Grigor puts a pot of water on the fire; when the water is warm enough he dips the chicken into it and begins to pluck it. In the light from the fire, he looks small and dark and fairy-like. Grigor does his job properly, singeing the last remnant of down off the chicken before he starts roasting it.

We get our food, which tastes first-rate, but already during the meal we're so severely bitten by bedbugs that we have to stop eating before we've finished. The beasts crawl up on us from the settle beds we sit on for lack of chairs. We'll have a lively night of it! comes the thought, and we decide to go to bed as late as possible. We go out again.

Grigor has a store downstairs; he's a businessman, and when he's not waiting on us he stands in his shop selling an assortment of pricey German merchandise, of which he has plenty. It's not without pride that he shows us this merchandise, which has come from so far away, from pocket mirrors to wallets and penknives. But there is a tall pile of Caucasian rugs in the shop, and we are more interested in looking at these. If only we weren't so far, far from home! And if only the rugs weren't so heavy! But they're not expensive. They are woven with great art. The women who created them had plenty of time, an infinite amount of time.

Outside it's quiet, no traffic on the road anymore, but people have by no means gone to sleep. Here and there men sit talking together at the roadside, behaving the way neighbors would at home: they rest their arms on their knees, fiddle with a straw, and smoke their pipes. The station's horses are nibbling here and there on the grounds, and some distance away, by the wall of a house, somebody is playing a string instrument and singing to the music. We listen and draw closer. A young boy sits there and sings; his song is monotonous but captivating in the calm of evening. The melody makes us think of the ballads that Thor Lange[32] has published; now we can understand his texts with the heart, and we realize what a fine poet this Dane in exile is.

It's getting late, but the boy goes on playing by the wall, and young and old sit talking beside the road. The people take their time; an hour or two doesn't make any difference to them. There is a heavy dew and the ground is wet, but the people here bear with the humidity, being brought up to do so from their youth. When they stand up and walk, however, it's as though steel springs are walking. The men are like that throughout Caucasia; even the herdsmen and the ox drivers walk light and straight, with elastic movements and their chests thrust forward. But one doesn't see much of the women; they keep mostly to themselves. Mohammedanism is still maintaining its grip.

When we get back to the inn, our settle beds have been made, with a pair of Caucasian rugs on the bottom of each bedstead. To please us, Grigor has given us new rugs from his shop. It will no doubt be a bit hard to sleep here, but the beds are amusing and the rugs gorgeous.

Then, seeing that we haven't brought sheets with us, which is customary, Grigor has the inspiration that my traveling companion ought to have one. Grigor is a cultivated man, his life as a businessman has given him a strong sense of cleanliness; he's plagued by an inability to endure the sight of a bed without sheets. To show him how generals deport themselves in the field, I wrap myself in the rugs and go to bed in my clothes, without undressing. And Grigor lets it happen as a matter of course; he doesn't interfere with the general's filthy habits—however, he flutters down into his store and tears off a couple of ells of canvas, which he presents to my traveling companion for a sheet. When he has done so, he bows and leaves. For a while we wonder whether to take the rugs outside and shake them thoroughly before using them, but abandon the thought in order not to hurt Grigor. And so we go to bed banking on our luck.

Then someone taps on the window.

Going out, I find Kornei outside. He wants to arrange the time for our departure in the morning. I grab Kornei by his collar and walk him down the stairs. Once we can see by the light from the store, I point at my watch to let him know we would start at five o'clock.

Kornei sticks to six o'clock.

Then a voice addresses Kornei in his mother tongue; turning about, I stand face to face with the officer. So that damn police officer was pursuing us after all, as he had said. He greets me lightly, before again turning to Kornei with unparalleled authority and saying a few brief words. Then he takes out his watch, points to the number five and says, "Five o'clock, as the prince has decided!" Next, he points down the road and says, "Go!" Whereupon Kornei tips his coachman's hat and instantly waddles off.

I was left alone with the officer.

"I hope you've found satisfactory lodgings," he said. "I'm staying at the station. I reproach myself for having reserved a room there, which you and your companion could otherwise have had. I didn't know the place was that full."

"We've obtained good lodgings," I replied, staring at him.

"Fine. Good night!" he said and went off.

He kept his promise and followed us. Once again my confidence began wavering. He could very well be a police officer, of course, even if he wanted me to come to terms with him. From what I'd read about Russian government officials, taking bribes was not an unheard-of thing among them; his hint of a way out was perhaps the very best indication that he was a police officer. It was no fun to know you were followed and persecuted this way, and tomorrow I would have to ask the man, in God's name, how much he demanded to let us go; otherwise he was capable of apprehending us the moment we entered Tiflis. I would go to him at the station early in the morning and purchase our freedom, so that our day would be without worries.

With this frailty in my heart I went to bed.

X

A very unpleasant night. The hard wooden bedboards and the terrible bedbugs kept us in a state of uninterrupted restlessness. Kornei came and knocked on our door at half past four, just after we had finally fallen deeply asleep.

However, Kornei had no intention of routing us out just then; far from having the horses ready outside, he came solely to find out if we couldn't delay our departure until six o'clock. Kornei was a pest and always would be.

I vacillated between smacking his face and giving in to his demand. I chose a middle course: I again seized him by the collar, led him down the stairs and out on the road, shook him, pointed in the direction of the horses and ordered him to fetch them. Kornei waddled off, but my imitation authority didn't exactly seem to have pierced him to the quick.

I could now use the wait to seek out the police officer, ask his pardon for coming so early, and hand him whatever sum he might demand. I wondered whether I could ask for a receipt, but that might offend him; such things were unnecessary between gentlemen. Lord only knows how much I would have to fork out! But I shall file a complaint and ask for the sum to be refunded, and if nothing else helped I would let the Russian government know that they could expect diplomatic complications.

But after a cold shower and an excellent breakfast of lamb that Grigor brought, my courage rose. The last hour's sound sleep hadn't hurt either; in short, my nerves were calm and strong—I was going to defy the officer. And if there was no getting out of it, let him catch me on entering Tiflis. What a tormentor, a real bloodhound! Catch me? He! Heh-heh, he was a swindler, a Jew who was having a stab at blackmail. I would report him to the police. If he came within my reach in this moment, I would chasten him! He would be wise to keep away.

I went about girding up my loins and feeling swell.

"Grigor, hey!"

Grigor comes.

What did I owe him for our stay?

"Six rubles."

"What's that?" I offer him two rubles. And get away with three. And even so we part as friends. There see, nobody could hold a candle to me when I really put myself out!

But Kornei doesn't come. At half past five I went out to look for him. I found him in a quiet, cozy chat with the Russian family's coachman, who had driven past us yesterday. Kornei's horses were hitched up, but he simply let them stand there while jabbering on.

When he caught sight of me he got a move on, jumped onto the box, and drove up. Ho-ho, how I would have it out with Kornei once we reached Tiflis.

By the time our things had been loaded onto the carriage, it was six o'clock; Kornei had forced his hour through. I was loath to leave the place like a tramp and went into the store to say good-bye to Grigor. As it happened, the police officer was in there, too. He surprised me once again. I abandoned my plan to chasten him and said a mechanical good-bye to Grigor.

The officer tipped his hat and addressed the following words to me: "You will take a rest at Chilkhany, where I too will rest. I'll be an hour behind you."

And I didn't knock him down on the spot; I was paralyzed by him and couldn't have taken care of anyone at that moment. How much courage could be expected anyway from somebody who had been awake for two nights in a row and was flush with Caucasian fever! I was excused on every count. God knows whether this almighty Russian chief detective didn't have handcuffs in his pocket into the bargain. After all, he *had* earlier on stopped all post horses in Vladikavkaz with one telegraphic word.

On the whole, my position was such that I had to capitulate and clear out. . . .

It's a calm, warm morning, still before daybreak. We drive past the monastery with the copper domes, but I tell myself that it's too dark to take a closer look at it. However, the truth is that I feel uneasy after my fresh encounter with the police officer. I'm not in the mood for anything. If only I could buck up and show some guts at our next meeting!

We drive uphill for a great many versts. I sleep for an hour; we are both asleep in the carriage—even Kornei himself is nodding on the box. After my sleep I'm brave again and ride in sheer joy.

It's getting more and more fertile around us every minute, though we are again gaining considerable altitude; there are woods on both sides of the road, woods of wild apple trees. The apples are small; taciturn brown men walk about here and there bagging them as the day is breaking. It's an enigma to me when the Caucasians sleep. Here these men are picking fruit at the crack of dawn, as if they haven't been doing anything else all night. I suppose they've lain in the woods overnight, to be up and about early today on account of the heat.

It's now full daylight and the road doesn't rise any longer; we are again going down. We are passing fairly large cultivated fields and there are wider vistas; women are carrying water up from the Aragvi River in jars on their shoulders. Again, it looks like Sunday morning to me; the landscape and the women are enveloped in an aura of festivity that greatly elevates my mood. Caucasian women are supposed to be small and unimpressive, I've read, and this may possibly be true in general; but these women were tall and slim and their walk was incomparable. They are mostly several together, but we can hear only subdued conversation among them. They come one after another up from the river, in a row, single file, the jars on their shoulders and one hand akimbo, in the Greek or Italian manner. We haven't seen anything resembling this; the women stride, or glide, in their blue-and-red sarafans and with silk kerchiefs on their heads.

Every time we saw these processions we did everything we could to get Kornei to drive more slowly so we would meet the women as they crossed the road. But that damn Kornei, who was a Molokan and had abjured the world, didn't pay attention to our gestures and signs. Anyway, as far as we could see, the women were anything but beautiful. Their complexion was muddy, with blue spots. But they were tall and slim like willows, and they had high bosoms.

Farther ahead, groups of young boys are playing along the road. They are as many as ten or twelve together, all under twenty. They leap and plunge lithely and recklessly in their play; when crossing a creek, they don't use the bridge but fling themselves over beside it. On the whole, they like to seek out obstacles. Though we drive straight through one of the groups, we don't hear any catcalls behind us; the boys are interested only in their game. Their faces are bright and lively. Only one of them is old and wealthy enough to have gotten a shiny belt; no wonder he walks among the others like a proud colt.

We arrive at the Dusheti station. Here the vineyards begin again—we are that far down. The station is situated a short distance from the town, which we can see half a verst away; it's supposed to have about four thousand inhabitants. There is an old church, big and tall; the stone walls of a fortress and a massive tower are reminders of times past when the princes of Aragvi were at war with the Georgians.

We pass the station.

Our road doesn't run between mountains anymore; there are wide tracts of grassland and grainfields. Some mountains can still be seen behind us and on our left, but they don't look high anymore, being so far away.

We can now see the road up to three versts ahead, and on both sides people are everywhere at work in the fields; some are plowing, others are mowing the yellow short-strawed grain. They plow with eight to ten or twelve buffalo to every plow, two and two together, in a long procession. We once saw eighteen buffalo hitched to one and the same plow, with four men to drive them. Every time the furrow was done and the plow had to be turned around, it was quite a trick to get the buffalo straightened out again. The drivers have long whips that they use to flick any buffalo that has it coming; moreover, they shout at the animals, using an assortment of sounds and howls, and make a lot of noise.

Here where the people are chiefly farmers, the houses they

119

live in are taller and the vineyards around them larger. There are groves of wild plum and cherry trees; the hills are covered with scrub to the top.

The sun is scorching hot—what will it be like later in the day?! It's dusty on the road, and that too will probably get worse later on. We can again see the road several versts ahead; it runs across a wide plain on the floor of the valley. It's so flat here that the Aragvi River doesn't go anywhere, but flows back and forth in the oddest twists and turns, back and forth looking about for a way out.

After a two-hour sleep, we are in Chilkhany; it's noon. We get off. Kornei demands a four-hour rest period like yesterday because of the heat. We are still thirty-five versts from Tiflis, but half of the road is downhill and the other half is flat. Good, Kornei can have his four hours.

XI

Here, too, the innkeeper brings a live chicken that he offers us for dinner, and we nod again, indicating that chicken is fine. We learn later, incidentally, that the innkeeper was born of German parents here in Caucasia and that his mother tongue is German. He also speaks English. So here we don't have to use signs.

An officer of the gendarmes turns up at the station. Scrutinizing us, he engages in a suspicious conversation with the innkeeper. The officer has two soldiers with him, to whom he talks now and then.

My deep anxiety returns, depriving me of my desire for chicken and food and everything; these gendarmes must have shown up at the request of the police officer in order to apprehend me here. What an obstinate, arrogant fool I was not to come to terms with that horrible person yesterday! Now it was too late. On the whole, one ought to come to terms with horrible people, make up with them instead of fighting them for the rest of one's life.

As it was, I might have to spend the rest of my days in a Russian prison, be brought to St. Petersburg in chains, and get buried alive in the Peter and Paul Fortress. I would wear a hole in my stone table with my skinny elbow as I sat brooding, my head cupped in my hand, and I would cover the walls of my wretched cell with maxims that would later be studied and published as a book. I would be given every possible rehabilitation after my death, but what good did that do me now? I've never had a passion for the honor implied by the existence of large bronze statues of me in cities around Norway; on the contrary, every time I've thought about these posthumous statues, I've wished instead to have what they are worth right away—hand over the cash! But now the hour of fate had struck. What would happen to my scientific notes for the Geographical Society? Get destroyed, be burned by the executioner before my eyes in the stony backyard of the fortress. And soldiers would stand round about with fixed bayonets, and the sentence would be read and I would mount the fire and repeat until the end: And yet the earth is round! Then a herald blows his horn before the gate of the fortress and waves a flag and bursts in on a horse in a lather, crying, Mercy, in the name of the Emperor! And my sentence is commuted to incarceration for life. Then I ask for death—standing in the flames with an erect carriage beyond compare, I ask for death instead of life. But those inhuman executioners take me down despite my protest and lead me back to the stone table, which I've worn thin with my brooding. . . .

While we are having lunch, the officer of gendarmes, using the innkeeper as interpreter, asks whether we saw an officer on our way.

I neglect answering and neglect chewing my chicken, all at once feeling completely full. So there was a connection between the gendarmes and the police officer.

The innkeeper repeated his question.

"Yes," my traveling companion answered, "we did see an officer."

"What was he like? Of medium height, rather stout, with a Jewish appearance, a Jew?"

"Yes, precisely."

The officer of gendarmes shows us a photograph of the man as he appeared on the train, in an officer's uniform. "Was it him?"

"Yes."

The officer of gendarmes bows and leaves; he goes back to his two soldiers and speaks softly to them. Then he walks onto the veranda and looks up the road; he is obviously expecting the police officer any moment.

"You're so pale," my traveling companion says to me.

I get up from the table and go out on the veranda as well. But I didn't descend the steps, to avoid being stopped by a thundering "Halt!" I sat down in my distress, breathing audibly.

On the veranda sits, besides the officer of gendarmes and myself, a young Englishman who plans to cross the mountains to Vladikavkaz. I begrudge him his indescribable calm. The young Brit is, like all traveling Brits, complacent, mute, indifferent to everybody; smoking his pipe, he smokes it empty, taps it out, fills

122

it again and goes on smoking, his conceit meanwhile preventing him from even noticing the two of us who are also present. I laugh a little at him to vex him, but he pretends not to hear it. "Hm!" I say, but he doesn't turn his head. However, having got a piece of dust in his eye, he takes out a pocket mirror and examines his eye while still smoking. I feel good about that piece of dust in his eye. True, the officer of gendarmes was my enemy and would soon apprehend me, but in what way was he personally to blame for it? It was the fault of the system. He was a cultured man who looked at me occasionally and seemed to deplore my fate. But there sat the Englishman looking down his nose at me.

Then we hear a carriage rolling on the sandy road; the officer of gendarmes jumps up and slips through the door, as if wanting to hide. The carriage comes to a halt in front of the veranda, and the police officer alights from it. He came, as he had predicted, one hour after us. He tipped his hat as usual as he passed me and remarked with a smile, "As usual, an hour behind you."

He went into the dining room and ordered food.

So I'm reprieved until he has eaten, I think to myself, but then he'll utter a word and point his finger, and the gendarmes will step up and seize me.

But the gendarmes were by this time gone; both the officer and the soldiers seemed blown away. Where were they? What a strange country Caucasia was! There I sat on the veranda and, though captive, was free to walk down those stairs if I wanted to. They gave me both time and opportunity to steal a march on justice, put a noose around my neck, and shorten my life. They felt so assured. But they shouldn't feel assured about anything, but expect everything from me.

My traveling companion comes out and reports that apparently something is up: the officer of gendarmes and his two soldiers are standing in the corridor of the second floor, listening down the stairs and behaving suspiciously. "Perhaps they're going to arrest someone," I answer, half senseless.

The innkeeper is waiting on the chief of police with the greatest courtesy, addressing him as His Excellency; he must

IN WONDERLAND

understand he's dealing with an all-powerful man. His Excellency's orders at the table are abrupt and authoritative, and when he has finished his dinner, he pays just as abruptly and authoritatively and joins us on the veranda.

He sits down beside the Englishman—who naturally doesn't move one millimeter. He takes out a handkerchief with a coronet on it and wipes the dust off his face; afterward he takes out a cigar case with a coronet on it and lights a cigar. Then he sits there smoking in silence.

My traveling companion descends the steps and goes into the field to pick some flowers. The three of us are left sitting there.

Then I see the officer of gendarmes, with the soldiers in tow, walk stealthily down the stairs from the second floor. A mute cry comes from somewhere inside my chest, and I get up and remain standing. Now it would come! The innkeeper himself appears in the doorway of the dining room in order to watch. The officer of gendarmes steps out on the veranda and stops before the police officer. Did I see correctly? And did I hear correctly? He places his hand on his shoulder and arrests him. Arrests him. "You are my prisoner!" he said in French.

The police officer looks up at the gendarme with a momentary shudder. Then he flicks the ash off his cigar and replies, "What are you saying?"

"That you are my prisoner."

"Why—? What do you want to—?"

A carriage that has been held in readiness rolls up, and the two soldiers grab the police officer under the arms and lead him onto the road; the officer of gendarmes follows them. I hear the Jew maintain that this will be a dangerous affair for the officer of gendarmes, he had papers and could establish his identity, just you wait! The four men take their seats in the carriage, the coachman cracks his whip, and the carriage rolls toward Tiflis.

There I was.

I turned here and there, looking about me for an explanation. The Englishman hadn't bothered to look up; he was again using his pocket mirror to examine his eye. As soon as I recovered

124

my power of speech, I asked the innkeeper what the whole thing was supposed to mcan. Had an arrest just taken place?

The innkeeper nodded, unruffled.

"But God help you, man!" I say. "You nod as if the whole thing was nothing at all. Didn't they just now arrest a living human being?"

"Surely. On a report from Pyatigorsk," the innkeeper replied.

I couldn't fathom this unheard-of action before our very eyes. "If something like that had happened to me, I would've sunk through the ground," I said.

The innkeeper looked indifferent.

"You still don't think that this was anything," I then said. "How do you imagine I could've lived through something like that? And how do you imagine my traveling companion would've lived through it?"

"Yeah, sure. But it didn't happen to you," the innkeeper replied, giving up at once.

At this point the whole affair gave me a feeling of rapturous joy. Though the fever again raged inside me and my whole body trembled in a cold sweat, every single part of me was filled with joy.

When my traveling companion returned, she said, "You've got some color in your face again."

"Yes," I replied, "I'm fed up with moping around and thinking about that ox. The ox that we saw, remember, it had gotten the yoke between its horns and walked with a twisted neck. Now it feels comfortable."

"It feels comfortable? How?"

"The officer just told me. The officer from the train, you know. He came just after we did; he also saw the ox."

"Well?"

"He got the yoke straightened."

"Thank God!" said my traveling companion.

I also felt content. I mentioned a couple of things I could eat now, and although I met with good advice to skip this or that and choose something else because of my fever, I persisted in my lunacy and ordered the dangerous things. For my appetite had become enormous.

In the same vein, I didn't like the Englishman to be so taciturn and forlorn anymore, the more so as my traveling companion now went off, giving me a free hand. To make him sit up, I turned to him and said, "There is plague in Oporto. Do you know that?"

He stared at me.

I repeated that there was plague in Oporto, but he didn't seem daunted and smoked away.

Then I fetched my issue of *The New Press* and said to the Englishman, "I'm just noting that, in the last report on market prices from Finland, chickens there cost one mark to one mark seventy-five penniä apiece."

The little Brit persisted in his attempt to treat me as if I weren't there; but he was too young, he couldn't hold his own, and it was amusing to see him struggle with his unpracticed dignity.

"The chickens?" he asked. "In Finland? How?"

"You'll cross the mountains," I said, "and then you'll go through Russia and finally get to Finland, from where you'll go home to your happy and thoroughly charming people, the English. I wanted to prepare you for the prices in Finland, so you would know them when ordering food. Remember that the price quoted is apiece, not for a pair of chickens."

"How much, did you say?" he asked.

"One mark to one mark seventy-five."

"How much is that in English money?"

I knew roughly how much and was able to tell him.

"I'm not going to Finland," he said.

It wasn't possible to get him involved in a dispute.

Maybe I could catch his interest with something else, I thought, and began to read from the paper about "the rumors of war from Transvaal." After reading the item aloud I translated it for him, torturing him with not knowing the simplest words in his language and asking his advice. In the end he was completely listless and answered yes to all my suggestions. Then he got up and ordered his telega to be driven up; I had worn him out. He tried to save the remnants of his British hauteur as he left: he again cut me dead. Then I said, "Have a pleasant journey! Remember to be courteous and greet people when you come and go. Those are the ways of the world."

He turned scarlet, and in his confusion he touched his hat. Then he drove off. . . .

I once saw an Englishman in a Munich streetcar, an artist most likely, a painter; he was going to the Schack gallery. As we come down the street at great speed, a child, a little girl, is nearly run over; she falls, gets in between the horses and is trampled, hurt. But we manage to pull her out alive. Meanwhile the Brit is smoking his pipe. When it's all over and the driver delays a moment before going on, the Brit looks at his watch in irritation. We cast a glance at him one and all, but we don't mean a thing to him; in his priceless Englishman's German he asks for his money back, he wants to get off. A child that has been run over doesn't concern him. A passenger offers to reimburse him for his ticket. He casts an indifferent glance at the passenger; slowly and indifferently he withdraws his eyes, declining the offer. He's not bothered by the indignation that is smoldering around him, and this staunchness would no doubt have won the applause of all his countrymen: that's right, John, just stand pat! He remained on the streetcar until his destination. Then he got off.

Often, of course, it's just as well and even preferable that not too many people crowd the scene of an accident. But everyone can stop smoking his pipe without special permission, everyone can raise his eyes, everyone perceive a light shock. Everyone. Without special permission.

If I were king of England, I would whisper a small piece of advice into the ears of my people. And my people would become the world's most splendid people. . . .

The carriage that drove past us yesterday is now overtaking us here. The Russian family eat, let the horses rest for only three quarters of an hour and prepare to be off again. Wanting to leave at the same time, Kornei, too, drives up with his carriage. There still remain three quarters of an hour of the four hours he had request-ed, but now Kornei can be less demanding, since he wants to take the opportunity to have company. He lines up behind the other carriage and waves to us. We let him wave. Then, starting to shout and scold, he even has the Russian come and speak with us in European tongues to get us going. But we are immovable. The Russian drives off.

Kornei remains behind, watching the carriage as it rolls away and ranting and roaring at us. We leave him to his ranting. There was a perverse streak in Kornei: if he hadn't been granted those four hours, he would have taken them; now that he could have them he didn't want them. But if he expected to be paid extra for not driving in the dust from the previous carriage, he fooled himself. He would not be paid anything extra. He had been trou-blesome all along.

Still, we don't torment Kornei more than half an hour before getting into our carriage. Kornei is sullen and angry and drives hard, as if he wants to overtake the carriage and annoy us. And we let him drive. If we know Kornei, he'll soon be bored with driving his horses too hard.

Riding across wide plains, we can see the road, long and yellow, running through the green landscape. After a while we come across corn. We are now at the altitude of Tiflis, approxi-mately 450 meters above sea level, and from now on our road will be flat. It's fertile here; corn, which according to an old adage must have one hundred days of warmth, ripens well here. The road is lined with Lombardy poplars, willows, and wild fruit trees; the hills are low. Ahead of us the mountains show blue far away, but they too seem low.

At a watering hole Kornei gets off, inspects each horse in turn and pours water on their heads. He has recovered his Molokan caution, since he understands that his forced driving won't even bring a protest from us, and from now on he drives evenly as before. It's none too early, the heat is terrible; we have to keep our hands under the mudguard, or the sun will burn through our gloves.

In the distance we see a castle with huge towers; in addition, we see meadows, fields, now and then a few trees, small Georgian houses of flint stone and clay, and plowing oxen.

A couple of times we meet carriages with canvas roofs, pulled by buffalo trudging ahead with sluggish steps. The carriages are occupied by sitting and lying people of a different type, Gypsies, reddish-brown migrating tramps. One carriage had ten people in it; a young girl, attractive and straight and with a red kerchief on her head, smiles at us, showing her white teeth.

We arrive at a huge ruined castle of stone and clay, a chaos of massive walls. The walls are cracked, but some of them may still rise to a height of about fifty meters; two of the many wings look as though they could collapse any moment. Possibly one of Queen Tamara's many palaces round about Georgia and Caucasia. A short distance from this ruin we come upon two temple-like buildings surrounded by a great many human dwellings: they are a monastery and a church, both very much alike in their ancient and unfamiliar appearance but situated on opposite sides of the road. The many surrounding houses spoil the impression; some have two stories, and all are in the modern style, with casement windows and tile roofs, all boring, all stupid and shameless, hybrids.

We are approaching the large castle we saw in the distance. This is not a ruin, but a complex of wings, some round, others square, with a huge main part that is round and resembles the Castle of St. Angelo in Rome. The castle, which is inhabited, is well maintained; it's the Arma Tsike Castle, the oldest seat of power in the country. We were told it is now used as a monastery, but I don't know any particulars in that regard.

We are now passing a sawmill. It doesn't run on steam or water, but on manpower. Standing two on each side of a huge saw, four men are cutting boards; they are bareheaded, clad in red flannel woolens from top to toe. Their appearance and their perpetual nodding, up and down, over the saw cause them to resemble figures cut out of wood and painted red.

Finally we reach the station Mtskheta.

Here Kornei tries for the last time to squeeze a small

advantage out of us: he turns around on the box and suggests that we take the railroad from here to Tiflis. But then we would first have to get to the city and the railroad station, which is situated some distance away, then wait for a train, then struggle with our suitcases and other luggage in the heat, then incur an additional expense for tickets! I point Kornei's nose straight ahead and utter the word that decides everything: Tiflis! And Kornei is sullen and angry and again drives faster.

We saw practically nothing of the town Mtskheta. Situated where the Aragvi joins the Kura River, it is one of the oldest places in Georgia and, before Tiflis, was the country's capital. I've read that the city is poor and in ruins; its most important building is supposed to be a cathedral from the fourth century. Here the kings of Georgia are buried.

A short distance outside Mtskheta we again come up against a bar, where Kornei has to present the receipt for toll already paid. Up the hill, a train from Baku passes by; we count forty-six of the gray cylindrical petroleum cars in the train. We are picking up an awful smell of oil.

By now the telegraph poles have twelve wires. We are approaching Tiflis.

We follow the Kura River all the way. The Kura is majestic and beautiful. We are about to cross the railroad track, but a barrier is lowered due to an approaching train and we have to wait. The train comes, with forty-eight more oil cars, making a roar like a waterfall between the hills. Then the barrier goes up and we continue.

We can now see Tiflis far away, like a collection of dots, a world apart. Smog hovers above the city. So this is Tiflis, which so many Russian writers have written about and where so many things in the Russian novel have taken place. For a moment I feel like a youth, looking forward in wonder and hearing my heartbeat. I have the same sensation as the first time I was to hear Georg Brandes give a lecture.[33] That was in an auditorium at the University of Copenhagen. We'd been standing on the street in the rain for ever so long, crowding one another before a closed door; then the door opened and we galloped up a flight of stairs, down a hallway and into an auditorium where I found a seat. Then we waited for a long time again, while the auditorium filled up amid a buzz and a roar of voices. Suddenly it's still all around, deathly still, I could hear my heart throbbing. Then he mounted the rostrum. . . . Not that I wouldn't have spoken far better myself! Of course I would.

Riding across a barren and infertile sandy plain, with thick, motionless dust hovering above the road, we meet the mail coach. The armed driver is playing a trill on his surna; I tip my hat, and the driver bows in answer while continuing to play as he passes us. We meet more and more oxen, donkeys and drivers, equipages, horsemen and loaded wagons. We also meet drunken men, a sight unseen during our whole trip through the mountains. We drive into the city. It's already getting dark, and in the houses and on the streets, where crowds of people are milling about, the lights are turned on. Now and then a long-bearded Persian in a large turban strides along the street with imperturbable calm. He sticks to his course like a camel.

We settle with Kornei. After receiving his pay he asks for a tip. I have the interpreter reply that Kornei hasn't deserved any tip. But when it is explained to him what his undeservingness consists of, he looks as though he has never in his life driven a more difficult princely couple. He doesn't understand a thing. He gets a ruble for milk all the same. But Kornei Grigorevich isn't satisfied with such a small tip, and he fusses and fumes so hard that he ends up being escorted out of the hotel.

XII

The heat was just too much last night, and my sleep was broken. I woke up any number of times, wiped myself, breathed and snorted, and slept again.

One time when I woke up, my traveling companion was reading a book by the lamp. I was too sleepy and wretched with fever to try to find out what that sort of extravagance was good for. Besides, had books been brought along on the sly, while I languished all the while over an old issue of *The New Press?* One should never go on a trip with someone else; one's companion thinks only of number one and puts away the best mouthfuls!

After a restless semi-slumber I wake again and look about me. It's fairly light, five o'clock. I jump up and get into my clothes. Then I turn to the room, direct a word to the other wall and suggest it's impossible to sleep any longer.

At that point my travel companion asks, "Who is this police officer you ran into on our way?"

"Police officer?" So that was it! My diary had provided the night's reading! I had disclosed nothing about the police officer; indeed, I had spared everyone else and kept the secret in my heart. Didn't that deserve some appreciation?

"How can anybody lie so blatantly?" the voice from the wall goes on. "And I don't believe in your ride into the mountains from Kobi either."

I had kept mum about the ride, too. I had undertaken that ride in behalf of science, had gladly sacrificed a night's sleep to promote the work of the Geographical Society, enduring all the hardships with a silent heart—that's how a true explorer comports himself.

"And besides," says my traveling companion, "and besides, I think you're writing down too many trifles."

That was the last straw. My good companion had used a quiet hour of the night when, through illness and fever, I was prevented from defending myself and my belongings, to poke her nose into my traveling archive. All right! But my good traveling companion also tried to make me feel uncertain of my ability to keep an excellent diary. That was the last straw.

"I'm going out," I said, leaving the room in an unforgiving mood. . . .

The hotel was still asleep, but when I came down into the vestibule, a doorman emerged, rubbing his eyes. He was one of those adventurers in the hotels of the Orient who know the fastest French you ever came across. I remain speechless because I cannot answer one word to a thousand; I merely wave the door open. When I'd gotten out into the street, I put together what the man had said: he had in one swoop wished me bonjour, remarked on the weather, inquired how I had slept, and offered his services as a city guide. That is only what I understood, but I missed out on a great deal. Oh yes, now I remember that he also wanted to shine my shoes.

However early in the morning it is, people sit in front of their doors chatting or wander about the streets; the Caucasians do not sleep. The sun hadn't risen, but it was a warm, clear morning. Directly opposite the hotel lies a large park; I enter, walk straight through it and come out on the other side. Most of the people I see wear Caucasian attire, with weapons; some wear European jackets and stiff felt hats. The officers sport Circassian uniforms. I see practically no women outdoors.

I had intended to study the city from one end to the other before breakfast, but I soon realized that this would be impossible. Feeling hungry, I got myself a bagful of grapes to fortify myself with, but as a Scandinavian, I needed, of course, to have meat and some slices of bread to be satisfied. I walked around the park and came back to the hotel.

Nobody had yet gotten up. In the vestibule the doorman began again to parleyvoo, so I pushed a door open to escape and found myself in the hotel's reading room. Here, on a table, I found a Baedeker of Russia and Caucasia; I looked up Tiflis and started reading.

My own hotel, "London," had one star. The city had 160,000 inhabitants, among whom there were twice as many men as women. Seventy languages were spoken in the city. The average temperature in the summer was twenty-one degrees Celsius, and in the winter one degree Celsius. Tiflis has been under Roman, Persian, and Turkish supremacy and is now under that of Russia. The city owes its progress in recent times to its favorable situation as a point of intersection for the commercial traffic from the Caspian and the Black Sea, from the Armenian highlands, and from Russia across the Caucasian mountains. Tiflis has a magnificent museum, theaters, art collections, a botanical garden, and a fortress; the city also has the castle of the Georgian kings, now used as a prison. Finally, it has a statue, that of a Russian general. But high, high above the city sits the David Monastery. It is situated on Mt. Mtatsminda, which is sacred to the Georgians. Near the monastery is the tomb of Griboyedov.

I close the Baedeker and consider what I may have read about Griboyedov. It's not much, only that he wrote *Gore ot uma*, this lone social satire that made him immortal in Russia. These strange words, "*Gore ot uma*," are beyond my comprehension, but the book has been translated under the title *The Curse of Genius* or similar titles, depending on the particular language.[34] Griboyedov married a princess from Tiflis, only sixteen years old. He became an envoy to Persia, where he was murdered by a mob at the age of thirty-five, whereas his widow lived another twenty-eight years, turning away all suitors. She erected this beautiful monument to her husband at the David Monastery. Her inscription on the tomb says he will be remembered forever.

Other Russian writers who have been here in Tiflis come to mind, such as Pushkin, Lermontov, Tolstoy, and many more. In consequence, I sit for a long while framing to myself a humble opinion about Russian literature in general. It's so early in the morning, and I still have this little room to myself; it is just right for framing a humble opinion in, being so nice and tight, without even a window opening onto the street.

Russian literature is, everything considered, very large

and very difficult to get a hold on. It's rather broad, due to the wide expanses of the Russian land and the expansiveness of Russian life. There are no borders that set bounds on the sides. I place Ivan Turgenev slightly on the side. He was a European, a Frenchman, at least as much as a Russian. His characters are not governed by the spontaneity, the aptitude for derailment, for the "irrational excess," that are unique to the Russian people. Would you in any other country see a drunkard about to be arrested go free by embracing the police constable in the middle of the street, kissing him and asking for mercy? Ivan Turgenev's characters are gentle and strikingly straight; they don't think or act sufficiently by Russian fits and starts. They are so engaging and logical and French. Turgenev was not a great intellect, but he had a good heart. He believed in humanism, belles lettres, Western European progress. His French contemporaries had the same beliefs, but not all his Russian ones; some of them, like Dostoyevsky and Tolstoy, deviated from straightness. Where the West Europeans saw salvation, they saw hopelessness. And in the seventies they abandoned themselves to the most unmodern worship: the worship of God. Ivan Turgenev was steadfast; he had once and for all found the clear, broad way taken by every mediocrity at the time, and the way suited him and he walked it. It is said about him that, when he returned home after his university studies in Berlin, "he brought with him a fresh breath of culture." And when he was on his deathbed he wrote a touching letter to Tolstoy and implored him to return to his straightness and produce more belles lettres. He would be so happy, he wrote, if this plea was heard.

When Turgenev died, it was a genuine believer who died.

Dostoyevsky, on the other hand, died a fanatic, crazy, a man of genius. He was as torn and disproportionate as his characters. His Slavophilism was rather too hysterical to be deep, the irritable obstinacy of a sick genius; he screamed and hissed about it. And his belief in Russia's god was perhaps no firmer than Turgenev's belief in that of Europe, that is, they both believed like mustard seeds. Where, as in *The Brothers Karamazov,* he wants to be philosophical, he betrays a strange confusion. He talks, chats, writes with a brush. Until he again gets hold of the needle—which is his pen. Never has human complexity been dissected as by him; his psychological sense is overwhelming, clairvoyant. Appraising him, one lacks the measure to mete with; he is in a category of his own. His contemporaries tried to size him up but failed; he was so immodestly great. For example, there was a man named Nekrasov, editor of a journal entitled *Sovremennik*.[35] One day a young man comes to Nekrasov and delivers a manuscript; the man's name is Dostoyevsky, and he had called his manuscript *Poor Folk*. Nekrasov reads it, is startled, runs out into the streets in the middle of the night and wakes up the great Belinsky,[36] crying, "We've got another Gogol!" But Belinsky is skeptical, as behooves a critic; only after reading the work does he share the other's joy. At his first meeting with Dostoyevsky he acknowledges the young author very warmly, but the latter immediately alienates the great critic by seeing himself as a genius. No less. Little great Belinsky found no trace of ordinary modesty in Dostoyevsky. He was without measure, by himself. But then Belinsky became reserved, I've read. "What a misfortune!" he wrote. "Dostoyevsky is no doubt talented, but if he already now imagines he is a genius, instead of working on his development, he won't get anywhere!" And Dostoyevsky did imagine he was a genius, and he worked on his development and advanced so far on the path he chose that nobody has yet caught up with him. If Dostoyevsky hadn't imagined he was a genius, God knows whether he would always have tackled the *greatest* tasks. Anyway, there stand his twelve volumes, which cannot be compared with anyone else's twelve volumes. No, not with anyone else's twenty-four volumes. There is, for example, a short novella called *Krotkaya*.[37] A tiny little book. But it is too great for all of us, too unattainably great. Let everyone acknowledge it.

But what a priceless remark that was by Belinsky, I think sitting there, namely, that Dostoyevsky wouldn't get anywhere if he already imagined himself a genius, instead of working on his development. Belinsky had read and learned what was the prevailing view in the Western Europe of his time. So many pounds of English beefsteak a week, so many books to be read, so many paintings to be looked at, so much "breath of culture"—that is "development" toward genius. Dostoyevsky ought to have learned something, first and foremost some modesty, which in ordinary people's eyes is a virtue. . . .

And I think of Tolstoy. I cannot overcome my suspicion that something inauthentic has come into the life of this great writer, a heavy artificiality. It may originally have occurred out of sincere perplexity; the strong man had to come up with something, and since the pleasures of this world were exhausted, he came down, with his natural heaviness, on the side of religious bigotry. At the beginning, to be sure, there was an element of playacting in it, but he was too strong to stop, and so it turned into a habit, maybe even second nature. It is dangerous to start playacting. Henrik Ibsen went so far that, for years, he sat sphinx-like on a particular chair in a particular Munich café at a particular time of day. Afterward he had to go on playacting; wherever he went, he had to act the sphinx for the people, sitting in a particular chair at a particular time. Because people expected him to. It may have felt like an awful nuisance at times, but he was too strong to stop. What strapping fellows they are these two, Tolstoy and Ibsen! There are many who wouldn't be capable of keeping up an act like that for more than a week. And those two would possibly have demonstrated greater strength if they had stopped doing so in time. As it is, they unfortunately become fair game for me and other ordinary humans. Well, they are probably great enough to endure that; we will ourselves be mocked in return. But if they had been a little greater, perhaps they wouldn't have taken themselves quite so seriously. They would have smiled a bit at their age-long folly. The fact that they lead others, and finally even themselves, to believe that their playacting is a necessity for them, betrays a flaw in their personality that makes them smaller, drags them down. A great literary work is required simply to repair the damage. To stand on one leg is an affectation; the natural posture is to stand on two, without putting on an act.

War and Peace, Anna Karenina—nobody has created greater works of literature of their kind. It is no wonder that an impressionable colleague asked for more such on his deathbed. But as I now sit and think about it, I can easily understand and easily forgive Tolstoy's boredom at contriving fiction, however magnificent, for humankind. Others can take care of fiction, such as feel good about doing so, who value the vocation highly and find the honor it confers great. What to my mind seems objectionable is the great man's fruitless attempt to write philosophy, to be a thinker. This is what distorts his position into a pose. He shares the fate of Ibsen. Neither is a thinker, but they both stand on one leg trying to be one. Supposedly there is more to them that way, they think it is grander. And the rest of us are small enough to make fun of them—which they are great enough to tolerate. Thinking is one thing, argument is something else. And brooding, something else again. They are brooders; but so are very many. A Gudbrandsdal[38] peasant brooded his entire life; he was such a brainy fellow that he became a legend to many. He had a forehead that was just as high as that of any writer. Among other things, he hatched on his own the idea of a clock that would show the time on all four sides simultaneously. He was in the mountains carting home moss for the cattle at the time he hatched this idea. When he related what had happened to him, he wept broodingly; but he used to add that he still carted the load of moss home from the mountain that day also. He was the talk of the villagers as well as of himself.

Tolstoy's philosophy is a mixture of old commonplaces and his own astonishingly imperfect whims. It's not for nothing that he belongs to a people that hasn't produced a single thinker in its entire history. No more than Ibsen's people. Both Norway and Russia have produced much that's good and great, only no thinker. Not until those two great writers appeared, Tolstoy and Ibsen.

I do not find it incomprehensible that the writers have become thinkers in these countries: we had no one else who was. And it's not an arbitrary choice, it makes good sense that it turned out to be the writers and not the shoemakers. I could also explain it the way I think it occurred. But I must check once more whether the windows are well shut before I elaborate on this.

Those who have lived long enough to remember the seventies will know about the changes that writers began to undergo at that time. They had until then been singers, purveyors of moods, storytellers; then they were caught up in the Zeitgeist and became workers, educators, reformers. It was English philosophy with its practical quest for utility and happiness that began to prevail among people and to transform literature. What resulted was a literature without much imagination, but there was much diligence and much common sense in it. One could write about anything that lay at everyman's feet as long as one was "true to life," and this gave rise to a multitude of great writers in many countries. Literature swelled up. A popularized science treated societal problems and reformed the institutions. In the theater you could see Doctor Rank's spine and Osvald's brain dramatized, and the novel had a still freer hand, allowing even for discussions of errors in Biblical translations.[39] The writers became people with opinions about everything; people asked one another what the writers thought about the theory of evolution, what Zola had found out about the laws of heredity, what chemical discoveries Strindberg had made. In consequence, writers advanced to a place in life they had never occupied before: being know-it-alls who liked to dispense their knowledge about everything, they became national leaders. Journalists interviewed them about universal peace, about religion and about world politics, and if it ever happened that a foreign paper printed a notice about them, the domestic papers saw it as a sign of how great their writers were. In the end, people couldn't help getting the idea that their writers were world celebrities, powerful individuals who exercised an overwhelming influence on the intellectual life of the time: they set the nations brooding. Eventually this daily bragging couldn't help having an effect on men who already had a penchant for posturing. What a helluva fellow you've become! they probably said to themselves; you can read it in every newspaper and hear it from everybody, so it must be true! And since the nation had no one else to do it, the writers became thinkers as well. And they accepted the position without objection and without a smile. They had, most likely, no more of a background in philosophy than ordinary educated people have, but with this as a foundation they got on one leg, wrinkled their brows, and dispensed philosophy to the age.

This, in short, must have been the way it happened. And once the game had begun, it had to go on. Though it would have demonstrated every bit as much strength to stop it.

That great writer Tolstoy—it would also fall to him to establish himself as a thinker. I suspect that his natural aptitude for this profession appears less to many others than it does to himself; I do not know what others think, but I assume this is so. Off and on there appear in the papers various samples of his thinking, and besides, he writes a book now and then in which he records his opinions about this life and the life to come. A few years ago he proclaimed his famous doctrine of total chastity, total sexual abstinence. When the doctrine met with the objection that it would spell the end of the human race, the thinker replied, "Certainly, that's the point, the human race must go!" St. Augustin's ancient doctrine, alas! Oh, that wise Manichean philosophy!

A little story by Tolstoy is entitled "How Much Land Does a Man Need?" It's about a peasant, Pakhom, who finds that he doesn't have enough land and buys an additional fifteen *desyatinas*.[40] After some time he gets into a dispute with his neighbors, whereupon he decides to purchase their land too, so that he actually becomes a small landowner. But after some more time has passed, a peasant from the Volga region visits Pakhom, and he tells him what a wonderful life peasants enjoyed there, how much land they could have for free, and how many thousand rubles they sold wheat for every year. Pakhom travels to the Volga region. Here he encounters no difficulty whatsoever in acquiring land, and he helps himself very generously; but through his efforts to acquire more, always more, Pakhom works himself to death. One day his servant finds him dead in the field. There he lay. The servant dug a grave for his master, and the grave was six feet long. That, says the thinker, is exactly how much land a man needs—six feet for a grave.

It would perhaps be more correct to say that six feet of land is far too little for a man; that is what a *corpse* needs. In the same vein, one might say that a man doesn't even need those six feet. First, because a corpse has ceased to be human; second, because a corpse can dispense with burial. So the thinker can have his six feet of land returned to him.

Here is another little anecdote by Tolstoy. A man was dissatisfied with his lot and complained to God. "The good Lord gives riches to others," he said, "but me he gives nothing. How can I cope with life since I don't have anything?" An old man who overheard these words said, "Are you really as poor as you think? Hasn't God given you youth and good health?"—Oh yes, the man couldn't deny it, he had youth and good health. Then the old man took the man's right hand and said, "Would you let this hand be chopped off for a thousand rubles?"—No, the man would not.—"How about the left one?"—"Oh no, not that either."—"But would you permit the light of your eyes to be put out for ten thousand rubles?"—"No, God help me." The man didn't want that either. Then the old man said, "There you see," he said, "what riches God has bestowed upon you, and even so you're complaining!"

Let us assume that there was a poor man without a right hand, without a left hand, without the light of his eyes at ten thousand rubles, and that there came an old man to him and said, "You poor? You who have a stomach at fifteen thousand rubles and a spine at around twenty thousand!"

The name Tolstoy is said to mean *thick*. . . .[41]

He does not lack logic. What he gets hold of he spins out to what, in his judgment, it should be spun out to. He does not lack the instruments. But the very seat of thought in him is empty. The boat has oars and equipment, that it has; but it lacks an oarsman.

Or it is I who lack all ability to understand the matter. In any case, what I think is only an opinion without general validity; it's only mine. But I do mean one would be hard put to find a worse philosophical penury anywhere than in Tolstoy's treatises.

But he is more sympathetic than some of his colleagues who play at being thinkers. Because his soul is so tremendously rich and so willing to give. He doesn't shut his mouth after the first ten words, leaving you to guess at the unfathomable depths behind them; he speaks on and on, with lofty words and warnings, and verily I say to you. It's not his greatest concern not to say too much, so that the world can get to know him; he speaks most willingly. And his voice is without affectation, deep and large. He's an ancient prophet, that he is. And he has no peer in our time.

People can hear his words, study them and put them in their right place. Or they can learn from them and live by them. That, too, they can do. If, that is, people don't mind having their concepts of what is possible and reasonable here on earth so shamelessly turned topsy-turvy.

XIII

We went sightseeing in the city without the company of the fast-talking doorman nor of anyone else. The city was anything but enjoyable, but there was a small corner of it to which we returned time and again and never got tired of seeing, namely, the Asiatic quarter. Shops with plate glass windows, streetcars, vaudeville theaters, and gentlemen and ladies in European dress dominated the city; but here in the Asiatic quarter there were none such, barely even streets, only alleys, nooks and corners, steps up and steps down from one house to another.

Here peoples from all over the world sat in their shops and had curious things to sell. In Teheran and Constantinople the traders were Persians and Turks; here they were an assortment of Caucasian peoples, Georgians, mountain people, Ural-Altaic tribes, all kinds of Tatars, besides Indo-Europeans such as Persians, Kurds and Armenians, people from Arabia in the south to Turkestan in the north, from Palestine to Tibet. And everything went peacefully, no one was in a hurry, the people were imbued with the calm of the Orient. White and motley turbans predominated; only an occasional green or blue one was seen crowning a gorgeous long-bearded head. The belts were either of chased metal or, as among the Persians, of many-colored silk. Caucasians, Kurds, and Armenians carried weapons.

It was extremely hot at the noon hour, but in many places the streets were roofed over and provided a nice shade. Donkeys, horses, and dogs mingle with the people. A horse stands in the broiling hot sun when we arrive; it is saddle-chafed and has big sores with countless flies in them. The horse doesn't pay attention to anything; nothing but skin and bones, its head hung low, it lets the flies just sit there. It is completely listless; if we chase the flies away, it doesn't seem to find any relief from it but simply stands there in the sun, getting scorched and blinking drowsily. Since it is hitched to a wagon, it is probably waiting for its master. Its sores smell. . . . It's a superior horse, a stoic horse. By walking a few steps it could get itself in the shade, but it just stands there. It isn't concerned about the flies sitting there either, so extreme is its ruin.

Side by side with donkeys, horses, and dogs, the artisans do their work in the street; the blacksmiths make the iron red-hot in their small forges and hammer it out on small anvils. The metal workers file, chop, chisel, and engrave; now and then they do inlays with turquoise and other stones. The tailors are sewing long cloth burnouses; armed to the teeth and with huge fur hats on their heads, they tread the sewing machines of the West. Until two hundred years ago, our Scandinavian tailors and shoemakers were girded with their swords too when they worked; here that custom has been retained.

In the stores there are mostly silks, embroidered goods, rugs, weapons, jewelry. If you decide to shop, you are welcome to look at everything even if you don't buy anything, but if you make a purchase it's OK that way too; these tradesmen maintain a blessed calm in everything. Though the shops are quite dirty, in the carpet stores precious rugs lie on the floor and in the doorway, down the steps into the street and up to another house. They are precious Persian and Caucasian rugs. And people and dogs trample on them and mess them up, a painful sight.

Here and there a scribe sits in a small shed writing for people whatever they require. He's surrounded by books with quaint characters in them, and it's no wonder he has grown so gray and venerable, we think, since he has learned such characters and can decipher them. We also saw earnest young people with documents under their arms, most likely the disciples of theologians and jurists on their way to or from their master. When they get to the scribe's place, they bow and greet him respectfully. The art of writing is a sacred art; the very paper used for writing is sacred. The illustrious sheik Abd al-Qadir al-Jilani[42] never passed a stationer's shop without first having purified himself by several washings, and in the end he became such a holy and ethereal person that he could live for weeks on a single olive. Paper serves to duplicate the sacred book, that's why it is so highly regarded. One chooses paper for one's copies with the greatest care, cuts one's pen and mixes one's ink with grave attention. On the whole, the art of writing and reading is still thought to be in high esteem in Islam, but a scholarly culture of the sort exemplified by the time of greatness in Samarkand no longer exists. This I've read in Vambéry.[43] Whether we turn to Constantinople, Cairo, or Bukhara, the universities, he says, are in decline, and where formerly Arabic scholars gathered students from everywhere, there now sits a teacher who instructs children with a long stick in his hand. And yet, an old culture dies slowly: some places in the Middle East have institutions of higher learning of such prestige that they attract students from Arabia, India, Kashmir, and China, even from the banks of the Volga. And one can, of course, come across extremely erudite individuals occasionally.

We, too, walk respectfully past these shops with books and paper. The men inside them are so fascinatingly dignified.

Dignified—who is not dignified here? If we stop at a shop and the owner is absent, he doesn't come running up to get us to enter. He just leaves us standing there. He may himself sit and talk outside at his neighbor's, and he will continue to sit there. Then someone calls from another part of the street that there are customers at his shop, and then he gets up, slowly and majestically, and comes over. Why didn't he come before? Why not right away? Because he mustn't be the first to spot his client, though he may have seen us all along. An Oriental is never all agog—unless he has become corrupted by westerners. If we then go further up the street and come to another shop where the owner is absent, the first tradesman will reciprocate and call to the other one that there are clients at his table. Whereupon the other one comes. To us "English," their nonchalance appeared refreshing and without an equal anywhere.

While we are out here in the Asiatic quarter, the hotel doorman pops up under our very eyes, despite everything. He has nosed out our way and found us. He chats with and greets every turban, calls our attention to weapons and rugs and ruins the entire street. But it has to be admitted, he knew about hideouts that we hadn't discovered yet. He led us coolly straight through a shop into the backyard of another that promised to be far more remarkable. That's how he dragged us about with him. From time to time we sat down, and then coffee and cigarettes, or a pipe, were brought us. And we didn't have to buy any of the merchandise, but we could look at everything.

Those we came to might be the owners of green turbans. They could have made their three journeys to the grave of the prophet, they had seen Mecca, were meek and pious; we were in exclusive company, so to speak. And here the dignity was sublime.

"Don't take it amiss," we might say, "but would you let us take a look at these rugs?"

"As long as you please!" is the answer.

"Maybe these foreigners will like to buy this rug," says the interpreter.

"I'll give it to them," is the answer.

The interpreter informs us of the answer and says thank you on our behalf.

Then we have to reciprocate. The interpreter says, "These foreigners are from so far away, but they're good people and would like to give you a present. They're poor people and have no jewels and no horse; but they do have a little money, money that was to pay for a long journey but that they now wish to give to you. How much money do you yourself think they should give you?"

The dignified Muslim is tired to death of money and doesn't reply.

The interpreter repeats his question, earnestly and respectfully.

Then the Muslim shrinks from being discourteous to strangers any longer by not accepting their gift, and he answers that he can accept one hundred rubles.

The interpreter relays the answer. "That is at least two-thirds too much for the rug," he says, adding, "Now I'm going to tell the old man that, if you gave him one hundred rubles, that would be to *pay* for the rug, and that, of course, was not the idea."

After we understand that this is the sequence and the manner in which a deal is to be closed here, we let the interpreter take over and say whatever he pleases.

A long conversation takes place between the two of them.

We step up to the doorway several times, wishing to leave, but there is still bargaining and chatting going on, and the end result is that we get the rug for what we ourselves are willing to pay for it. We part from the pious man in the most courteous and friendly way.

But time—well, we had all been generous with that.

The tradesmen's turbans are multicolored; that is why one sees so many motley turbans here. But there are almost just as many white ones, because the white turban is that of the nobility, of learning and piety—which often means that of humbug. Who wouldn't gladly be of noble birth, learned or pious? Anyway, many try to make others believe they are precisely that. The turbans of Jews and Christians are black and made of coarse woolen fabric, a sign of their servitude; in Persia, these pariahs are altogether prohibited from wearing turbans.

But what sort of people are those brick-red men whom you see now and then in the streets? They have dyed their beards, the palms of their hands, and all ten nails on their fingers with henna. They are Persians, Afghans, as well as a few Tatars. They stride along proudly, as though brick-red were the only color in the world. A European opens his eyes wide the first time he comes across this marvel; later he gets more accustomed to the sight and views it the same way as, say, the turbans. And if you have seen American Indians in full war paint and Parisian cocottes in gala, you think to yourself: these oddballs are not the only ones who paint themselves, and henna is just another color.

In Tiflis we were told by people who ought to know that the right to paint oneself with henna depended on a certain degree of piety. This proved to be incorrect: in Persia women paint themselves with henna and, as Vambéry reports, even babies are colored with it. To say nothing about the horses from the Shah's stable, which are recognized by their henna-dyed tails. But it's possible that in Tiflis a local custom has developed, according to which only the pious have a right to use this embellishment, for we saw only grave men sporting it here.

In any case, here is the Asiatic quarter, a good, quiet place in the world. It is surrounded by the modern American noise of a commercial center, but here it's quiet. You rarely hear a loud word spoken, rarely an unnecessary shout. Only quiet conversation and thoughtfully nodding turbans. There are few women to be seen, but now and then a couple of them may stand side by side, each with a child on her arm, and they too speak quietly. The Armenian shopkeepers are an exception to this, offering their weapons for sale and vociferously cheating their customers here as elsewhere. A Jew can swindle ten Greeks, but an Armenian swindles both Greeks and Jews, we were told in the Orient. But then the Armenians have both Mt. Ararat and the land in which the four rivers originated and Eden was located. And then they are Christians, of course, so they are considerably grander than the Mohammedans. When they had fraudulently obtained economic dominance, they occasionally showed their great superiority by not answering the greeting of a poor Muslim who passed by. Not that the Muslim appeared to take it to heart; nothing could disturb his calm—unless perhaps when an infidel offended his religious views, profaned his shrines, or a rival approached his woman. Then he yelled like a camel stud and took violent action. Only then. If he has enough to get by and fate hasn't deprived him of his health, he's content and grateful, and if he suffers privation and loss, he even then endures the vicissitudes of life with dignity. He doesn't write complaints to the newspapers. Nothing can change Allah's decision anyway, and so he puts up with it. Fatalism, this ancient, tested philosophy with its simple absolute system, has its home in the Orient. And even if there are countries and peoples who profess other systems, many individuals revert back to fatalism and face up to its validity afresh. It's so simple and so tried, it's iron. . . .

When we were about to leave, the horse still stood stoically in the sun. And the smell of its open wounds was attracting innumerable flies. . . .

We returned to the Asiatic quarter in Tiflis day after day, because here was a world different from our own. But in the end we didn't open our eyes quite so wide; looking at things with small eyes, we found that life here also had some familiar traits. Henry Drummond[44] tells a story about one of his black bearers in Africa,

148

a dandy who refused to carry burdens on his head in order not to spoil his precious coiffure. We saw dandies here too, among a turbaned population. And we also saw jealousy. If a veiled woman was talking with an older one in the street, she couldn't refrain from removing her veil a bit occasionally. Then an admirer coming along might whisper a few quick words passing by, whereupon the beauty would answer by bending one or two or three fingers of her hand. Meanwhile, the older woman just stood there as an innocent intermediary, completely unaware of what was going on. But sometimes the owner would come, the woman's owner, and he would scream like a camel stud, even though he was dignified and brick-red with henna. Then the women suddenly disappeared and ran off to their daily cage with the barred windows.

XIV

We are on the train to Baku.

We had intended to travel second class, but there it was so crowded with passengers that it became impossible; we could at best find seats for ourselves, but there was no room for our luggage. Only after much going back and forth did we finally get ourselves and our bags installed in first class. Once this had been done, we collapsed. The thermometer in the compartment stood at above thirty-one degrees Celsius.

There were three men in the compartment ahead of us. Two of them looked at us with great displeasure when we entered, whereas the third, who was quietly smoking through his huge beard, even pulled up his legs a little to let us pass to the window.

How one always has the same experiences in a railroad compartment all over the world: only reluctantly does anyone make room for another entering passenger. He's seen as an enemy and is hated; one tries to hinder him from getting to his seat and doesn't answer when he tips his hat in greeting. But at the next station this roughly treated passenger is equally rough on a newcomer!

One more experience. If a lone gentleman enters, he is usually modest and sometimes even asks whether they think there is room for one more. And he sits down quietly. This makes a conciliatory impression. But if he is accompanied by a second gentleman, a comrade, he immediately throws his bag into the net and says to the other, "There is plenty of space, you know." He brazenly pushes all other luggage aside and even expects to be helped in doing so by the previous arrivals. Therefore, the greatest fear of a traveler is to share the compartment with two gentlemen who are acquaintances traveling together. . . .

On this line, too, the locomotive is fueled with crude oil, so the smell is pretty awful in the heat. However, it isn't too bad for us smokers; cigarettes in particular seem to taste very fresh. There is smoking in every compartment, none are reserved; there are ashtrays even in the women's compartments. And the filth is egregious, with bedbugs crawling on the seats and up the panels.

The conductor knows a few French words, and when I hand him a bill to pay for the difference between first- and second-class fare, he brings us our supplemental tickets and the change on the bill. Then the long-bearded passenger sticks his nose into the affair. Giving the impression that he knows the supplemental charges in and out, he starts to quiz the conductor. They exchange several questions and answers, and I have to put down the change received to be checked; it turns out that a ruble is missing. The conductor says something: he was shortchanged at the station, that's where the mistake was made. But the long-bearded man retorts with a couple of strong words, and the conductor takes a ruble from his pocket and adds it to the change. But now the long-bearded fellow gets really puffed-up and long-winded, to show the sort of man he is; he demands that the conductor wait until he has checked the change once more. I make a bow and say "merci" numerous times to them both, for now everything was in order, after all. The long-bearded man seemed to be a senior railroad official; he had gotten many printed railroad papers out of his pocket and presented the conductor with a fare schedule.

The landscape is pitifully poor; everything is burned and buried in desert sand, steppe sand. No forests. We arrive at the Akstafa station, where there is a restaurant. I've had a fever all along and been drinking *pivo,* mild Russian beer, to quench my thirst, but since *pivo* seemed to excite me, I switched to Caucasian wine. This wine tastes like a certain kind of Italian table wine, and it helped me superbly for a moment. For a moment. Then it was as bad as ever again. What I ought to have had was tea. It's not for nothing that the natives take their samovars along and mess around with tea-drinking all day. Here at Akstafa I went to the opposite extreme and drank water. Water from the Kura River. And that was the worst of all. For once someone has drunk from the Kura River, he will always long to go back to Caucasia. . . .

Evening is falling. The travelers have got off; we are alone. The conductor knows so little French that he takes us for a French couple, and there is much good will toward the French in these parts after the alliance in Kronstadt. The conductor informs us that we shall have the compartment to ourselves all night; he simply locks our door. And although he doesn't do so without the hope of a reward, it betrays a great deal of natural kindness.

In any case, at night we heard the conductor fight like a bodyguard outside our door, to prevent an inspector or whatever he was from entering the compartment. It was expressly demanded that the door be opened, but the conductor interceded for us and replied feelingly that we were French and that I had a fever. And the door was not opened. We could have slept in peace and quiet if it hadn't been for those dreadful bedbugs. I left the compartment at the first light of dawn.

It was daybreak with a moon, cool, still.

There are plains on every side, endless plains without a tree. On our right there seems to be a lake, but there is no lake. It sits there hour after hour and doesn't change; it's a salt steppe we are on. From over there it doubtless looks like a lake where we are, too, and like we are traveling on this lake. It's becoming lighter. The salt lies in layers, one after the other, along the steppe. The salt is sacred, and Caucasia does have salt. This marvelous country has salt, too! From here, this precious merchandise was at one time carried in small bags all the way to Baghdad, all the way to India. Don't spill salt, it's sacred! Leonardo da Vinci's Judas overturns the saltcellar, and Judas came to grief. The Jews speak about salt from the Books of Moses to the Epistles to the Corinthians, and in all nations it was equally expensive and sacred. But in Tibet it was more expensive than sacred; there it was used as money in the form of cakes.

We had never seen a salt steppe before.

And here we saw, also for the first time, a caravan of camels. The animals walk one after another in single file, twenty of them, with heavy loads on their backs, swaying, striding steadily onward along the steppe. Some of the people in the caravan walk behind, others ride high, high up on the animals' backs. Not a sound reaches us from the caravan. Silent and majestic, the animals and people pursue their course south, toward Persia.

152

XV

It's half past six in the morning. Baku is situated in one huge cloud of white dust. Everything here is white or gray; the lime dust settles on people and animals, on houses, windowpanes, and on the few plants and small trees in the park. It looks like a completely insane world in which everything is white. I write characters in the dust on the tabletop in the hotel, but in a short while they are buried under fresh dust and smoothed out.

Then there is the smell of oil throughout the city. It's everywhere, in the streets and in the buildings. The oil intermingles with the air one breathes, and until one gets accustomed to this air one has to clear one's throat continually. The oil also mingles with the dust in the streets, and when there is a wind—which happens nearly all the time here—the oil-saturated dust can leave greasy stains on one's clothes. It seemed to us to be the most unpleasant place we had visited, although we could see the Caspian from our windows.

Baku has approximately 125,000 inhabitants and is one of the most important commercial centers on the Caspian Sea. Down by the harbor there is a great traffic of ships and boats and trains and many kinds of steam engines. It makes an odd impression, in the midst of this modern commotion, to see rows of kneeling camels getting loaded with merchandise in front of every warehouse. A camel can sometimes have a mysteriously vicious expression in its eyes. One day a camel was forced to rise when half loaded, then was forced to kneel down again. It obeyed, but with an air as though it swore revenge. It had huge yellow molars that it displayed, and its dark eyes grew hard, full of rage. Then it got a smack on its muzzle and closed its eyes. But as I was watching, I noticed that it opened its eyes a crack and followed its tormentor with a squinting look.

We were going out to Chornyi Gorod, the black city, a suburb of Baku and headquarters for the petroleum firms. We are being driven by a Persian; all the cabmen here are Persians. They drive like demons, and since they cannot be made to see reason and refuse to understand a Christian's gestures and signs asking them to spare the horses, there is only one thing to do: sit still. And one more thing: get off.

I told our driver by clear signs that horses were our fellow creatures, that according to the most recent investigations they even had a soul and therefore were almost human beings, but that devil of a Persian laughed me to scorn for my Occidental theories and continued to speed ahead, taking us to the black city now on one wheel, now on another. Then we stopped the man, paid him, and waited for the steam streetcar. Do you think the driver learned a lesson from this talking-to? Not at all. He had driven "Englishmen" before and knew that they were queer. He sat down to breakfast on the box. Fetching a few slices of wheat bread and a cluster of grapes from the carriage chest, he took bites from each by turns. We couldn't help thinking of the cabmen in our own dear carnivore climate.

The steam streetcar brought us to our destination. Under the black city runs a system of pipes that carry oil; the streetcar crosses small greasy puddles wheezing out of the ground and scintillating with the loveliest metallic pigments. Here there is an even worse smell than in the city of Baku. But however oily and sandy everything is, there is still a patch of garden before a dwelling here and there—unlike the petroleum centers in Pennsylvania that I've seen. And the people were differently dressed here, in silk, Persian raw silk for rich and poor.

We asked about Nobel's house,[45] and it was like asking about the Royal Palace when you were in Kristiania. We found our fellow travelers from the train journey through Russia, the engineer and his family; their house was nice and pleasant, and they had a garden in the back where the wife herself had planted acacia trees. These excellent people were living in a comfortable and attractive place, but sometimes they had to shut the windows when the smell from outside became too strong. And it could be trying enough to sit with shut windows in this heat. The engineer had suffered from Caucasian fever in all the years he had lived here. It left him during the summer when he vacationed in his native Finland, but caught up with him as soon as he returned to Baku. His Caucasian-born wife, on the other hand, was in her element and defended Baku lovingly.

The engineer showed me around the many apartment buildings, workshops, and offices of the gigantic business. The firm has its own forges, foundries, carpentry, and pattern makers' shops, and drafting rooms. Several of these establishments employ Finns, Swedes, and Danes. The engineer also showed me around in the factories. Here were furnaces so tremendous that I felt bewildered; the heat was brought up to 400 degrees Celsius. It was white heat, and from the raging fire, which seemed to spin like wheels, there emerged a weltering noise. Pursued by this white roar, I hurried back to the door and stopped only in a workshop, where I again could see and hear in human fashion.

The engineer gave me information about everything. But when I wanted to take notes, he asked me kindly not to. He didn't know whether his bosses would like it. So I avoided writing in sight of everybody, holding the notebook behind my back when I wrote. However, this was a difficult job and went very slowly, and I missed a good many answers to my questions because I couldn't write fast enough. And besides, the characters became preposterous, resembling in their absurdity the signs in the books of the scribe in Tiflis. Finally I had to be so concise that my notes became unintelligible also for that reason.

What, for example, does the following sentence mean: "261 steam boilers?" I certainly don't know. To be sure, this number of steam boilers can give an impression of the firm's huge size, but, I'm sorry to say, I don't know where they are, what they are used for, or why they are continually being stoked. Nobel was a rich man, so naturally he could afford to get himself a reasonable number of steam boilers. He liked steam boilers and loved fueling them. When he saw that Sully Prudhomme[46] had no fire under his kettle, he gave him 100,000 kroner for fuel.

Another sentence in my notes runs: "13 varieties in vials indigo dye."

This note is equally unintelligible. I understand very well that Nobel was dreaming of dyes. This accursed city of Baku is, after all, so chalk white that it could drive a person out of his mind. But to deck it out with thirteen different varieties of indigo is excessive. That Mr. Nobel cannot afford. That is foppishness.

Let me confess that I believe there is something wrong with my notes. The lines run so up and down that it breaks my heart just to look at them, and I believe the indigo dye has gotten into the wrong line. One mustn't accuse me of carelessness, for the way I study my diary, I'm conscientiously deciphering the obscure parts and am as delighted as any scholar when I discover the correct reading.

The correct reading, in my opinion, is as follows.

First, the engineer dragged me about with him in a certain building. There a brownish-green soup that seemed no more valuable than any other mud came pouring in; but that was the raw material, crude oil. And in that building the soup was distilled to produce benzene, gasoline, ligroin, etc. Then he dragged me over to another building and showed me what else could be made of petroleum, enumerating a great many oils that I find it impossible to decipher in my notes. It was difficult to take down all this behind my back, and I bluntly expressed the opinion that the distillates from the mud were getting to be quite many. "Many distillates?" the engineer replied, whereupon he showed me a shelf marked *13 varieties in vials*. At that moment I backed off several meters and was unable to stick to the lines in my diary.

But the engineer continued to tell me all about the petroleum. "And when everything has been extracted," he said, "this is what's left." Then he showed me some huge containers of something that he called metal fat. I had heard of many kinds of fat, leaf fat and herring fat and dead man's fat, but never of metal fat. Here it was. To be quite frank, it looked like a horrible ointment. But this thing, which looked so pitiful that both the engineer and I got tears in our eyes, was now—the chief product. "Previously we used to dump it in the sea," he said. "Now we use it for fuel; we fire our boilers with it, run our steamships and trains with it, supply the steamers on the Caspian, transport it to Astrakhan and furnish the river boats on the Volga with it."—"God help me!" I said. "And now, lately, we've begun to distill *indigo dye* from it," he continued. It was then that I wrote "indigo dye" anywhere I could find in my book and hit the wrong line.

~

The engineer takes us on a drive into the city and shows us around. The heat is intense, and I pick up a ready-to-wear yellow silk jacket in a shop. It made me look rather odd, to be sure, but life became easy as soon as I rid myself of my Nordic doublet. And I got a fan in my hand into the bargain.

All people were more or less oddly dressed here; the town is so Persian that it's not European, and so European that it's not Persian. There are silk clothes in abundance; we saw ladies wearing dresses of hand-embroidered silk, occasionally tricked out with some awful Berlin baubles. Gentlemen in Persian suits of raw silk sported multicolored German cotton ties around their necks. The floors and stairs in the hotel were covered with expensive Persian rugs, and sofas and chairs had Persian upholstery; but the sofas and chairs themselves were Viennese work, so-called, as was the dressing table with the marble top. And the proprietor wore gold-rimmed glasses.

We are going to the castle. Situated in the middle of the old city, it is colossal, Persian-Byzantine, ornate. It encloses the khan's palace and two mosques. The palace is now a military depot, and the commandant's permission is required to step inside the walls. But to obtain this permission we had to present my card. And I didn't have a card.

I am in a quandary as I stand there beside the officer on duty. But since Wentzel Hagelstam's card worked so well in Vladikavkaz, you could now try his wife's card, I think to myself. And I present the officer with my card, which read: "Mrs. Maria Hagelstam." He nods and asks me to show him my passport. God help and preserve me now! I think, but I hand over my passport. He looks at both documents, compares the names and apparently finds the letters to be identical. He knocks on a door and enters the commandant's office with both the card and my passport. Now we would see whether my dirty trick would work. I wasn't very hopeful.

The officer returns, hands me the passport and orders a young lieutenant to show us around. I was saved. The lieutenant bows and comes with us. A Cossack with a loaded rifle follows at our heels.

Meanwhile, my companions had been standing outside, free from all anxiety.

The khan's palace is supposed to be from the fifteenth century. Its exterior isn't much to look at, and we aren't allowed to go inside. There are no locked doors, of course, for all these gates and portals have no doors, but we were not admitted into the inner-most halls and holes of the dethroned ruler. The lieutenant knew only Russian, so it was good to have the engineer with us.

We were shown the gala entrance. It wasn't up to much, except for the fine Persian ornaments over the portal. The entrance to the harem was narrow, as is meet and proper for an Oriental entrance for women; the special entrance for the favorite wives was somewhat grander. Inside the long corridors, openings led to small rooms, cells, and there were many of these small rooms. The last khan of Baku had fifty wives, the lieutenant tells us, and when the Russians conquered his country and occupied his city in 1808, he escaped with all of them. But that same Hussein Kuli-khan was a great scoundrel: at the moment the keys to the city were handed over to the conqueror, General Tsitsianov, he had him stabbed to death with a *kinzhal*.[47]

Here we were at the palace of an Oriental ruler. The extant surrounding wall with the embrasures showed that it was built in a not very peaceful time. This home had to be defended with arms. The building has no windows, but large arched openings through which an abundance of light enters the halls. Inside, among the columns, the shade turned the place into a veritable Eden for us who came from the burning sun outside. We went as far as we could go: here people were received, here was the courtroom where the sen-tences were proclaimed, here a hall with a sort of platform where the ruler may have sat on his throne. Our steps reechoed against the brick walls. Only a hundred years ago, we couldn't have moved so freely in there, for the khan of Baku was a mighty potentate.

There were two mosques inside the walls of the castle; one in particular had extremely fine ornamentation around the portal. We expected to hear a mullah summon the believers for prayers from the cornice of the minaret, but twelve o'clock came around and he didn't appear. When we spoke to the lieutenant about this, he immediately called to some turbaned men sitting near the mosque, and finally he was able to make himself understood. They shook their heads: the mullah was ill.

The Russian lieutenant with his Cossack in tow had shown us everything inside the castle walls, and when we parted from him and thanked him, he smiled and answered that it had been a pleasure to be of service to us. And he stood a long while with his hand to his cap.

We had intended to drive to Kiz Kale, the Maiden's Tower, about which there is a romantic legend, but the heat was so intense that we gave up on it. We drove to the park. Here everything was wilted in the sun, burned, coated with dust, pale gray. It was a painful sight. There were some small trees, acacias, almond trees, fig trees; there were also some miserable flowers that had learned to survive from one rainy season to another. But altogether it made a dismal impression. When I moistened some leaves with saliva and wiped off the dust, I had to be gentle, for they would crack, being so burned by the sun and the lime dust. Soon after I had opened their pores and made it possible for them to breathe, they shriveled to pitiful curls in the sun, so I had to strew lime dust on them again. If it weren't for the heavy dew at night, they wouldn't survive.

But thistle lives on the salt steppes under conditions that are still worse. The soil in which it grows consists of clay, and salt and wind and sun singe it—but there it is, clusters of it. It's hard, bristling, like a metal wire with shag on it. One looks at these small spots of thistles with great joy. They stand there like little people, defiant. Defiant. If they get rain they bend, just as people bend in gratitude for a kind word, but during the long and intolerable drought they just raise their heads higher and become upright, unyielding, hard—like people during a drought.

Only a camel's jaws, which have the strength of a machine, can snap this thistle in two.

XVI

A steamship from Nobel's fleet is placed at our disposal for an excursion to the oil wells in Balakhany. It was not the first and only time that the ships of the great firm carried visitors out there; it is undertaken with alacrity year in and year out and is nothing special. A good many of the Scandinavians were kind enough to come along and explain everything to us.

It was a quiet, moonlit evening. After half an hour's ride outside Baku, the water is seen to boil in black swirls. The swirls change, move, and merge with other swirls; the incessant movement makes you think of the northern lights. A handful of cotton waste is kindled and tossed down into the swirls, and at once the sea in that spot is ablaze. The sea burns. The black swirls are natural gas. Then we have to ride back and forth in the flames, letting the propeller wipe the fire out.

We arrive and step ashore. The ground is damp and fatty with oil, the sand feels like soap when you walk on it, and there is a sharp smell of petroleum and kerosene that gives us foreigners a headache. The petroleum area is divided into basins, lakes, surrounded by sand banks. But it's not much use trying to block out the oil, which seeps into the banks, making them fatty and damp along with the rest.

Crude oil was known by the ancient Jews and Greeks, and out here, on the Apsheron peninsula, it has been used by the population for fuel and lighting for a very long time. But only during the last thirty years have they been making kerosene from it. Not to mention the "13 varieties in vials," which are still more recent products. Now a city of derricks extends as far as the eye can see, the world's most unpleasant and incredible city of black, greasy, crudely built derricks. Inside, there is a roar of machinery day and night; the workers shout to one another to drown out the noise, and the derricks shake from the huge drills that are sunk into the ground. The workers are Persians and Tatars.

We go inside one of the derricks. My hat bumps against a beam and looks ruined for life, it's that greasy and black; but they assure me that in the Baku factories it won't take a minute to get the oil out again by chemical means. The noise is terrible. Swarthy Tatars and yellow Persians stand each at their machines, minding their work. Here the crude oil is drawn up; a contrivance goes down into the ground and returns after fifty seconds with 1,200 pounds of oil, then goes down again, is away for fifty seconds and returns with another 1,200 pounds of oil—around the clock, all the time. But the hole has cost money; it's five hundred meters deep. They used a year to drill it and it cost 60,000 rubles.

We go to another derrick, where they are drilling. The hole is still dry, the drill is working night and day in sand and stone, in rock. This hole is a capricious hole, it's known for its viciousness throughout the city of derricks. The place was discovered last year, when it showed clear signs of oil like all places around here, and drilling was started. Fifty meters down, almost no distance at all, that is, the oil suddenly shoots up in a mighty fountain, killing people as it gushes forth and shattering the derrick. The fountain is without order and moderation, it's wild, forcing up oil in such excessive amounts that it creates lakes around itself and floods the earth. They make dams and throw up banks, but the dams are too narrow and fresh banks have to be thrown up outside the initial ones—the fountain spewed oil to the tune of one and a half million rubles in twenty-four hours. For two days and nights. Then it stopped. And no earthly power has managed to make it yield another liter of oil since. It corked the hole. It has probably found a rock in the earth's entrails down there and hurled it before the opening. Since then they have drilled and drilled without interruption, but to no avail; they have now got down as far as 650 meters, all in vain. And they are still drilling; some day, I suppose, they will get through the rock. The yellow Persians and the swarthy Tatars stand there with their hearts in their mouths; if this madcap begins to lash out like the last time, Allah will squeeze them all through the derrick's roof and tear them to pieces in a second. But then Allah would have ordained it that way. La illaha il Allah.

The noise of machinery wasn't originally part of this place; America has desecrated it and brought its roar into the sanctuary. For here is the seat of the "eternal fire" of antiquity. There is no place hereabouts where one can escape America: the drilling method, the lamps, even the distillate gasoline—it's all America. The Maccabees burned "the thick water" only for the purification of the temple. And when we have become tired of the noise and half blinded by the natural gas and prepare to leave the place, we go back in a Robert Fulton kind of boat.

Tomorrow we shall visit Surakhany. Thank goodness, it's said to have a Parsee temple.

~

We supposedly received quite many of our religious ideas from the Iranian peoples. The old Israelites did by no means remain uninfluenced spiritually by the neighboring peoples; they got something from Egypt during the time they lived there, something from Assyria, Babylon, Persia. Thus, the writings of the Old Testament mention the activities of evil spirits, demoniacal possessions that were unknown among the Israelites; but among the Persians there were evil spirits in great numbers. Then, according to the inscriptions, the Mesopotamians received these ideas from the Persians and brought them westward to the people of Assyria, and at the time of Christ there was, at least in Judea, a flourishing lore about spirits and demons. And so it became part of Christianity. Whereupon it spread to many peoples and lighted many witches' pyres. Whereupon it even got to Finnmark, burning up many women who were so possessed that they stayed on the surface of the water "like a float."

And here we stand on the spot from which Christianity received its poetic notion of the "eternal fire." There was a fire in the earth that required no fuel, it burned all by itself and never went out; such a fire was sacred. The ancients were very poor scientists; they didn't know that petroleum stems from the prehistoric vegetable kingdom, like coal. They didn't even know that science afterward abandoned this theory and adopted another: that petroleum is due to animal matter in the earth—frankly speaking, fish. The ancients were very stupid scientifically. They only got to know this thick water and set fire to it, making it burn, burn eternally. They connected it with Mithra, the sun, which also burned eternally and was God's image. And the water became sacred to them; they worshiped it and made pilgrimages to it. And when someone even erected a temple over this source of fire, their gratitude was very great.

But then the good Iranians gave birth to the great religious innovator called Zardusht, Zarathustra. He thought his people was worshiping strange gods—which all founders of religions think about their people—and so he taught that they shouldn't have so many gods anymore. He decided that there should be one good god, to be called Ormuzd, and one evil god to be called Ahriman. That sufficed. But in the course of time he needed one more god, and he would be above all the others and be called Mithra. And Mithra became truly great in Iran.

It was the same Mithra they worshiped here, before the eternal fire at Baku.

And Zarathustra continued to lay the foundations of his religion and succeeded quite well. Besides the three gods, of which Mithra was the highest, there were, he taught, three kinds of good supernatural beings, angels, who were higher than man. Then there were three kinds of evil supernatural beings, demons or devils. In short, Zarathustra taught Christianity many good things.

And everything was just fine.

But then it turned out that the Iranians couldn't make do only with gods; they also had to have a goddess. *Où est la femme?* they said. And so they installed a woman as their goddess, and her name was Anaitis. But once they had begun to change and improve on Zarathustra's teaching, they picked up gods galore, even from Babylon, even from Greece, and the people again fell into idolatry and polytheism. The Iranian kings despised Zarathustra's teaching; since it was not foreign, what was there to make a song and dance about? The kings favored Hellenism, while the people themselves found a gap in their religion, called attention to the gap and grumbled about it. Zarathustra had never managed to explain the origin of good and evil, and the relationship between the good and the evil god. The Iranians said: If both good and evil have their source in Ormuzd, that is, in the same fundamental being, then they lose their character as complete opposites—figure out that little conundrum, they said; we call it a gap. You see, the Iranians were unaware of our knowledge on this question: we take care of a trifle like that with a serpent and an apple.

After this, the reputation of Zarathustra's teaching greatly declined, and when the Mohammedan caliphs took over the country, it was almost completely eradicated. But a few faithfuls emigrated to India with the teaching intact and have lived there to this very day under the name Parsees, while others remained in Persia, a few thousand, the so-called Ghebers, fire worshipers. Of the latter, there also lived a few at the fire temple near Baku until quite recently.

Here Parsees from India and Ghebers from Persia came to pray. To these pious ones, Mithra was the same as before, the god of all, eternal as the sun and the eternal fire. No people had a more sacred place. Those upstart Mohammedans had only Medina to go to, and in Medina there was only a grave; but here was a living fire, a kind of sun inside the earth, God. Already from afar, at the first sight of the white temple, the pilgrims threw themselves on the ground in trepidation, and they approached the temple humbly, with repeated prostrations. These people had become poor and miserable, the upstarts had made themselves masters of their nation and pushed them into a remote corner of their country; but in their hearts they were mightily comforted by the thought that it was they, and no one else, whose belief in God was right and true. The Mohammedan caliphs and shahs of Persia pursued them unsparingly when they were on their way to their white temple, but their faith was so great that they preferred to put on the unclean garb of the upstarts and travel in disguise rather than give up their perilous journey to Baku.

And when they came to the temple, there were small cells and other rooms all about this blessed house where they could stay. And in every cell there burned a low petroleum flame, a small sun that never went out. And here Ghebers and Parsees lay on their faces, leaving the world behind.

But then America, with its roar, invaded the place. On their arrival one year, the pilgrims discovered that a petroleum factory had been constructed near the sanctuary. All the little suns in the cells had been extinguished; every stream of gas led to the factory.

Then, little by little, the Ghebers and the Parsees abandoned the shrine. The upstarts from the Orient had fought with them, but it was the upstarts from the West who vanquished them. Defeated, they withdrew to their remote corner of the country. Their Baku shrine is now a mere legend. But the living fire will be sacred to them until the last of these faithfuls is dead. For they are fire worshipers.

XVII

We are unable to get money on our letter of credit, this French document that is for such a blessedly big sum. Not even the Baku branch of our bank in Tiflis had seen such a paper before or dared pay out any money to us on it, but referred us to Tiflis.

We have no choice but to go back to Tiflis.

But we needed money right away; the hotel bill was due and we also wanted to make some purchases in town. On the engineer's advice, I then went to the head of the Nobel firm, Mr. Hagelin, who is also Norwegian and Swedish consul in Baku, and received from him one hundred rubles. I got the money at the first word, and the offered receipt was turned down. Mr. Hagelin was a fine, amiable man; he even gave us a letter of introduction to a big shot in Tiflis. He was in no hurry, but took the time to listen to a brief explanation—that I needed this money now and that I would return it to him from Tiflis. "Thanks, that's fine," he replied, putting his hand into his desk for the bills. I wanted to show him the letter of credit, but it wasn't necessary, he said, and only after I had unfolded it did he take a quick glance at it. But at that point the business had already been concluded. It felt rather agreeable to be trusted this way, instead of first being asked about the letter of credit. And yet it didn't occur to me for a moment to doubt that I was in the presence of a great businessman. The glance he took at my paper no doubt hit the entered sum, the essential thing, the point.

On the way back to Tiflis there are two strangely clad men in our compartment, brownish-yellow Asiatics, one in a white, the other in a gray caftan on top of a silk gown. Their trousers are wide, like skirts, their tall boots of red shagreen; the bootlegs go outside the trousers and are embroidered at the heel. They wear a belt but carry no weapons. Both have a turban-like cap on their heads and rings with turquoise stones on their fingers.

A Tatar-looking gentleman in European dress speaks with the two of them. That same Tatar knows some German, and he tells us that the two gentlemen are from Bukhara and are on their way to Medina. Pilgrims traveling second class on the railroad! Being wealthy merchants, they can afford the journey.

The two merchants behave very strangely—pulling off their boots and sitting barefoot because of the heat. Incidentally, they had clean and very beautiful feet. When the Russian conductor passed by, he ordered them crisply to put their boots back on, and they dutifully did so. Dutifully, but without embarrassment: they obviously had to defer to the custom of the country, but the Bukhara custom was the best. They were proud of Bukhara, there was no place like Bukhara. They got their dinner, consisting of stone-hard wheat rusks with small holes in them and dried currants, out of a bag. They also offered us of their food, saying proudly, "Eat, it's Bukhara food!" Their teapot had a pretty shape and was no doubt valuable; its sides were enameled and set with precious stones.

The Tatar, who is himself a Mohammedan, gives us some information we ask of him. "Why do these two travel such a distance? After all, they have a sacred tomb in Bukhara."

The Tatar asks the merchants and is told that, yes, they do have the tomb of Bahaeddin. But they do not have the tomb of the prophet. And they have no Mecca, nor do they have Mt. Arafat.

"Which way do they go?"

"Via Constantinople to Damascus, where they will join a caravan."

Wasn't it supposed to be more deserving to travel by land? I had read that somewhere.

The prophet hadn't forbidden travel by sea.

"Where are you from yourself?" I ask the Tatar.

"I'm from Tiflis."

"Where did you learn the Bukhara language?"

"I haven't been to Bukhara."

"But where did you learn the Bukhara language?"

"I haven't learned the Bukhara language. I'm from Tiflis."

"But you speak the language of the two merchants, don't you?"

"No, they speak my language. They are merchants, they've learned it." And he adds with great contempt, "I have not learned the Bukhara language."

"But you have learned German, haven't you?" I ask, unable to understand his thinking.

"I also know Russian and English," he answers proudly. And as it turned out, he knew a few English words.

We were obviously in the presence of a *modern* Tatar. He treated the two pilgrims very superciliously and laughed when they were ordered to put their boots back on. One thing that certainly surprised us a bit was that he carried a modern revolver in his pocket. He took out the revolver and showed it to the pilgrims, but we had the impression that he was really putting on airs for us. He, too, was an interesting man to meet.

Now and then when the train stopped, the two pilgrims would rush out of the compartment and down to a certain car of the train where they started to assume various postures: stooping and standing up and curtsying with both hands on their breasts. The Tatar explains that the emir, or khan, of Bukhara is on the train; it's for him the two are posturing.

"The emir of Bukhara in person?"

"Yes."

Was he, too, going to Medina?

No, he was going to Constantinople, to the sultan.

We talk about this briefly. So we were in really genteel company. The emir sat in a first-class car far back in the train, the Tatar explained, and his whole retinue traveled in second- and third-class cars, according to rank. We were no longer surprised that the train was so long. But how come there had been no great stir in Baku, with the emir of Bukhara being there? The Tatar finds this quite natural: the emir of Bukhara is not the tsar. But he did rule over a great and renowned country with millions of people, right? Yes, but the tsar ruled over him again; the tsar ruled over many lands and over 120 million people.

I defended the emir of Bukhara in the most disinterested manner, but the Tatar stuck to the tsar.

Eager to see this genuine Oriental ruler, we began our-selves to take walks down to the only first-class car in the train to get a glimpse of him, if possible, but we didn't succeed. At last we were getting alarmingly close to Tiflis, and we still hadn't seen the emir of Bukhara. And so I decide to enter the first-class car and look around.

There is no guard at the door, and since all cars are walk-through, I get in without hindrance while the train is moving. I look into every compartment in first class, but find no one who can be an emir; the few seats taken are occupied by white-breasted Europeans. I then go all the way down to third class, looking for the emir's ret-inue, but while all sorts of men and women sit on the wooden bench-es, no one has the looks befitting an emir's attendants.

The Tatar had fooled me.

I work my way back again through all those cars; during my long walk the train blows its whistle for Tiflis, and I got back to our compartment the very moment the train stopped. The two pilgrims were readying their mattresses and their bags. The Tatar had disappeared. The Tatar had obviously pulled our legs, having made up the story about the emir of Bukhara. This was the second Oriental ruler we didn't get to see, if I include the khan of Baku, who had been done away with.

We now understood why the pilgrims had made those trips to the first-class car: they had performed their devotions there, choosing to do so in front of a quiet car where nobody was hang-ing out of the windows.

Pilgrims? Perhaps they weren't even pilgrims; that accursed Tatar had no doubt lied about that too. If I could get at him with a little finger, I would knock him into a cocked hat! But why had he played a trick on us in the first place? Probably just for his own amusement. I've read somewhere that Orientals occasionally play the most priceless pranks on traveling "Englishmen," writhing with the most delighted laughter when they succeed. And all things considered, it's no wonder that Orientals try to requite some of the importunity and curiosity of the westerner. They themselves con-sider it beneath their dignity to show surprise at anything whatever, while we gape at unusual things, show them to one another and crow over them. I saw an Arab who had come to Paris. He walked the streets in his fluttering white garment, and the Parisians, that exceedingly silly race, were of course promptly bewildered by such a singular sight. But the Arab walked quietly on.

You were right to teach us a lesson, my good Tatar!

But we had to clear up whether we had traveled in the company of pilgrims, in any case. I get hold of the white-clad man from Bukhara, point straight at him and then toward the south and ask, "Medina?"

He doesn't understand.

I consult my dictionary and find the name in Arabic. Then his face lights up; the one in gray also joins us, and both point at themselves and nod and point south and reply, "Medinet el Nabi, Om el Kora," Medina and Mecca.

Then I take my hat off to them and bow. And this seemed to make them respect me, though I hadn't been able to speak a word or wish them a pleasant journey.

I walk to the bank in Tiflis to take out some money and promise to be back in a little while. But in the bank I'm told that it's too early in the morning, the officer concerned doesn't come in until ten o'clock; I had to wait. So I stroll into town, look at people and into the shop windows and buy photographs. Among others, I bought the emir of Bukhara and his premier, both on the same picture. The sun rises quickly and grows hot, it's a beautiful morning, and in the park the small birds are singing their familiar tunes. When ten o'clock came around I went back to the bank, found the right window and the right officer and handed him my letter of credit. While I stand at the window I've pushed my hat onto the back of my head on account of the heat.

Then there is a message from the manager's desk that I must take off my hat. I cast a glance at the little Tatar who sends me this message—it's, God help me, the same man who bamboozled me with the emir of Bukhara. As I look at him, he makes emphatic gestures and signs to me to bare my head.

Suddenly I no longer feel that the supercilious Tatar has the right to teach me any more lessons; on the contrary, I again wanted to knock him into a cocked hat. I'd seen as soon as I entered the bank that there were plenty of Tatars and Georgians and Russian military men sitting around with their heads covered, so why should I bare my head? To entice the manager to come up to me, I tip my hat ironically low to him and put it on again. I even twirled it a few times near the floor to emphasize how low I bowed. Then the clerks nearby started snickering. The manager abruptly rose from his seat and came toward me. Hadn't I seen that he carried a revolver in his pocket? Did I dare stand up to such a man? But already as he was beginning to get close to me, he didn't walk with such a firm step anymore, and when he reached me he said, quite amiably, that it was customary to take one's hat off when entering somewhere. He was right about that to some degree, of course, and I couldn't knock him into a cocked hat when he took it that way; secretly I was glad that I didn't have to. But I told him straight out I didn't feel like being lectured to by him. Here he was my servant: I'd done him the honor of having my letter of credit made out to his little bank. At length he became friendly and invited me to sit down while waiting.

Here sat this Tatar, bent on playing more tricks on his "Englishman." But when the trick doesn't come off anymore, he gives up right away. He doesn't even trust the respect for his revolver, this little thing that is supposed to be so highly regarded in Europe; he simply gives up. His superiority was not inborn; he had acquired it, decked himself out with it. It was European depravation.

He had no doubt also learned in some European bank that one must be lofty and strict in a bank. A bank is not a shop—here you must bow! God knows how this loftiness originated; it probably stems from subservience to money, gold. When you enter a bank, you first read the directions on the windows to find out where to go. But when you come to this window you're often referred to another window "straight across," and among all the windows straight across you must try to find the right one. And here you present your little blessed paper, a check to be honored, and this is entered into books and then sent on to a second and third window, where it is also entered into books and verified, and in the end the client must himself find the last window, where he may be lucky enough to get his money paid out. During all this loftiness and fuss, the client stands there like a veritable supplicant; even at the first window, where he is referred to the window "straight across," he understands by the tone that the work being done here is very onerous. And through the entire transaction he is helped with a deadly slowness that bears no comparison with any other business.

What if a bank were just a shop, a general store, where things are bought and sold? And what if the officers were clerks, counterjumpers, as in other stores? But you just try to believe it!

What if the banks learned a little from the postal service? After all, the postal service handles a thousand times more money and monetary values than most banks and yet dispenses with antics. You write your name on a slip of paper, hand it in and get your registered letter with the money.

I know of no easier and happier way of receiving money than through the mail. The money arrives in the morning before you get up, you are awakened by it, it comes from heaven. And all your bad nocturnal dreams about someone who comes and carries away your furniture are at once forgotten. . . .

We wander about Tiflis for many hours, visiting the Asiatic quarter where we look at metalwork and rugs and turbaned Orientals. And time passes. When I finally get to the post office to mail Consul Hagelin those one hundred rubles, it's too late in the day; the registry section is closed. That gave us a good reason for revisiting the Asiatic quarter.

In the evening we came to realize that we couldn't very well leave Caucasia yet. Being once again in Tiflis, we had to see some of the country to the west as well, Gruzia, Guria.[48] The following afternoon we found ourselves in the train bound for Batum on the Black Sea.

XVIII

One doesn't get to see very much of a country from a train window. If we could afford it and had the time, we would have undertaken this journey on horseback, in the saddle, and made long side trips into the branch valleys. Now we were limited to watching the landscape we rushed through from a window and to observing our fellow travelers. For that matter, doing both was far more than we could handle.

We travel for many, many hours and the landscape is barren, but gradually it changes and eventually we are in one of the most fertile regions of Caucasia. The vegetation is so luxuriant, I've never seen anything like it. The forests appear impenetrable, and when we stop at the stations and can look more closely, we see that the trees are intertwined with a continuous web of creepers. There are chestnuts, walnut trees, and oaks; the underbrush consists of hazel thickets. On small cleared patches, corn, grapes, and all kinds of fruit are cultivated; everything seethes and grows and ripens on the stalk, and there is a fragrance of apples. We look out upon this wonderful landscape without a peer; it's so beautiful and rich, and we have seen it! The moon rises before the sun goes down, and here too the stars come out in drifts, while the train sails into a silver sea above the earth.

We cannot see much more than outlines by now, but the outlines are fine. There are ridges, hills and dales, and silhouettes of mountains. A bonfire in an occasional village appears like blood in the white light. And the evening and night are unwaveringly peaceful and warm. I notice that there is a heavy dewfall; my gloves stick to my hands, and my yellow silk jacket darkens a shade from the moisture. And the fever chases me in from the platform.

But the dreary compartment is pretty unbearable; the light is so poor, too, and my reading was the same as ever, that old newspaper. I passed an hour or so trying to get my watch to run; it had stopped. And I wasn't surprised that it had finally grown tired, with my having constantly moved the time back and forth, back and forth during the last few weeks. St. Petersburg had one time,

Moscow another; when we got down to the Don, there was an entirely different time, and in Vladikavkaz we had to set our watches ahead half an hour. But on the way to Tiflis, traveling through the mountains, the time changed every day, to give way to a fixed time during the days we spent in the city. But no sooner had we arrived in Baku than all the oil people smiled at our wretched Tiflis time and made us adopt theirs. And when we again came to Tiflis, Baku time was unusable both for meals and for train departures. My watch had previously put up with everything; now it had stopped. It was actually quite amusing to discover it was that independent, after I had led it by the nose for so long.

After struggling with the watch for an hour or so, taking it apart and being unable to put it together again without more tools, I packed it all into my handkerchief. Then I took a stroll back to third class. Here people were still up. Caucasians don't sleep. I look for a place as though I belong there, and two Imeretians[49] move apart a little and offer me a seat. In return, I give them cigars, for which they thank me; but I had no more cigars left for those sitting directly opposite us.

There was an inexcusable amount of bedbugs; it was better to stay up than to sleep in such squalor, and I smoked and observed my fellow travelers to my heart's content. They all appeared to be poor folk, but everyone was dressed in the uniform of the Circassians, with weapons and accessories. A few of the men had bedizened themselves with a flat embroidered cloth on their heads, a kind of runner that was held together by ribbons around their back hair. They were handsome people. There were no women.

Still, in a while it became rather boring for me to sit there without understanding a single word of what was said, and since there was no music or singing, I got up and went to the next car. Here, apart from a couple of Persians, who were sleeping, they were all awake and quietly chatting. On one seat, among other luggage, lies a balalaika, and I ask those sitting nearest to me to play, but they don't answer. They look unfriendly, as if they knew I didn't have any more cigars on me. So I walked away from them.

I wander from one car to another most of the night, and when the train stops I jump off and enjoy myself mingling with people on the stations. Meanwhile, the fever is running riot inside me, and I know full well that I feed the flames by the senseless nightlife that I lead; but I would also feed it by going to sleep—that is, giving in—and so I choose to stay up because it's more fun. But I did eventually make it back to my seat and got some sleep.

I'm lucky enough to wake up just as the day is breaking, so I can take another look at this fabulous country. We are up in the mountains going down, down through a landscape of riotous fertility. Here fruit and grapes grow wild, and there is a lively bustle of birds and animals everywhere in the woods.

It's getting light; in a moment the sun appears on the horizon at the same time as the locomotive blows a loud whistle. We are going around a curve, and leaning out over the platform I can see the shiny limbs of the machine in operation. I have an impression of being lifted high up, that I'm flying—everything is marked by a proud grandeur. The screeching locomotive, invincible and roaring, passes between the cliffs like a god.

We will soon be at our destination. Farther down and to the right, we see ocean, the Black Sea.

XIX

Batum is a city of 40,000 people, or a little more, and looks approximately the same as Tiflis and Baku, with a random mix of large modern stone buildings and amusing small stone sheds from the Turkish era. Its streets are wide but not paved; people drive and walk in sand. The port is teeming with ships, small sailboats from the towns in the south, as far away as Turkey, and large European steamers, packet boats with runs to Alexandria and Marseilles.

The city is situated in an unwholesome area, marshy but fertile, surrounded by forests, cornfields, and vineyards. High up in the mountains, the trees have been burned down here and there, and on the bare spots Kurds graze their sheep. Some ruined castles rise above the shaggy woods. In this landscape Batum sits on a marsh.

Here my fever got worse than ever, whether it was due to the food in the hotel or the city's air. I even found it very difficult to walk to the post office with Consul Hagelin's money. A man from the hotel takes me there. The office is dark and not very clean. When I go up to the window, my guide whispers, "Take off your hat!" I looked at him—he was carrying his cap in his hand. Then I took off my hat and likewise carried it in my hand. Evidently it was customary to appear at a window with bared head in this country; that Tatar in Tiflis had perhaps been more right than I, despite everything. Subsequently I've learned that it is the tsar for whom they bare their heads.

I handed in my letter and was given a receipt. But I don't understand a word of this receipt. I'm still hanging on to it, because I don't know even today whether the Consul has received his money.

Then the man from the hotel takes me to a watchmaker. He is an Armenian, like my guide. The watchmaker cries out when he sees that I've taken the watch apart and begins to express his doubt as to whether it can still be repaired. Then I explain that I'm a watchmaker myself, so cut out the rubbish! I'll give him one—1—ruble to brush out a grain of sand that has gotten into the watch and is now blocking the wheels. But the watchmaker smiles and shakes his head; he won't repair the watch even for five rubles. I take the watch back with a vigorous gesture, and my guide and I go to another watchmaker.

He is an old man, a Russian, sitting in front of his door basking in the sun. My guide takes the lead, explaining on his own that I am a great foreign watchmaker who simply wants to borrow a few tools to screw his watch together with. The Russian is all agape, his blue eyes fixed intently on me. How could he lend out his tools? What, then, should he use himself if someone brought in a watch? No, that he couldn't. "But come in, let me look at the watch. Is it the spring?"

We stepped into the shed. I wished this man could earn his fee. When he took the watch into his hand and looked into it with the help of a magnifying glass, he had blue veins in his temples, as if he were thinking. He was no longer a stranger to me; I recognized his facial expressions from other people who had taken pains to find out something. "It's not too bad," he said. "It's not running," I said. But he repeated that it wasn't too bad.

He put a long, narrow tube to his mouth and blew into the watch from a certain angle. So it was a grain of sand, I thought. He again looked into the watch with a magnifying glass, then picked up a pair of tweezers and pulled a tiny little stub of hair out of the watch and held it up. The watch had started instantly. Then he screwed it together again. How much did it cost? Thirty copecks.

I'd never heard of a fee that small.

But now I was barely able to stand on my legs, and I found myself a place to sit in the shop. When the old Russian learns what is the matter, he sends my guide over to the pharmacy for medicine. Meanwhile, he entertained me and called me watchmaker in good faith. This word was about the only one I understood.

When the medicine came, the watchmaker indicated with his finger on the vial that I could take half of it. If it contains quinine it's no use, I thought. It tasted faintly of peppermint, but was fat, oily, and I had to smoke intensely afterward to keep it down. But it really helped me a little, reviving me sufficiently to be able to leave with my guide after a quarter of an hour, and I grew better and better as I walked.

~

Life in Batum has a South American air about it. People who enter the hotel's dining room wear modern suits, silk dresses, and jewelry. And they eat choice food and drink champagne. Two Jewish ladies, ostensibly mother and daughter, complain to the waiter that their napkins aren't clean. They are presented with new napkins on a platter, but these do not look clean to them either, and they have to be given fresh napkins for the third time. Then they wipe their glasses, knives, and forks before using them; their fingers are dark and pudgy, covered with diamond rings. Then they eat. They are no doubt very wealthy; they use their thick fingers so daintily. When they are through eating, they order bowls of water and wash their hands; it's as though they do this every day at home, when they take a meal with their Abraham or Nathan. Then they each pick up a toothpick and clean their teeth, meanwhile screening their mouths with the other hand, as they must have seen other genteel people in Batum do. Etiquette differs in the different parts of the world; this is how it appeared to be here. One is just as good as the other. A certain French king did many things that the emperor of China would never do. And vice versa.

People behave differently at every table in this Caucasian dining room. There was even a young Japanese here, a man with a long, thick braid down his back who was dining with two ladies. He was deeply engrossed in courting one of them, who seemed to be his fiancée; he would run out and return with flowers for her even during the meal. He had already become somewhat of a non-Japanese; his deportment was so confident, and he showed off before the fair one by spouting French phrases. That he had kept his Japanese costume made him a rare bird on the premises, and the young lady seemed to be proud of the attention he attracted.

The South American air of the guests runs true to form when the time comes to pay the check. They are quite apt to present a needlessly large bill, which the waiter has to get the proprietor himself to break. And they give big tips and leave wine in the bottle and in their glasses. The two Jewish ladies left their bottle only half empty, they were in such a hurry to get away. Because over there, at the table of the Japanese, they had laughed and talked in loud voices, and that was not genteel. They cast many sullen glances at the yellow gentleman. Then they walked out and climbed into their waiting carriage. . . .

The shops in town are full of German and Austrian merchandise, all mixed up. One can also purchase Turkish and Arabian textiles, besides Persian rugs and Armenian weapons. The population seems inclined to put on European clothes; even authentic Tatars may here be wearing a jacket and a stiff hat. But deep down they were Tatars all the same: one day we observed a Mohammedan religious service where several such gentlemen in European dress participated in the ceremonies. However, the old Persians completely upstaged them with their ankle-length tunics and their turbans.

Now and then we met such an old Persian in the street. Though old, he could be very tall and erect, and his walk expressed a wise quietude and dignity, though he might be quite ragged. One day I stalked such an old man to see how he conducted himself along the way. He went home. He had been out basking in the sun, and now he went home to rest. We came to a small flat-roofed house with a flight of steps outside; he walked up the steps, came into a hallway and to another small staircase, a couple of steps, which he climbed. I had been observed by several people outside, so I didn't act bold, but I did manage to get myself into the hallway and over to that last flight of stairs. There was no door in the doorway and no glass in the window opening on the wall, so the place was quite drafty and cold. I no longer heard the old man's steps, nor did I see him anymore, but when I climbed the few steps right in front of me I noticed the oldster lying on the bare floor with one arm under his head. It was a hard bed for such an old man, it seemed to me, but he was satisfied with it. And he didn't fetch an inspector to make an estimate of the draft in his house. He didn't cry out when he saw me, but his face assumed an idiotic expression, and when I noticed that I bothered him I placed my hands on my breast and bowed. This was meant as a kind of greeting before I left.

So that's the way things are for those magnificent old men we meet now and then during the day, I thought to myself. They don't seem to have an easy time of it, but they resign themselves and grow old with it. And if they have lived their lives in such a way that they can paint a green turban on their tombstone, there is nothing, nothing at all, lacking in their existence anymore; then Allah has been good to them. And they have no human rights or the right to vote or labor unions. And they don't carry an issue of *Vorwärts*[50] in their pockets. Poor Orient, we Prussians and Americans should feel sorry for you, shouldn't we! . . .

Batum has also a main drag. Around sunset the shore boulevard swarms with people, riding and walking. And there are spirited horses and rustling silk and parasols and smiles and greetings just as in a South American city. The street dandy, or fop, is here too, dressed in an embroidered silk shirt with a collar as high as a cuff, his hat perched at a rakish angle and his cane thick as an arm. The dandy is here as elsewhere a kind soul. If one gets to know him a bit, one will find his good nature and his helpfulness to be very attractive. It's not out of arrogance that he decks himself out, it's just that he too likes to be grand, and he chooses this rather outward way of being so, which quickly leads to the goal and entails little inconvenience. A hat can make a man known in town more quickly than a book or a work of art. The dandy takes advantage of that; why not? Perhaps he also experiences an *inward* joy from being dolled up, and then he is simply a dandy out of sincerity, of course. God knows whether even his mission in life isn't great and justified. He is the guinea pig of fashion, an outpost, pulling fashion along with him, validating it, introducing it. What's more, one cannot shut one's eyes to the courage he often has to show in the process, with a cuff around his neck.

I just saw here in Batum a dandy who had the longest and most pointed patent leather shoes in the world. People looked at those shoes and at the whole man and laughed at him. He didn't slip

181

into a side street and disappear, he went on and put up with the world. Some lout wanted to spit on his shoes, but then the dandy just displayed his monstrosity of a cane and was left in peace. When I tipped my hat and asked for a light, he too tipped his hat and was very glad to give me a light. Then he walked on in all his finery and with his amusing Swedish back hair parting. . . .

Now and then there appeared at the door of the hotel a Persian dervish, a monk and student of theology. He was wrapped in a motley rag rug, walked barefoot and bareheaded, and had long hair and a full beard. Occasionally he would gaze fixedly at a stranger and begin to say something. In the hotel he passed for a lunatic; Allah had touched him and therefore he was thrice holy. Unless his lunacy was just an act. He seemed to have acquired a taste for displaying himself, for popping up, strange and holy, to be observed and remembered with alms. Moreover, his portrait was for sale at the photographer's, which shows what a remarkable person he was. It was as though he had become accustomed to the veneration he inspired everywhere, and he felt good about its continuing to come his way. He was a handsome man with exceptionally fair skin, ash-blond hair and smoldering eyes. Even the servants at the hotel, who were Tatars, left everything to look at him, and they treated him with veneration when he came. What was he talking about?

"Get him to say something," I said, "and then tell me what it was."

The doorman asked what he could do for him. The dervish replies, "You all walk with your heads down, and I walk with my head up. I see everything, all the depths."

"How long has it been since he began to see all the depths?"

"It's been very long."

"How did it happen?"

"I saw another world, that's how it happened. I see the only one."

"Who is the only one?"

"I don't know. He tires me. I'm often on the mountain."

"Which mountain?"

"The birds fly toward me."

"On the mountain?"

"No, here on earth. . . ."

I, of course, had to be clever and know all about it, and since I felt suspicious of him I snorted rather scornfully at his simulated lunacy and went off without giving him anything. But when I saw that he didn't, for that reason, send me a dissatisfied glance, which I had expected, I grew less confident, turned around and gave him something. If this man was playacting, he did so brilliantly. But there was, of course, this matter of the portrait, in which he seemed to pose for effect. And those staring hypnotic eyes of his, which I thought were somewhat affected. And this matter of the attention he seemed to expect because he was mad. This was the man I would have liked to observe as he climbed the stairs in his shed and lay down in solitude. . . .

The fever is draining my strength. The watchmaker's medicine, which I've acquired more of, doesn't help me anymore. I shall probably have to leave this place before I've seen everything, and before I've been in the forest and inspected a Kurd's house. Last night, when the fever was at its worst and I didn't want to awaken anyone in the hotel, I dragged myself across the street to a shop where I saw some bottles in the window. A man was standing behind a small counter, and some swarthy men sat on the floor drinking from tin cups.

I walk up to the counter and ask for cognac. The man at the counter understands and plunks down a bottle. It has a label I'm not familiar with, and it says Odessa on it. "*Pfui!*" I say, doesn't he have something else? He doesn't understand. I reach up into the shelf myself and pick out another bottle of cognac. It proves to be the same Odessa label but has five stars. I look at it, scrutinize it, and find it to be common. Doesn't he have something better? He doesn't understand. I count the stars for him, five of them, and add a couple more with a pencil myself. That he understands. He actually brings an Odessa bottle with six stars. "How much does it cost?"—"Four and a half rubles."—"And the previous one?"—

"Three and a half." So one star was a ruble. Well, I took the one with five stars, and it turned out to be a smashingly strong cognac that enabled me to sleep.

And today, in defiance of the sage counsels of all wise women and all tourists, my fever is better, although I drank cognac last night.

~

It's late afternoon. I sit at the open window watching some naked men water their horses in the Black Sea. Their bodies show dark against the blue sea. And the sun still shines upon the ruins of Tamara's castle, which rise above the shaggy woods.

Tomorrow we again go to Baku and then onward to the Orient. So we won't be in this country much longer. But I will always long to be back here. For I've drunk from the waters of the Kura River.

EXPLANATORY NOTES

1. Hamsun was traveling with his first wife, Bergljot, whom he had married in May 1898; she is usually referred to as "my traveling companion." From November 1898 to September 1899, the Hamsuns lived in Helsinki, Finland. Their travels in Russia and the Caucasus were begun on September 8, 1899, and lasted for two to three weeks. By September 30, they were in Constantinople. See *Knut Hamsuns brev* (Knut Hamsun's Letters), ed. by Harald S. Næss, II (Oslo: Gyldendal, 1995): 129–30. Hereafter this publication will be referred to as *Brev*.

2. The Dual Monarchy refers to the Kingdom of Norway-Sweden. Norway became an independent nation only in 1905.

3. The Finnish engineer's name was Björckman (*Brev*, II: 129).

4. William Brede Kristensen (1867–1953) was born and educated in Norway but spent most of his life abroad. In 1901 he was appointed professor of the history and phenomenology of religion at Leyden, Holland. In his research he emphasized the study of Old Egyptian and Ancient Greek literature and religion. Hamsun spent most of the period from April 1893 to May or June 1895 in Paris.

5. Tsar Alexis (1629–1676) was the second tsar of the Romanov dynasty, which ruled Russia from 1613 to 1917. He ascended the throne in 1645.

6. Literally, Tsarpushka means "The Tsar Cannon." Hamsun's spelling of the few Russian words that occur in the text has been reproduced as closely as possible, regardless of whether it is correct Russian or not.

7. Tsarkolokol means "The Tsar Bell."

8. Ivan III (1440–1505), Grand Prince of Muscovy and called "the Great," liberated Russia from the Tatar yoke. From 1480 on he refused to pay tribute to the Kazan Khanate, and subsequently

he claimed the title of tsar.

9. Count Helmuth von Moltke (1800–91), Prussian field marshall, is famous chiefly for developing the strategy that led to the Prussian victories over Denmark, Austria, and France between 1864 and 1871.

10. My translation of this sentence makes no attempt to reproduce, in English, the liberties that Hamsun here takes with Norwegian, turning the German words *Bier*, *verdammt* (misspelled "verdamt"), and *famos* into verbs by compounding *Bier* with the Norwegian "prate" (to make "bierprattle") and adding the Norwegian present tense verbal endings to "verdammt" (damned) and "famos" (capital, splendid).

11. The verse of Aleksey Koltsov (1808–42) deals with nature and peasant life and resembles folk poetry in style and form. Hamsun's statement of his age when he died is incorrect.

12. In the 1830s, Nikolay Stankevich (1813–40) was the leader of the principal Moscow philosophical circle, to which both future Westernists and future Slavophiles belonged.

13. "Khan" was formerly a title given to the rulers of Mongol, Tatar, and Turkish tribes who succeeded Genghis Khan; now it is used as a title of respect for important persons in India and some central Asian countries. "Pan" here means a Polish landowner. The "boyars" were the upper nobility in Russia from the tenth to the seventeenth century. The rank was abolished by Peter the Great (1672–1725).

14. Contrary to Hamsun's admiring description of Nikolay I (1796–1855), most scholars see him as a repressive monarch. It seems significant that on his first day as tsar in 1825, he crushed the Decembrist Uprising. While some improvements were made in Russian economic and social life during his reign, political progress was hampered and minorities were persecuted under the slogan "autocracy, orthodoxy, and nationality."

15. Kazimierz Waliszewski (1849–1935) wrote numerous

studies about Russian history and Russian literature. The work referred to by Hamsun appeared in English translation in 1887. Friedrich Wilhelm von Bergholz (1699–1765) was a high official of the Duchy of Holstein, which since 1460 had been part of Denmark and remained so until 1864. Bergholz wrote a diary about his travels in Russia from 1721 to 1725.

16. The Lezghians are one of the indigenous peoples of Dagestan. A folk dance of the Lezghians, the lezghinka, is known throughout the Caucasus. To the Georgians, Chechens are known as Kists.

17. Hamsun deeply admired the poetry of the Dane Holger Drachmann (1846–1909), which at its best, as in *Sakuntala* (1876), combines a passionate intensity of feeling with a brilliantly evocative rhythm and form. The poem's title is taken from one of the plays of the Indian dramatist Kalidasa (fl. 5th cent.), *Shakuntala*. Hamsun knew Drachmann personally.

18. The religious sect of the Molokans developed in the late eighteenth century in Tambov Province southeast of Moscow and spread to a number of other regions of Russia. The Molokans rejected the church hierarchy, fasting, icons, and the Eastern Orthodox ritual. Their forms of worship, which took place in houses of prayer, were influenced by the Baptists.

19. Helsingfors is the Swedish name for Helsinki, the Finnish capital.

20. Jean Sibelius (1865–1957) is the well-known Finnish composer. Albert Edelfeldt (1854–1905), also Finnish, was a painter whom Hamsun had met in Paris during the spring of 1895. Wentzel Hagelstam (1863–1932) was a bookseller and editor when Hamsun made his acquaintance during his ten months in Finland. Later he published a number of poems, stories, and novels. Forced to leave his native country during the reign of terror (1898–1904) of Nikolay Bobrikov, the Russian governor-general of Finland, he was the Paris correspondent for the principal

Swedish-language Helsinki daily until 1922.

21. During the visit of Nikolay II (1868–1918) to Paris in 1896, Franco-Russian ties were reinforced, and an alliance was officially announced during a return visit by French president Félix Faure (1841–1899) to St. Petersburg. Kronstadt is located fourteen miles west of St. Petersburg.

22. Shamil (1797–1871) was a religious and political leader of the North Caucasian Muslim mountain peoples in their resistance to Russian conquest. After several major victories in the 1840s, he surrendered to the tsarist armies in 1859. Subsequently, Dagestan and Chechnya were annexed by force.

23. Pliny the Elder (c. 23–79 A.D.) was a Roman naturalist, whose *Historia Naturalis* deals with a wide range of subjects, including geography and anthropology.

24. The Jotunheimen Range is located in the central part of South Norway, the Hardanger Plateau farther south, east of Bergen.

25. All the names that Hamsun enumerates, with the possible exception of one, refer to real people and belong to scholars who published works about Russia and the Caucasus. Roderich von Erckert (1821–1900) wrote, in German, "The Caucasus and Its Peoples" (1887) and "The Language of the Caucasian Tribes" (1895). Marie Félicité Brosset (1802–1880) published and edited a great number of studies about the Caucasian region. Hamsun's Opfert, who eluded my search, may be a misspelling for Jules Oppert (1825–1905), an extremely prolific writer on the Middle East. Friedrich Martin von Bodenstedt (1819–1892) published many studies on Russian literature and society, including "The People of the Caucasus and Their Fight for Freedom from the Russians" (1849; in German). One of the essays in volume 12 of his *Gesammelte Schriften* (1865–69; Collected Writings) is entitled "The Position of Women in the Orient and the Occident." Elisée Reclus (1830–1905) published, among other works, *The Earth and Its Inhabitants* (New York: A. Appleton & Co., 1892–95), which, in

volume 6, has an informative chapter on Asiatic Russia, including Caucasia.

The inclusion of Nestor (ca. 1056–1113) in this group of nineteenth-century scholars is anomalous. A hagiographer and annalist of Kievan Russia, he is best known as the likely author of *Povest' vremennykh let* (The Tale of Bygone Years), usually referred to as *The Primary Chronicle*. The authoritative English edition is *The Russian Primary Chronicle, Laurentian Text,* trans. & ed. by S. H. Cross & O. P. Sherbowitz-Wetzor (Cambridge, Mass.: The Mediaeval Academy of America, 1953). The *Chronicle* covers the period from the beginning of Russia to 1110. Nestor starts by tracing the genealogy of the Slavs "from the generation of Japheth" and follows this with an account of their early history.

26. The Order of St. Olav was established in 1847 by Oscar I, King of Norway and Sweden, for the purpose of rewarding "outstanding service to the fatherland and humanity."

27. The same year in which *In Wonderland* appeared, 1903, Hamsun also published *Queen Tamara,* a play inspired by his experiences in the Caucasus. It was performed at the National Theater in Kristiania (now Oslo) in January 1904.

28. Hamsun's account of the incidents involving Håkon I of Norway, usually called Håkon the Good (r. 934–961), is taken from *Heimskringla, or the Lives of the Norse Kings* by the Icelandic historian Snorri Sturluson (1178–1241). Håkon had been brought up at the court of the Anglo-Saxon king Athelstan (r. 924–939) and was known as Athelstan's foster child. The two places mentioned, Lade and Mære, are both located in the region around Trondheim, where political power in Norway was concentrated at the time.

29. "Good evening!"

30. Tiberius (42 B.C.–A.D. 37), who succeeded Augustus as emperor in A.D. 14, developed a marked suspicious streak in his later years, when he ruled Rome from the island of Capri.

31. This is the horse of Napoleon Bonaparte (1769–1821).

Legend has it that the horse named Marengo was captured during the Egyptian campaign in 1798 and that Napoleon rode it throughout his career starting with the second Italian campaign, in which the French defeated the Austrians at Marengo in Lombardy on June 14, 1800. Napoleon was in the habit of naming his horses for victories in the field. After the French defeat at Waterloo, Marengo was reputedly captured and taken to England, where it was exhibited. Later it was put out to stud. Marengo died in 1831. Its skeleton is on display in the National Army Museum. For more information about the fate of this horse, which remains something of a mystery, see Jill Hamilton, *Marengo: The Myth of Napoleon's Horse* (London: Fourth Estate, 2000).

32. Thor Lange (1851–1915) taught classical languages in a Moscow school and was Danish consul in Moscow 1887–1906. He was a translator of poetry as well as a poet in his own right. In 1899 he was made a nobleman by the Russian government.

33. Georg Brandes (1842–1927), Danish literary critic, is best known for his six-volume *Main Currents in Nineteenth-Century Literature* (1872–1890). Hamsun and Brandes knew one another well, but their relationship was not without occasional frictions.

34. The classic comedy of Alexander S. Griboyedov (1795–1829), *Gore ot uma* (1825), is usually translated under the title *Woe from Wit* in English. The sixteen-year-old Georgian princess Griboyedov married was Nina Chavchavadze. Judging by his dates, he could not have been over thirty-four at his death, and his wife outlived him by thirty rather than twenty-eight years. See D. S. Mirsky, *A History of Russian Literature from Its Beginnings to 1900,* ed. by Francis J. Whitfield (New York: Vintage Books, 1958), p. 114.

35. Nikolay Nekrasov (1821–1878) was an important poet and editor. In 1845, however, when the manuscript of Dostoyevsky's *Poor Folk* was submitted to him, he was not yet editor of *Sovremennik* (*The Contemporary*); his editorship began only in

1847. *Poor Folk* appeared in January 1846 in Nekrasov's *Petersburg Miscellany*.

36. Vissarion Belinsky (1811–1848) was the first in a long line of Russian critics and literary journalists who promoted progressive opinions and championed a realistic literature dealing with contemporary issues in a spirit of social idealism.

37. English translations of Dostoyevsky's title, *Krotkaya* (lit. the "meek" or "gentle" one), range from *A Gentle Heart* to *The Meek Girl*.

38. Gudbrandsdalen, the Gudbrandsdal Valley, is about eighty miles long and runs in a northwesterly direction between the towns of Lillehammer and Dombås. Hamsun was born at Vågå, in one of its branch valleys.

39. Dr. Rank, a character in Henrik Ibsen's *A Doll's House,* and Osvald Alving in *Ghosts* are both afflicted with syphilis, attributed in the play to their fathers' dissolute lives. Dr. Rank's major symptom is a spinal condition that leads to his death; young Alving undergoes a mental collapse, caused by general paresis, at the end of the play.

The reference to "errors in Biblical translations" relates to a novel by Bjørnstjerne Bjørnson (1832–1910), *På Guds Veje* (1889; *In God's Ways,* 1890), which Hamsun had reviewed in the first number of the journal *Samtiden* (*The Contemporary*) in 1890. There are several allusions to differing interpretations of Biblical verses in Bjørnson's novel.

40. One *desyatina* is 2.7 acres.

41. The Russian word meaning "thick" or "fat" is spelled somewhat differently, *tolstyi*.

42. Abd al-Qadir al-Jilani (1077–1166) is one of the most celebrated members of the Sufi movement in Islam, which emphasizes the personal union of the soul with God. There are also poets of Sufism, mainly Persian, among them Omar Khayyam (fl. 11th century).

43. Arminius Vambéry (1832–1913) wrote extensively about the Near East, Central Asia, and India. His works, including books of travel, were widely translated.

44. Henry Drummond (1851–1897), a Scottish clergyman, was also a traveler and travel writer. His *Tropical Africa* was published in New York in 1891.

45. Alfred Nobel (1833–1896), the inventor and philanthropist, grew up in Russia. However, it was his brother, Ludvig Nobel (1831–1888), who, starting in 1874, developed the petroleum industry in Baku into a vast enterprise.

46. R. F. A. Sully Prudhomme (1839–1907), French poet, received the Nobel Prize for literature in 1901, the first such prize to be awarded.

47. General Pavel Tsitsianov (1754–1806) was indeed treacherously murdered during negotiations with the khan of Baku, Hussein Kuli-khan. Fearing a Persian invasion, the khan had requested admission of the Khanate into the Russian empire, a request that was granted in 1803. Three years later, in 1806, the Khanate became a part of Russia. The word *kinzhal* means "dagger."

48. According to a Russian historian of my acquaintance, Gruzia is the region around Tiflis; thus it makes no sense to speak of it as being "to the west" of Tiflis. Guria, on the other hand, is in Western Georgia; its inhabitants speak Georgian. In the past, the Gurians, or Guruli, were known for their distinctive culture and way of life.

49. Imeretians are Georgians living in Imereti, a historical region in West Georgia whose center is the city Kutaisi. Having been an independent feudal kingdom since the end of the fifteenth century, in 1811 Imereti became the Imeretian province of Russia. The population speaks the Imeretian dialect of Georgian.

50. *Vorwärts* (1891–1933) was the central organ of the Social Democratic Party of Germany.

HOW TO
TASTE
COFFEE

HOW TO
TASTE
COFFEE

DEVELOP YOUR SENSORY
SKILLS AND GET THE MOST
OUT OF EVERY CUP

JESSICA EASTO

A SURREY BOOK

AGATE

CHICAGO

First printed in October 2023

P. 170, The Coffee Taster's Flavor Wheel by the SCA and WCR (©2016–2020) is licensed under a Creative Commons Attribution-NonCommercial-NoDerivatives 4.0 International License.

P. 100, Source: World Coffee Research *Sensory Lexicon*, 2017.

Printed in China

10 9 8 7 6 5 4 3 2 1   23 24 25 26 27

Cover design and illustrations by Morgan Krehbiel

Library of Congress Cataloging-in-Publication Data

Names: Easto, Jessica, author.
Title: How to taste coffee : develop your sensory skills and get the most
    out of every cup / Jessica Easto.
Description: Evanston, Illinois : Surrey, an imprint of Agate Publishing,
    2023. | Includes bibliographical references and index. | Summary: "Home
    coffee-making authority introduces you to the wide world of coffee
    flavor"-- Provided by publisher.
Identifiers: LCCN 2023007844 (print) | LCCN 2023007845 (ebook) | ISBN
    9781572843295 (hardcover) | ISBN 9781572848795 (ebook)
Subjects: LCSH: Coffee tasting. | Coffee--Sensory evaluation. |
    Taste--Physiological aspects. | Smell--Physiological aspects. |
    Touch--Physiological aspects. | Flavor--Analysis.
Classification: LCC TP645 .E117 2023 (print) | LCC TP645 (ebook) | DDC
    663/.93--dc23/eng/20230221
LC record available at https://lccn.loc.gov/2023007844
LC ebook record available at https://lccn.loc.gov/2023007845

Surrey Books is an imprint of Agate Publishing. Agate books are available in bulk at discount prices. For more information, visit agatepublishing.com.

CONTENTS

LIST OF
PALATE EXERCISES

INTRODUCTION

WHY DO WE ENJOY COFFEE? It's a mild stimulant, sure. It's inspired the thoughts of Great Minds over the centuries, fueled hard work and innovation, lubricated the exchange of ideas and culture, and played wingperson for countless first dates around the globe. But its unique, complex flavor is also a symphony for our senses, an opportunity to be surprised, to remember, and to savor.

Modern growing, processing, and roasting techniques—which tend to celebrate the character of the coffee bean itself, in all its raucous variety—have provided coffee lovers a world of multilayered flavor to explore and appreciate. Perhaps you, like me, took the stepping-stone path from diner coffee ("first wave") to big specialty chains ("second wave") to small independent purveyors (still "specialty") of what I call craft coffee ("third wave," "fourth wave," who knows anymore) and, in doing so, discovered delightful notes of fruit, nuts, or cocoa in your cup.

Birders often talk about their "spark bird," the bird that ignited their interest in bird watching. Coffee enthusiasts tend to have a similar experience, a spark brew, if you'll allow me, that hits us over the head and shows us that coffee can taste like more than, well, coffee—something distinct and different from every other cup we've had before. Maybe it was a coffee so well balanced, there was no characteristic bitter bite. Maybe it was a cup that was so complex, it tasted like three different cups, all delicious, as it cooled. Or maybe a naturally processed Ethiopia walloped you with an unmistakable note of blueberry. *Does this coffee have additives? No.* It was a mind-blowing moment, and you now search for the sublime in every cup.

In the introduction to *Coffee Sensory and Cupping Handbook*, authors Mario Roberto Fernández-Alduenda and Peter Giuliano write, "It is no exaggeration to say the specialty coffee industry is founded on the concept of flavor."[1] The specialty coffee industry distinguishes itself from commodity coffee by quality—and flavor *is* quality. Over the past several decades, the industry has worked to help producers cultivate and sell flavor, and it has developed and standardized ways to evaluate quality and train professionals to recognize and articulate it. In recent years, the industry has partnered with sensory science researchers to bring academic rigor to this growing body of knowledge, data, and protocol. The goal, as Fernández-Alduenda and Giuliano put it, is to "reach valid interpretations about how a product is perceived through human senses" by reducing the bias and error that come with using human beings as instruments of evaluation.[2] In other words, the industry is codifying the wondrous experience of drinking coffee and substantiating it with science.

The handbook, published in 2021 by the Specialty Coffee Association (SCA), is a product of this collaboration, as are other industry standard resources, such as the World Coffee Research *Sensory Lexicon* and Coffee Taster's Flavor Wheel, both of which revolve around sensory attributes, the words we use to describe the sensation of tasting coffee. A more consumer-oriented term is *flavor notes*.

Ah, flavor notes. I'm sure you've seen them in the craft coffee shops you frequent and on the bags of coffee you buy—*chocolate, walnut, strawberry*. They hope to describe the indelible flavor experience we're often chasing in our high-quality brews, and they frequently play into our purchasing decisions. That being said, I'm fairly certain that you, coffee lover, have been at times misled by flavor notes, if not disappointed, if not utterly betrayed. Perhaps you've given up on them completely. Perhaps, already understanding coffee's fickleness, you dismissed them from the start.

Many of you have read the words *toasted marshmallow* and thought that sounded swell, only to taste none of it in your cup. Perhaps your first reaction was to blame yourself. You wouldn't be the first person. Your palate simply isn't refined enough, you thought, or you or the barista brewed the coffee poorly. Has a flavor note ever tarnished your experience of enjoying coffee by not delivering on its promise? Are we doomed to quest for the sublime without the benefit of reliable signposts? If all of this research has been done to codify the experience of drinking high-quality coffee, why is it so dang hard to spell it out on the packaging?

I've become convinced that "what we've got here is failure to communicate."* Yes, the industry has done an immense amount of work to understand coffee sensory science and train professionals to evaluate and recognize high-quality coffee. The *Coffee Sensory and Cupping Handbook*'s primary goal is to help sensory scientists and professional coffee tasters communicate effectively among themselves. The *Sensory Lexicon*, which includes both sensory references and vocabulary, standardizes coffee's professional trade language. However, I'm not so sure this information is trickling down to us—coffee consumers who appreciate the high quality the industry peddles—in a way that helps us purchase and appreciate coffee to the fullest extent possible. Too much of the time, all we get are flavor notes, the crumbs of sensory science, or other scraps of information that don't quite have enough context to make sense.

I wish more of the industry would use the lexicon and flavor wheel to educate and communicate with consumers, which would strengthen

* Yes, I'm quoting Captain from Stuart Rosenberg's 1967 film *Cool Hand Luke*.

our appreciation of the product, invite us to explore the diversity coffee offers, and help us make purchasing decisions. In reality, standardized consumer education and communication currently aren't happening in any consistent, widespread way. Casually, I have observed a couple of possible reasons for this.

First, while the aforementioned tools do seem to be used widely by scientists, producers, green buyers, quality assessors, and roasters, many baristas—the faces (and thus mouthpieces) of craft coffee for most consumers—do not receive sensory training or even customer-service training, so they don't know the standardized language. US baristas, like many in the food service industry, are often underpaid and under-supported for the services they perform already, so this is understand-able in that regard.

Second, even some roasters and coffee shops that do have well-trained folks on staff simply do not use the standardized language. Some places have developed their own language, and more still take a decidedly poetic, subjective approach that does not appear—to me, someone who has studied language and written her fair share of marketing copy—to be based in consumer research or industry standard marketing strategies. In other words, it does not educate or appeal to consumers. This is not surprising. The craft coffee world is primarily a vast network of small independent coffee shops that have neither the time nor the resources to hire marketing professionals.

The result is inconsistent, subjective flavor language that, from a consumer perspective, is at best unhelpful and at worst actively confus-ing. If we are all using different language, and we don't agree on what the language means, we simply cannot effectively communicate. That is the reason the SCA teamed up with scientists to create a standardized coffee language that includes vocabulary tied to references (things you taste and smell). Flavor is experiential. We can't communicate effectively about coffee unless we have shared experience (the references) and a common tongue (the lexicon).

> Flavor is experiential. We can't communicate effectively about coffee unless we have shared experience and a common tongue.

I'm not saying that no one is effectively communicating with consumers. Some people and organizations are, and some researchers specialize in this. But we consumers simply do not yet have a widespread shared understanding when it comes to coffee flavor. We don't understand how it works, and we don't know how to talk about it. To my knowledge, the SCA does not offer marketing resources to help coffee shops with its consumer-facing language, nor does it offer many resources to consumers who are interested in self-educating.

That, in a nutshell, is why I wrote this book. I firmly believe that a solid foundation of knowledge stokes the fires of appreciation and enjoyment, particularly when it comes to coffee. When you understand the number of people and amount of work it takes to craft your cup, coffee becomes miraculous. When you understand the basic science of how coffee extraction works, delicious coffee starts to seem improbable, rare. And like any interest or hobby, it takes effort to learn this stuff. For those who want to take it on, I attempted to help you start your home coffee-making journey in my first book, *Craft Coffee: A Manual*. In addition to information about extraction and brew methods, it provides a basic overview of coffee flavor but without a ton of emphasis on it because "you don't need to know why you like it to enjoy it."

That's still true. But lately, I've been thinking of coffee flavor as the final frontier—and maybe some of you would like a roadmap. Maybe you *would* like to know why you like or don't like your coffee and how you can taste it with more thought and intention. Maybe you would like to

My mission is to make craft coffee accessible to more people by collecting everything in one place and translating barista-speak into everyday language.

understand where flavor notes come from and why they so often seem to fall short. Maybe you would like to know a little of the science behind coffee flavor. Maybe you would like to develop your palate and find joy in that journey. And maybe you would like to develop a sensory attribute vocabulary so you can talk the talk.

As with my first book, my mission is to make craft coffee accessible to more people by collecting everything in one place and translating barista-speak into everyday language. Language is frequently the barrier between coffee consumers and professionals—even when professionals attempt to speak directly to us. If you've spent any amount of time around specialty coffee, you know that bags of coffee and café menus are often strewn with words, presumably to set our expectations about what the coffee is and how we will experience it. In the beginning, it feels like you need a dictionary to place an order: "Ethiopia. Natural. V60." "Gesha. Panama. Filter." "Santafé. Colombia. Washed. Chemex."

In the most general terms, information about coffee variety, origin, and processing are signs of quality simply because they say, "I am a roaster who cares about how coffee is grown and processed, and I am being transparent with you." That's important. But at the end of the day, many of us want to experience delicious coffee, and we want to be able to discuss it with other people. Some information about flavor can be gleaned from the language of origin, processing, and so on, but it's complicated. Nothing seems consistent, there don't appear to be hard and fast rules, and there are so many unknowns left to explore. Where does that leave us? With many people taking their cues from those dang flavor notes. They are supposedly telling us what the coffee tastes like, after all.

This book is my attempt to bridge the language and knowledge gap between coffee professionals and coffee enthusiasts. It explains the science behind our sensory systems, provides a "state of the union" on coffee sensory science, and teaches you how to develop your palate with exercises that help you (1) gain sensory experiences and (2) name them using the vocabulary of the industry. In the process, it demystifies flavor notes and provides the tools you need to navigate the system, explore new coffee, and identify the coffee you like to drink. The book also spends a good bit of time marveling at the mystery that is flavor. I hope the information and insight I include here inspire you to taste widely and sip consciously, with more appreciation and a greater sense of wonder.

As part of my research for this book, I attended the Specialty Coffee Association's Sensory Summit and took coffee sensory courses. But I should be very clear about one thing: I am neither a scientist nor a professional coffee taster, and this book will not teach you how to become a professional coffee taster. As you'll soon find out, professional coffee tasting has very specific goals related to buying and selling green coffee, product development, quality control, and scientific research. Our goal here is very different. Our goal is to have fun. That being said, this book does rely on some tools of the industry—the World Coffee Research *Sensory Lexicon* and the Coffee Taster's Flavor Wheel—and some of the exercises are the same as or similar to what you'd find in a professional sensory class.

This book is your introduction to the coffee sensory experience and palate development. Get ready for a weird, winding, wonderful ride.

BEFORE YOU READ

One of the reasons I wrote this book is that, in general, it seems easier these days to choose craft beer or wine from a menu and know you're likely going to enjoy it than it is to do the same with craft coffee. If you're into fine food and drink, you probably know, for example, whether you prefer red or white wine, dry or sweet. You probably also know that IPAs are generally associated with a hoppy bitterness—and whether you like that or not. In other words, we have a general knowledge about certain terms and what they mean, and we can rely on those terms to mean those things no matter where we are.

But many of my friends and readers have told me that they often don't know what they're getting when they choose coffee. When they select coffee based on a description of flavor (or other attributes), there is little guarantee that it will match expectations. In response, some simply find a blend they know they like and buy that all the time. Others say "que sera, sera" and cheerfully let come what may.

When I set out to write this book, I wanted to unequivocally solve that problem. I wanted to give readers the tools they need to order from a coffee menu, confident in their choices, the way many of us are confident that we prefer Belgian-style beers to IPAs. My research has humbled me. While I know this book will help you become a better coffee taster, learn how to be a better communicator about what you're tasting, and deepen your appreciation for our beloved bitter brew, I don't think it's possible for me—or any person—to single-handedly solve the "problem." As it turns out, coffee sensory science is an extremely complex and evolving space, and there are lots of reasons why choosing a bag of coffee might be a little more difficult than choosing a glass of wine or beer. Coffee flavor is simply not so cut and dried—and it helps to understand why.

First, most (though not all!) flavor notes in coffee are subtle—there's no getting around that. They rarely hit you over the head the way the woody note of an oaked Chardonnay or the banana note of a Belgian-style beer does. You'll likely be able to identify some flavors in coffee, especially those you are most familiar with, without much of a concerted effort. But it takes practice to become a thoughtful taster. It's a skill you develop. The good news is that anyone can become a better taster, and the exercises and tips in this book help you do just that.

But there is an even bigger difference between coffee and wine or beer that complicates matters: coffee must always be brewed in the moment. It's made of only two ingredients—coffee and water—and both are fickle as hell. Basically, anything and everything affects the way coffee tastes, from where it was grown and how it was processed to how it was roasted to how old it is to how it was brewed. The flavor notes on café menus and coffee bags describe a moment in time. Whoever made those notes tasted the coffee brewed a specific way, for a specific amount of time, with a specific type of water. Even if there was a way to control for all other factors, it is still impractical to control for water. Different regions have different water, with different concentrations of minerals that affect how coffee is extracted and thus how it tastes. In other words, coffee flavor is a moving target, and it's difficult to label something that is constantly shifting in subtle ways.

The other point to keep in mind is that our ability to explore the expanded spectrum of coffee flavor that we discuss in this book is a relatively new opportunity, and not everyone has easy brick-and-mortar access to this coffee. Most people don't try their first cup of black coffee and think, "Hoo-ha! This is delicious." This is partly because many of us try low-quality coffee before we try high-quality coffee (remember, flavor is quality). We are simply inundated with low-quality coffee, and often it's the only thing available to us. It's also partly because coffee is by nature a bitter brew. Food and drink that people say are "acquired tastes," as they tend to do with coffee, beer, and wine, usually have some kind of characteristic—like bitterness—that tells our primitive brain, "Hey! This is poison! This is dangerous! Stop!" When we don't keel over, we "acquire" alarming tastes by desensitizing our palates to them. You, my friend, have already acquired the taste for coffee. You've jumped the first hurdle!

But before you go too far into this book, I want to make sure we're on the same page about the kind of coffee I'm going to be talking about and recommending you try. For the most part, that is high-quality coffee that has been roasted with what I'm calling modern roasting techniques. This coffee is roasted to emphasize the unique characteristics of the bean itself. Coffee is full of compounds that contribute to a wide range of flavor attributes, including those that are fruity, floral, nutty, cocoa, and more. Coffee has the potential to be complex in the way fine wine, beer, tea, cheese, and chocolate are complex. The processing and roasting can bring out coffee's inherent flavors as well as impart new ones. The result is "a product that is both diverse and variable."[3] I am generalizing a bit here, but this kind of roasting is largely happening at what I call craft coffee roasters. It's one of the traits that separates craft coffee from the rest of specialty coffee.

Traditional roasting methods, the kind most people are familiar with, emphasize roast characteristics—flavor imparted by the roasting process itself—which by nature are dominated by dark, roasted, and bitter notes. These notes are traditionally associated with coffee. They are potent and tend to overwhelm the other flavors present in a cup. Don't get me wrong: there are many traditional roasters who can craft a well-balanced bean, especially in countries—such as Italy—that perfected the art of coffee roasting long ago. However, they showcase only a portion of the coffee flavor wheel. If you choose this coffee as you exercise your palate in this book, you likely won't taste many of the flavors we discuss. They simply will not be there for you to find. Coffee roasted with modern techniques still tastes of coffee, of course, but there is more there to taste. And that's what this book celebrates.

Coffee has the potential to be complex in the way fine wine, beer, tea, cheese, and chocolate are complex.

Keep in mind, too, that coffee has long been enjoyed with dairy. In fact, lots of coffee is roasted specifically so that it pairs well with the fat and sugar of steamed milk—that's where your café au lait, latte, cortado, and so on come in. In this book, we are primarily concerned with the coffee itself, and we will be drinking it black, without additives.

There are other reasons for choosing high-quality coffee, even if you must seek it out.* The lower-quality coffee that dominates grocery store shelves in the United States may use coffee varieties that are more bitter by nature. To make matters worse, roasting coffee within an inch of its life has long been a quality control measure. Common wisdom dictates that most consumers want a product that tastes reliably the same no matter when or where they buy it. The easiest, most efficient (read: cost-effective) way to do this with coffee is to obliterate any unique attributes in the roaster. Some large US specialty coffee chains do this, too. The result is oily, extremely bitter, charred coffee. This kind of coffee— which is largely unrecognizable from the traditional Italian coffee that supposedly inspired it—has become ubiquitous in the United States and many other parts of the world. It has warped our thinking about coffee flavor, and in some ways, craft coffee must fight to reverse that expectation. As a result of all this, the potential of coffee flavor is largely misunderstood. I hope to rectify this misunderstanding.

Okay. Enough disclaimers. You can start reading chapter 1 now.

---

* Besides flavor, roasters who prioritize flavor often prioritize transparency and equity, which means they pay producers a fairer wage (often higher than so-called fair trade prices). Coffee producers have been historically exploited, so this is important. Get to know your roasters!

CHAPTER 1

Coffee Flavor:
A Multimodal
Mystery

C OFFEE IS AN INCREDIBLY COMPLEX PRODUCT. Science has pinpointed about twelve thousand compounds that contribute to our sensory experience of it.[1] And input from all five of our senses—taste, smell, touch, sight, and sound—contribute to that experience. Coffee flavor is a *multimodal* experience, as the scientists say. In this book, we focus on the first three senses: taste, smell, and touch (which we experience as mouthfeel when we drink coffee). Together, these three create the perception we call flavor.[*]

You will soon explore these three senses individually, but in practice, when you eat or drink something, it's difficult to separate the senses from one another. They all influence each other, for one thing.[**] Additionally, they are all processed and synthesized simultaneously in the brain and limbic system (our so-called primitive brain), and the result is "an instantaneous sensation of flavor" that science has not yet completely explained. We humans are very good at this. At the time of this writing, not even computers can replicate the human body's ability to analyze and identify flavor in such a speedy and precise fashion.[2]

Coffee sensory science, in general, has only relatively recently been studied with academic rigor, so there is still a lot we don't know about

---

[*] Some scientists don't include the sense of touch in flavor.

[**] This is why other scientists *do* include touch in flavor. There is some interesting science about crossmodal influence, or how sensory inputs impact our perception of coffee. Neuroscientist Fabiana Carvalho is a leader in specialty coffee sensory science. Her research, including looking at how sight impacts taste perception in coffee, is extremely cool. Look her up!

coffee flavor specifically. Science has shown that—no matter the bean, roast, and preparation—people can easily identify coffee as coffee.[3] It has a distinctive (though hard to describe) quality. And although it is making progress, science can't definitively tell us how coffee's twelve thousand compounds contribute to that distinct coffee quality—or why coffee can taste like so many other things at the same time.

What's more, our perception of flavor cannot be predicted by measuring chemical compounds with scientific instruments, or at least not the ones currently available.[4] The only way to measure flavor is through us—human beings! The field of sensory science uses human beings as instruments to study flavor perception, and some scientists, such as those at the UC Davis Coffee Center, are currently researching the coffee sensory experience specifically.

For now, let's break down the multimodal experience of drinking coffee into steps, using the terms coffee professionals use to articulate the journey. You can use this same tasting process when completing and thinking about the exercises in this book, as well as when you want to consciously sip your coffee. This will also serve as an introduction to the concepts that we explore in more detail later.

Fragrance

WHAT YOU DO: Take a good long sniff of freshly ground coffee.

Food and beverage experiences involve all five of our senses—in a restaurant, you might hear the tinkling of other diners' silverware on their plates, feel the cool heft of your water glass, taste the salty, umami qualities of your burrata appetizer. But whether you are brewing at home or walking into a coffee shop, the first thing that envelops you—before you ever bring the cup to your lips—is the distinct fragrance of coffee. And that's a bit unique. When you walk into a wine bar, you aren't hit over the head with the fragrance of wine. But when you walk into a café, that familiar, enticing coffee smell greets you every time. The smell is potent, it hangs in the air, it lingers. It's something we *must* experience while we stand there, waiting for our coffee to brew.

The proper name for our sense of smell is *olfaction*. And the type of smelling we do through our nose—you might think of this as sniffing—is *orthonasal olfaction*. Professional tasters call this first part of the coffee experience "fragrance." It specifically refers to the orthonasal olfaction of freshly ground coffee beans before they make contact with water. This is an industry-specific distinction (scientists usually call smells "odor," regardless of how, when, or why they happen), but for clarity's sake and because this is a book about coffee, I'll use this terminology, too.

If you've ever taken a deep whiff of a bag of coffee, you know that fresh whole beans are fragrant as they are, but grinding them up releases even more volatile compounds into the air because of increased surface area. In chemistry, something that is *volatile* is prone to vaporize—that is, change from a liquid or solid phase into a gas phase. Volatile compounds can be readily smelled (if they have odor) because they mix with air and travel inside our noses.

The most volatile compounds have the smallest molecular weight, which means they can easily become airborne and find their way to our nasal passages. These are the compounds we perceive when we experience coffee fragrance. They tend to be "the most delicate odor notes—buttery, honey, floral, fruity."[5] They are also the reason a coffee's fragrance is different from its aroma.

Aroma

WHAT YOU DO: Take a good long sniff of freshly brewed coffee.

For coffee tasters, coffee "aroma" is the orthonasal olfaction that happens when you smell brewed coffee. (Again, this distinction is unique to the coffee tasting experience; scientists would likely still use the word *odor* here.) The act of brewing—pouring hot water over ground coffee—releases heavier volatile compounds into the air through energy transfer, making the once inaccessible now accessible to our noses. This is why the aroma of brewed coffee is usually different from the fragrance of ground coffee—there are simply more volatile compounds at the party.

The new heavier compounds blend with the lighter compounds from the fragrance stage, sometimes overpowering them entirely. The compounds we tend to smell most intensely at this stage of the experience can be traced back to the Maillard reactions that happen during roasting. Maillard reactions are the series of chemical reactions that take place when food browns, such as when toasting bread, searing steak, or roasting coffee. It's no surprise, then, that the notes here tend to be "caramelly, nutty, or chocolatey in character."[6]

Flavor

WHAT YOU DO: Take a sip of brewed coffee, slurping (if desired) to spread coffee across your whole palate.

When we take a sip of coffee, several sensory perceptions combine into what we call flavor. Our sense of taste (gustation), working primarily through taste buds, detects the five basic tastes—sour, bitter, sweet, salty, and umami—among the coffee compounds that have dissolved into water during brewing. At the same time, we switch to a different kind of smelling, one that happens from within our oral cavity: *retronasal olfaction.* As we sip and swallow our coffee, volatile compounds become airborne and travel via the pharynx (where our mouth, nose, windpipe, and esophagus connect) into the nasal cavity as we breathe. This is why some people like to slurp while they sip. It spreads the coffee across the palate and helps vaporize volatile compounds, which are then free to travel up to the nose, where they can be identified.

Our sense of touch (somatosensation) is also working, detecting compounds that contribute to the weight and texture (known as body) and the temperature of the coffee. Depending on the coffee, we may also experience chemesthesis, an "irritation" caused by a chemical stimulus (as opposed to a physical one, such as heat). In coffee, this is most commonly the drying sensation we know as astringency. The heat sensation caused by capsaicin in chiles is another example of chemesthesis.

World Coffee Research, in partnership with the Specialty Coffee Association (SCA), has identified and codified 110 flavor attributes found in coffee, which are organized into nine broad categories: roasted, spices, nutty/cocoa, sweet, floral, fruity, sour/fermented, green/vegetative, and other (chemical and papery/musty). We'll explore some of these attributes in more detail in chapter 4.

As brewed coffee cools, its flavor changes. If you've ever set a cup of hot coffee down and forgotten about it for a while before sipping again, you likely already know this. Part of this is because our perception of taste, as we'll see, is impacted by temperature.[7] Additionally, the heat that energized the volatile compounds enough to become airborne in the first place starts to dissipate, so the mix of compounds detected retronasally changes, and thus our perception of flavor also changes.[8] And if you wait long enough, the compounds in coffee start changing on a chemical level, often due to oxidation (exposure to air), which further changes the taste—often for the worse.

Aftertaste

WHAT YOU DO: Pay attention to the flavor that remains after you swallow brewed coffee.

Coffee tasters call the final segment of the coffee experience the aftertaste: it's the flavor that lingers when you no longer have coffee in your mouth. This flavor perception comes from the residue on and around our tongues. In coffee, insoluble solids, including lipids, are often responsible for aftertaste, and the most common notes associated with these are nutty/cocoa, roasted, and chemical.[9] This makes sense, as soluble compounds—those that are easily dissolved in water—are more likely to be washed away in the swallow. The insoluble lingerers contain compounds that not only interact with taste and touch receptors in the mouth but also travel up into our noses to interact with smell receptors—the three sensations that are responsible for flavor. And since it's not the same mix of compounds as was experienced when the coffee was in your mouth, the aftertaste is distinct from the other segments of the coffee tasting experience.

~~~

Every time we brew and drink a cup of coffee, it takes us on a journey. Coffee flavor is constantly shifting and evolving, which means it can ensnare our senses in a way that not many other foods or beverages can. You can see why coffee tasters like to honor the coffee experience by breaking it into separate observational stages. There are new sensory attributes to discover at every stop on the journey, which is one of the reasons sipping and savoring a cup of coffee can be so pleasurable.

CHAPTER 2

Coffee and the Basic Tastes

I DRANK MY FIRST CUP OF COFFEE ONE AFTERNOON after high school in a local diner that was primarily populated with retirees at that hour. The boy I was with ordered coffee, and not wanting to look unworldly, I followed suit. When the server asked if I wanted cream and sugar, I said no. My parents didn't drink coffee, so we never had it in the house. I knew nothing about it except that my grandpa took his black, so I figured that was the preferred way to drink it.

Both the boy and the server asked me whether I was sure. I sensed I had overplayed my hand, but there was no turning back now. "Yes," I said. "I always drink it black." When the steaming mug came, I took a sip, hopefully looking as if I had done this hundreds of times before. It was intensely bitter and watery, what I now know to be classic diner coffee: weak and overextracted at the same time. I suddenly understood why the boy across the table was, without a thought, stirring creamer into his.

But now I was a black coffee drinker. It was my "thing." And I never did use additives, which came in handy when I had my first cup of high-quality coffee. The difference was stark. Where diner coffee tasted harsh, this other coffee tasted smooth. And where diner coffee tasted bitter, sometimes burnt, this tasted different, delicious even—it was hard to describe how or why. But I was hooked.

The words *taste* and *flavor* are often used interchangeably, but scientifically speaking, there is a difference. For the purposes of this book, we are going to observe that distinction because it adds a layer of nuance and appreciation to the coffee tasting experience. Taste (gustation) is one of our five senses. Flavor (which we will examine in chapter 3) is a combination of primarily three senses: taste, smell, and touch.

Taste is a chemical sense, meaning it responds to chemical stimuli—called tastants[1]—as opposed to physical stimuli. In contrast, our senses of sight, hearing, and touch all respond to physical stimuli (light, sound, and pressure, for example). Tastants correspond to the five basic tastes: sweet, salty, bitter, sour, and umami.

How Does Our Sense of Taste Work?

At the most rudimentary level, taste happens when specific tastants associated with the basic tastes interact with corresponding taste receptors. The tongue (and a few other places) is home to tons of taste receptors, located within taste cells. The tiny bumps that you can see on your tongue are called papillae, structures that house taste buds. Taste buds are bulb-like structures chock-full of taste cells, fifty to one hundred each.

Chemical compounds in food must be dissolved in water before they can interact with taste receptors—our saliva helps with this when there isn't already a liquid medium at play (as there is in coffee!). Once taste receptors are stimulated by chemicals in food, they communicate with sensory neurons, which in turn communicate with the brain, which then analyzes the information and prompts a response. This whole network is called the gustatory system.

For a long time, scientists didn't quite understand how the mechanism of taste worked. They're still fleshing out the details, actually. Aristotle first wrote about the basic tastes sweet, bitter, salty, and sour in 350 BC, but umami didn't hit the scene until 1908, when Japanese scientist Kikunae Ikeda described it (and it would take about another hundred years for Western science to accept umami). It wasn't until 2002 that the first receptor (bittcr) was discovered; discoveries of receptors for each of the other basic tastes followed over the next decade.[2] There may be other basic tastes, but it's not considered a done deal until scientists identify the corresponding receptor and describe how it works. As of this writing, scientists are debating about whether fatty ("oleogustus," if you're fancy) should be considered the sixth basic taste.

The taste mechanism is pretty complicated, so here is a very basic explanation of how we detect taste. Sweet, bitter, and umami work in a similar way, through what scientists call the "lock and key" principle. The sweet, bitter, and umami taste receptors each have their own locks—and they can't be unlocked until the right key (chemical compound) comes along and unlocks it.

Taste receptors detect salty and sour via ion channels. When dissolved, salty and sour tastants separate into positive and negative ions. (Remember from high school science: an ion is an atom or molecule that has gained or lost one of its electrons, resulting in a net positive or net negative charge.) Ion channels allow charged ions in and out of cells and are sensitive to changes in electrical activity. The ion channels that detect salt, for example, are sensitive to the concentration of positive ions. A low concentration reads as "yum" and a high concentration reads as "yuck." Scientists are still figuring out the mechanism behind sour—another taste that can be either yum or yuck—but believe it's similar.[3]

Dear Brain: Messages from the Gustatory System

As we've seen, the gustatory system detects information via taste cells in the mouth and transmits information through a neural network to the brain. The first bit of information is what is called the *quality* of the taste—are we dealing with sweet, salty, sour, bitter, and/or umami? But the brain is interested in two other types of information: the intensity of the quality and its hedonic value. The *intensity* describes the magnitude of the taste sensation—just how sweet, salty, sour, bitter, or umami is it? The *hedonic value* describes how pleasant or unpleasant the taste sensation is.

Like all our senses, the gustatory system is designed to keep us alive. Our brain synthesizes information about quality, intensity, and hedonic value and decides whether what we're eating or drinking has nutritional value and whether it is toxic. Based on the brain's assessment of taste, we want to either keep eating or stop. If the brain determines something is very toxic, it may make us involuntarily reject it or initiate some other protective response. This all happens instantaneously and, often, unconsciously. But we're trying to consume consciously here, so let's unpack some of the messages flying around the gustatory system and learn how we can intercept and observe them with intent.

First, if you pay attention to what you're eating and drinking, you can assess all three types of information separately (practice this with the exercises starting on page 29). At the same time, none of them exists in a vacuum. For example, different qualities can change based on how much stimulus is present in food, and one taste can influence our response to another.

Second, in general, humans (like many omnivores) tend to gravitate toward sweet and umami things and show aversion toward bitter things. Salty and sour can go either way, depending on intensity. Scientists generally believe that these responses are linked to "evolutionary pressures."[4] In other words, sweet and umami things have a tendency to give us the nutrition we need to survive, while bitter things tend to be toxic. Pleasantly salty and sour things tend to indicate nutrition, while overly salty and sour things tend to be spoiled or toxic. Information about the basic tastes can trigger automatic behaviors, such as gagging or licking, that appear to be hardwired in the "ancient" part of the brain—lingering evidence that our sense of taste plays a critical role in our species' survival.[5]

In sum, how much we like a taste often depends on both its quality and intensity. This is at the heart of why we perceive one cup of coffee as "good" and another cup of coffee as "bad." For example, an under-extracted coffee has an overabundance of molecules that contribute to perceived acidity, which makes the cup unpleasantly sour, while overextracted coffee has too many bitter-contributing molecules, making the cup unpleasantly bitter. A well-extracted cup has a pleasant balance of acidity and bitterness.

Last, and perhaps most importantly, our perception of taste is influenced by our genetics and life experience. This ultimately means that taste is not inherently objective. On a physiological level, we may physically sense taste—and thus experience taste—differently from our neighbor. In fact, our perception of and sensitivity to the five basic tastes can vary widely. At the same time, we can actively shape our gustatory system through experience, which is often a product of our environment, and through mindful observation. (So, yes, that means that what I described in the previous paragraph about over- and underextracted coffee is a generalization from a Western, specifically US, perspective.) We can become better tasters! And what we perceive as pleasant or unpleasant can change naturally over time—or by sheer force of will.

> ### FUN FACT
>
> The tongue map is a myth! Many of us grew up with textbooks that featured a tongue map that explained how taste is perceived on different regions of the tongue—sweet on the tip, for example. As it turns out, that map was just based on some misinterpreted data. In reality, we can detect all five tastes on all areas of our tongues.

The Basic Tastes in Coffee

Bitter and sour are the primary basic tastes found in coffee, but let's take a closer look at the biology and chemistry behind all the basic tastes and how they might express themselves in coffee. For each one, I identify a common reference—something you can consume that represents the taste attribute. You'll use these to practice identifying basic tastes in the exercises found in this section. I recommend preparing each of the five basic taste references and conducting a blinded tasting (see page 142) until you can distinguish each easily. This is the same exercise that coffee professionals use to pass introductory sensory courses.

BITTER

Common bitter references: caffeine, Epsom salt (magnesium sulfate), Goody's Extra-Strength Headache Powder

Primary bitter compounds in coffee: chlorogenic acid lactones, phenylindanes, caffeine, unidentified compounds

The bitter taste may be the most complex of the five tastes,[6] and there's still a lot science doesn't know about it. The chemical structure of bitter tastants can vary widely, and scientists have so far identified about twenty-five bitter taste receptors in humans.[7] These receptors can detect hundreds of different bitter tastants with wide-ranging structures, from tiny ions to relatively heavy peptides.[8]

You can think of bitter as essentially the opposite of sweet. Whereas sweet is innately pleasant, bitter is innately unpleasant, even to infants and other animals. Our brains read it as "poison," "toxic," or "dangerous." As such, many of the purest taste references, such as quinine, are not easily obtainable because they are toxic at certain quantities, and certainly too dangerous for me to recommend you consume for this book. The SCA recommends pure caffeine powder as a training reference for bitterness. Pure caffeine powder is difficult to come by, unless you are a business or institution, because it is dangerous to consume at higher quantities. Caffeine pills are widely available, but they usually contain additives to make them less bitter. You can also use magnesium sulfate (Epsom salt), a bitter-tasting salt that scientists discovered in 2019 was perceived by a receptor called TAS2R7.[9] Another alternative is Goody's powder, which is an over-the-counter medication that contains pain relievers and caffeine. Epsom salt and Goody's powder are widely available and useful around the house beyond sensory training, but they may not have as much of a "pure" bitter taste as pure caffeine. There really isn't a perfect reference for bitter.*

It likely comes as no surprise that of the basic tastes, bitter is the most present in coffee. And no wonder: there are seventy to two hundred bitter tastants found in coffee.[10] Caffeine is one of them, but it doesn't contribute as much (10 to 20 percent) to coffee's bitterness as other compounds. Recent research suggests that 50 to 70 percent of coffee's bitterness comes from chlorogenic acid lactones and up to 30 percent comes from phenylindanes, both of which form during the roasting process. Scientists believe that up to 20 percent of coffee's bitterness comes from unknown tastants.[11]

Oddly, you won't find bitterness on a coffee professional's evaluation sheet, and in my experience, coffee professionals tend to avoid discussing "bitterness" in coffee at all. Sometimes, it seems like it's regarded as a negative attribute, even though it is ever present—to one degree or another—in coffee. You can't have coffee without bitterness, and understanding your threshold for bitterness is important information when discovering what kind of coffee you enjoy.

According to the SCA, there is a level of nuance to how bitterness presents itself in coffee. Caffeine bitterness is "clean" or "unidimensional"; chlorogenic acid lactones are "round," "velvety," or "smooth";

---

* Choose a caffeine pill that is powder enclosed in a plastic capsule, as opposed to a compressed tablet. I found that the latter often has some kind of flavoring added, which throws off the reference. The capsules have filler, usually something like rice flour that dilutes the bitterness, so you many need to increase the amount you use, but be warned: caffeine pills are hard to dissolve in water, likely because of the filler. Goody's powder dissolves much more easily and contains three bitter components: caffeine, acetaminophen, and aspirin. At higher concentrations when dissolved in water, it can have a strange acidic taste.

Fundamental Taste: Bitter

Use this exercise to practice identifying the bitter quality on its own. Once it's in your memory bank, it will be easier to identify qualities of bitterness in coffee and other food and drink.

What you'll need

- digital scale (0.1 gram precision)
- Goody's Extra-Strength Headache Powder, powdered caffeine, or Epsom salt
- 1 liter hot filtered or spring water (no additives), plus room temperature water for tasting plain
- two equal-size (4- to 8-ounce) drinking glasses with lids (such as coasters)

Create a 0.05% caffeine solution by dissolving 0.5 grams of caffeine/1.5 grams of Goody's Powder/5 grams of Epsom salt in 1 liter of hot water, stirring or shaking until completely dissolved (none of these references dissolve well unless you use hot water). Cover the bottle and let the solution cool to room temperature.

Pour the bitter solution into one glass and cover to keep the aromatics in. Pour plain water into the other glass. Taste each and compare. What does the taste feel like? What does the taste remind you of? Describe it as best you can and/or connect it to a memory.

Tips

- For all basic taste exercises, try using 1-liter plastic or glass bottles. That way, you can easily store your samples for comparison and blinded tasting to test your identification skills. Once each reference is made, store them in the refrigerator and use within a couple of days. Let them come to room temperature before tasting.

- I conducted this exercise with the powder from inside caffeine capsules and with Goody's Extra-Strength Headache Powder. Although both contain additives, I think the Goody's powder makes the better reference. Keep in mind that I created the Epsom salt ratio myself, and I could not scientifically confirm it is the same intensity as the other references. Epsom salt also has complex basic taste qualities, so it isn't the purest reference, but it's better than nothing.

and phenylindanes are "harsh"[12] and appear to contribute to astringency, a separate sensation that is often associated with but distinct from bitterness (see page 65).

Whether bitter tastants provide additional distinct sensory qualities or subqualities (as sour and sweet tastants do) has yet to be fully demonstrated and articulated from a scientific perspective. Research from 2019 found that some bitter tastants significantly affect how tasters perceived retronasal coffee aroma, suggesting that specific bitter tastants do possess distinct sensory qualities. However, this may not be due to a specific difference with the bitter modality itself but rather the effect of the bitter tastant's combination of subqualities (salty, astringent, and metallic, for example).[13]

As a coffee lover, you well know that, over time, our natural aversion to bitterness can morph into an affinity for it. Coffee is a classic example. So are beer and dark chocolate. Scientists think this transformation is more likely to occur when bitterness is paired with something enjoyable. Keep in mind, too, that humans' sensitivity to bitterness can vary widely, and genetics, as we'll see later, is partly responsible. Culture also plays a role, and this is evident in the different coffee cultures around the world. Some cultures prefer intensely bitter coffee, while others do not.[14]

The quality and intensity of bitterness depend on both the concentration of compounds found in the green (unroasted) beans and their roast level. Some types of coffee, such as *C. canephora*, have more naturally occurring bitter compounds than other types of coffee, such as *C. arabica*. But even *C. arabica*, when heavily roasted, will be more bitter than less roasted coffees, due to the concentration of phenylindanes. Recent studies have also found that perceived bitterness in coffee is linked to its total dissolved solids (TDS), which is a measure of strength. High-TDS coffee is perceived to have more intense bitterness.[15]

SOUR

Common sour reference: citric acid

Primary sour compounds in coffee: chlorogenic acids, carboxylic acids, phosphoric acid

The sour taste is a bit of an oddball, as we humans can find it either highly appealing or highly unappealing—it can add a pleasant, tangy dimension to food and drink or it can revolt us, especially in high quantities. Our draw or aversion to it can change throughout our lives: infants tend to reject sour while children often gravitate toward it (did any of my fellow millennials have a Warheads phase in elementary school?). Although the mechanism is still being worked out, scientists have long known that acids are associated with the sour taste. They believe that sourness helps us detect acids and avoid ingesting too many of them, which can disrupt our bodies' pH balance. The sour taste is also associated with electrolytes, minerals that are essential to nutrition.[16]

Along with bitter, sour is an important basic taste in coffee. Coffee tasters use the word *acidity* to describe it, and it's a prized quality, especially in light and medium roasted coffees, so much so that it has its own section on professional evaluation sheets.

Sour tastants are always acids, and in coffee this includes three major types: chlorogenic acids, carboxylic acids, and phosphoric acid. Acids make their way into coffee in all sorts of ways. This includes during growing (absorbed through the soil, produced during photosynthesis), processing (formed during fermentation), roasting, and brewing.[17]

Sour tastants tend to have distinct sensory attributes and can thus present in many ways in coffee, in terms of both quality and intensity. You are likely already familiar with the carboxylic acids that serve as references in the *Sensory Lexicon*: citric acid (associated with lemons), acetic acid (associated with vinegar and ferments), butyric acid (associated with aged cheeses, such as Parmesan), malic acid (associated with apples), and isovaleric acid (associated with foot odor and cheeses such as Romano.)

Some sour acids provide additional sensory attributes because they are also volatile, which means that your retronasal olfaction gets involved. Acetic and formic acids, for example, are thought to be responsible for a "winey" character in coffee.[18] In contrast, studies have found that, in general, citric acid provides a "burst of tartness," and malic acid provides a "smooth tartness," both distinct qualities from the "tart and sour" character of acetic acid.[19] Additionally, you know from the bitter discussion that compounds formed from chlorogenic acids have a bitter dimension. Caffeic and quinic acids, also formed from chlorogenic acids, have a similarly bitter, dry quality.

"SOURNESS" VERSUS "ACIDITY"

The scientific definition of terms is often different from how we use them in everyday speech, when we are not so technically precise. From a chemistry perspective (and in the simplest terms) an *acid* is a molecule that donates protons (usually a positively charged hydrogen ion) in a solution. Strong acids (low number on the pH scale) donate lots of protons, and weak acids (high number on the pH scale) donate fewer. Many acids are sour tastants, but not all.

In coffee world parlance, these terms are used to communicate a quality judgment. *Acidity* is used to describe a pleasant, sought-after quality ("tanginess," "brightness," and other euphemisms are often used to describe sour qualities) in coffee, while *sourness* is used to describe an unpleasant sensation. Both acidity and sourness are references to the basic taste called sour. In the former, the perceived sour taste is in balance with the rest of the cup; in the latter, the sour taste is too intense for the drinker's palate.

Fundamental Taste: Sour

Use this exercise to practice identifying the sour quality on its own. Once it's in your memory bank, it will be easier to identify qualities of sour in coffee and other food and drink.

What you'll need

- digital scale (0.1 gram precision)
- food-grade citric acid
- 1 liter filtered or spring water (no additives), plus more for tasting plain
- two equal-size (4- to 8-ounce) drinking glasses with lids (such as coasters)

Create a 0.05% citric acid solution by dissolving 0.5 grams of citric acid in 1 liter of water, stirring or shaking until the citric acid is completely dissolved.

Pour the citric acid solution into one glass and cover to keep the aromatics in. Pour plain water into the other glass. Taste each and compare. What does the taste feel like? What does the taste remind you of? Describe it as best you can and/or connect it to a memory.

Tips

- Citric acid is sold at some grocery stores and online.
- Keep your solution, as it plays a role in other flavor attributes (see page 114). Store in the refrigerator and use within a couple of days. Let it come to room temperature before tasting.

You might think that the intensity of the sour taste would correlate with the pH of coffee. After all, green (unroasted) coffee is about 10 percent acid by weight, including citric, malic, and acetic acids.[20] However, a recent study found that wasn't the case. Recall that not all acids produce a sour taste: chlorogenic acids in coffee, for example, tend to produce a bitter taste. Likewise, not all strong acids (low pH) have a high intensity of sour taste. Sometimes, weak acids (high pH) have a greater sour intensity than strong acids. This led researchers to believe that something else might be at play.[21]

The resulting study found that perceived acidity did correlate with titratable acidity, the measure of the total acid concentration in food. (pH, on the other hand, measures only the concentration of dissociated acids, those that have released their hydrogen ions.)[22] Moreover, the perception of sourness changed the most based on the way the coffee was brewed—not on its roast level or anything else. The highest perceived sour intensity was found in coffee with a high concentration of TDS and low percent extraction (PE)—the brew with the lowest pH—and the coffee that lacked in perceived acidity had low TDS and high PE.[23]

TDS AND PE

Total dissolved solids (TDS) measures the *strength* of coffee. Strong coffee has more dissolved coffee compounds in it than weak coffee does. Percent extraction (PE)—also called extraction yield or extraction—refers to how much material from your coffee dose (the grounds you started with) made it into your cup. It has to do, primarily, with how long water was in contact with the coffee, as water is what extracts compounds from the grounds. Not enough time and you have *underextracted* coffee. Too much time and you have *overextracted* coffee. See page 86 for a summary of how brewing affects flavor.

That being said, during roasting, some acids are broken into other acids and carbohydrates—in general, the darker the roast, the lower the acid content of the coffee, but it's still there.[24] Still, roast does affect the perception of acidity in coffee. The sour tastants that remain after high levels of roasting are easily overwhelmed by bitter tastants, which increase as coffee is roasted.[25] This is why sour can shine in light roasted coffee and be completely obscured in dark roasted coffee.

SWEET

Common sweet reference: table sugar (sucrose)

Primary sweet compounds in coffee: probably none, since sweetness in coffee is a perception

The sweet taste is almost universally appealing to humans (even babies) and most other mammals, as sweet is associated with carbohydrates, which are a necessary part of our nutrition. It is perceived as pleasant at even very low concentrations (but very high concentrations can turn us off).[26] Interestingly, studies have shown that animals that eat strictly meat-based diets with no need for carbs, like big cats and house kitties, are categorically indifferent to the sweet taste.[27] Coincidence? Science doesn't think so.

Sweet tastants are detected with the help of two receptors. (Cats don't have the gene for one of these, by the way.) Mounting evidence suggests that we have sweet taste receptors throughout our body, including the gastrointestinal tract, nose, and respiratory system.[28]

Unlike some of the basic tastes, many different tastants can activate sweet taste receptors.[29] Of course, there are tastants like sugars (sucrose, glucose, fructose, maltose) but also sweet amino acids and sweet proteins. Scientists have also cracked the code on how to design certain molecule structures that activate our sweet taste receptors—enter artificial sweeteners such as saccharin and aspartame.

Sweet can reduce the perception of some bitter tastants,[30] which is perhaps why sweetners are so often added to coffee.

However, in specialty coffee, natural sweetness—not the added kind—is a highly valued attribute and an important part of a well-balanced cup. Professional coffee tasters often seek sweetness in a cup, and it has its own section on the cupping score sheet. But this is primarily *perceived* sweetness. In other words, the sensory perception of sweet in coffee is not strongly correlated with known sweet tastants, such as sugar.

As far as we know, there are very few naturally occurring sweet tastants in coffee by the time we are sipping it from our cups. There *are* sugars in green coffee (as much as 10 percent sucrose, according to the SCA), but they are degraded nearly to the point of absence during the roasting process. Recent research done by the UC Davis Coffee Center has found that the sweet tastants—such as sucrose and the simple sugars that form as the roasting process breaks down complex carbohydrates—are well below the human threshold for perception, confirming that natural sugars have little to do with sweetness in coffee.[31]

So, what are we tasting? Part of it is likely to do with compounds that contribute to aroma and/or other flavor attributes that "trick" our brains, giving us the sensory *impression* of sweetness.[32] These include compounds with sensory qualities reminiscent of caramel, nuts, chocolate, and fruit, which are common in coffee.[33] These qualities are actually aromas, perceived through retronasal olfaction. A true sweet taste would be perceived through taste receptors on the tongue.

Another theory is that some compounds in coffee may enhance sweetness, even when true sweet tastants are at a very low concentration. These enhancing compounds may give our taste buds the boost they need to detect sweetness in coffee.[34] During the writing of this book, the Specialty Coffee Association announced that its Coffee Science Foundation (CSF) had partnered with the Ohio State University to conduct new "sweetness in coffee" research, the results of which are still forthcoming at publication.[35]

Fundamental Taste: Sweet

Use this exercise to practice identifying the sweet quality on its own. Once it's in your memory bank, it will be easier to identify qualities of perceived sweetness in coffee and qualities of actual sweetness in other food and drink.

What you'll need

- digital scale
- granulated white sugar
- 1 liter filtered or spring water (no additives), plus more for tasting plain
- two equal-size (4- to 8-ounce) drinking glasses with lids (such as coasters)

Create a 1.0% sucrose solution by dissolving 10 grams of sugar in 1 liter of water, stirring or shaking until the sugar is completely dissolved.

Pour the sucrose solution into one glass and cover to keep the aromatics in. Pour plain water into the other glass. Taste each and compare. What does the taste feel like? What does the taste remind you of? Describe it as best you can and/or connect it to a memory.

Tip

- Store in the refrigerator and use within a couple of days. Let it come to room temperature before tasting.

SALTY

Common salty reference: table salt (sodium chloride)

Primary salty compounds in coffee: potassium, sodium

Salt—sodium chloride—is an important part of our nutrition. Sodium helps our bodies perform vital functions, such as conducting nerve impulses and maintaining the right balance of water and minerals. Like sweetness, saltiness is perceived as pleasant, even at low concentrations.[36] Humans and other mammals tend to gravitate toward salty food even when we already have enough sodium in our diets (hello, high blood pressure), which suggests to scientists that the salty taste is innately preferred by our gustatory system and not learned. (High concentrations of salt are generally off-putting, however.)

Infants don't immediately prefer salt the way they do sugar, but studies have found the preference starts developing around four to six months old. We can take action to moderate our sodium preferences by eating less salt, but as the innate allure of salt is so strong, it can be rather difficult for many people to do. Salt has more pleasing effects than just the salty taste.[37] It can affect texture, such as contributing to a sense of thickness in soup. In can enhance sweetness, sourness, and umami; neutralize some bitter tastants; reduce off-flavors; improve flavor balance; and boost flavor intensity. No wonder we crave it!

The salty taste is caused by a simple tastant: ions, and the sodium ion in particular (though potassium and magnesium salts can also taste salty).[38] Scientists would love to replicate salty in the lab, as they have with sweet—there is financial incentive to figure out a way to get us to eat less salt and thus reduce the health problems associated with high-salt diets. But so far? No dice.

Some outlets recommend adding salt to coffee, due to its neutralizing effects on some bitter compounds. In general, though, the salty taste in coffee is considered an off-flavor. Coffee does contain some sodium, a

Fundamental Taste: Salty

Use this exercise to practice identifying the salty quality on its own. Once it's in your memory bank, it will be easier to identify qualities of saltiness in coffee (should you be unlucky enough to come across it) and other food and drink.

What you'll need

- digital scale (0.1 gram precision)
- noniodized salt
- 1 liter filtered or spring water (no additives), plus more for tasting plain
- two equal-size (4- to 8-ounce) drinking glasses with lids (such as coasters)

Create a 0.15% salt solution by dissolving 1.5 grams of salt in 1 liter of water, stirring or shaking until the salt is completely dissolved.

Pour the salt solution into one glass and cover to keep the aromatics in. Pour plain water into the other glass. Taste each and compare. What does the taste feel like? What does the taste remind you of? Describe it as best you can and/or connect it to a memory.

Tip

- Store in the refrigerator and use within a couple of days. Let it come to room temperature before tasting.

common salty tastant, about 5 milligrams per 8-ounce (237-gram) cup, but that is generally below our threshold to taste salty. In order for us to detect salty in our brew, everything would have to go right (or wrong, depending on how you look at it): there'd have to be enough salty tastants in the brew and other tastes could not cover it up.

However, if the water you are using to brew coffee has high levels of sodium or potassium, it might cause your coffee to taste salty. Some claim that saltiness is a sign of underextraction.[39]

UMAMI

Common umami reference: MSG (monosodium glutamate)

Primary umami compounds in coffee: unknown, but maybe the amino acid l-glutamate

Umami is often described as "rich," "savory," and "mouth-filling"—the kind of sensations associated with foods like meat, seafood, seaweed, mushrooms, and tomatoes. Like sweet and salty, umami is generally perceived by humans as pleasant, even at low concentrations, and is associated with proteins, which are essential to our life functions.[40] Proteins contain amino acids, some of which are umami tastants along with many short peptides and some organic acids.[41] One amino acid that really sets off umami taste receptors is l-glutamate, which is close to its pure form in monosodium glutamate, or MSG. Another is aspartic acid.

L-glutamate is present in coffee—and the lexicon does include the attribute "meaty/brothy"—but there hasn't been much research related to umami and coffee. That's not surprising, since Western science rejected umami as a basic taste for a long time and has had to play catch-up in recent years. So far, science has identified two receptors for umami, although there may be more. One interesting feature of umami is that it seems we can detect subtle differences in umami, suggesting

Fundamental Taste: Umami

Use this exercise to practice identifying the umami quality on its own. Once it's in your memory bank, it will be easier to identify qualities of umami in coffee and other food and drink.

What you'll need

- digital scale (0.1 gram precision)
- monosodium glutamate (MSG)
- 1 liter filtered or spring water (no additives), plus more for tasting plain
- two equal-size (4- to 8-ounce) drinking glasses with lids (such as coasters)

Create a 0.06% MSG solution by dissolving 0.6 grams of MSG in 1 liter of water, stirring or shaking until the MSG is completely dissolved.

Pour the MSG solution into one glass and cover to keep the aromatics in. Pour plain water into the other glass. Taste each and compare. What does the taste feel like? What does the taste remind you of? Describe it as best you can and/or connect it to a memory.

Tips

- MSG is sold at most grocery stores, often in the spice section as "flavor enhancer" or "accent salt"; just check the ingredients to make sure it's pure MSG.
- Store the solution in the refrigerator and use within a couple of days. Let it come to room temperature before tasting.

there are several types of umami taste. Umami also has the remarkable ability to make food taste better—period.[42]

As of this writing, umami in coffee is a relatively rare profile but not unheard-of. In 2013, World Barista Champion Hidenori Izaki competed at the championships with a program that highlighted the umami profile in coffee. He took great care in explaining the concept to the judges, not taking for granted that they were already familiar with this coffee profile.[43] Still, the coffee-specific research related to umami is far less than that of sweet, bitter, and sour. Anecdotally, one of the best coffees I've ever tasted was a cold-brewed Kenyan coffee that had a distinct sweet, savory tomato note, which may sound strange but was delicious—I've never tasted anything like it before or since.

What Impacts Our Perception of Taste?

Earlier, I mentioned that individuals experience taste in fundamentally different ways. For example, two people can be drinking the exact same cup of coffee, and one might find its bitterness pleasant while the other might find that the bitterness is too intense, and thus unpleasant. How can that be? Well, genetics and culture both play a role. Understanding these differences is helpful when you are navigating the world of specialty coffee, developing your palate, and identifying your preferences. Sometimes, a kind of groupthink can happen in which certain flavor profiles are labeled objectively "bad" and others are labeled objectively "good." A lot of the time, that isn't true. A basic understanding of how genes and culture affect taste and preference will also prime you to appreciate coffee culture beyond your own, if you are lucky enough to have the opportunity to explore.

GENES

Genetics can affect our perception of and sensitivity to the five basic tastes. Remember how scientists believe that specific taste receptors detect specific corresponding tastes? Well, these taste receptors are influenced by our genes. As with eye color, hair color, height, and any number of physical traits that arc inherited from our ancestors, taste receptors are controlled by our DNA—and there is quite a bit of natural genetic variation afoot. Just as one sibling's hair might be one shade of brown and the other sibling's another, your taste receptors may also be genetically coded to express differently. For example, you may have more taste buds than other people, which may make you more sensitive to sweetness (studies have shown that genetics account for up to one-third of the variation in sweet taste perception).[44] In other words, how we detect and perceive taste—our taste physiology—is inherited, and researchers tend to believe that taste physiology influences our personal taste preferences and behavior.

Let's spend a moment with bitterness, the perception of which is quite variable among us humans. We have twenty-five known receptors for bitterness, but not all of us are able to detect all known bitter tastants.[45] Two tastants are often used as a measuring stick for so-called supertasters, or individuals who perceive the basic tastes with greater intensity than others in the population. One tastant is called phenylthiocarbamide (PTC) and the other is 6-n-propylthiouracil (PROP).

Supertasters can detect PTC and/or PROP as bitter while others cannot taste them at all, and studies have isolated the genes that control the perception of these chemicals (though this doesn't offer a complete explanation of supertasters).[46] Studies have also shown that the ability to perceive PTC and/or PROP often correlates to eating preferences and behaviors, such as picky eating. Supertasters tend to find certain foods, such as broccoli, spinach, and Brussels sprouts, unpleasantly bitter, and they often dislike dark chocolate and chiles. PROP tasters tend to drink less alcohol and—perhaps you know where I'm going with this—avoid black coffee and caffeine in general.[47]

Are You a Supertaster?

Use this exercise to see whether you are a supertaster based on the number of taste buds you have.

What you'll need

- food coloring
- cotton swab
- strip of paper with standard hole punch in it
- camera (the one on your phone will do)

If you don't have access to PTC or PROP, you can see if you're a supertaster by counting your taste buds. Squeeze a drop or two of food coloring on the cotton swab, then color a portion of your tongue with the colored swab. Place the strip of paper on your tongue, with the punched hole over the colored portion. Take a photo. Zoom in and count the papillae on your tongue. If you have more than thirty-five, you are a supertaster! If you have around thirty-five, you are a typical taster.[48]

COFFEE TOO BITTER? IT MAY BE IN YOUR GENES.

Researchers have specifically looked into genetics and how they relate to a person's proclivities toward sweetened or unsweetened coffee beverages. In a 2022 study of Italian coffee drinkers, researchers found that participants who were genetically predisposed to be sensitive to caffeine bitterness tended to prefer sweetened coffee beverages. Those who were genetically predisposed to be sensitive to sweetness tended to prefer unsweetened coffee beverages.[49]

About 25 percent of people are ultrasensitive to PROP and another 45 to 50 percent can moderately taste it, while about 70 percent of people can taste PTC. However, certain populations have a higher percentage of tasters than others. For example, one study found that the group with the lowest number of PROP or PTC tasters were Indigenous peoples of New Guinea and Australia, while the group with the highest were Indigenous peoples of the Americas. But there are supertasters and typical tasters in every community.[50]

There are simple kits you can purchase online to determine whether you are a supertaster—and if so, which kind. The kits contain paper strips with PTC, sodium benzoate, thiourea, and a control paper. You may be able to taste one or all three chemicals—or none at all. You can also find PROP test kits online, which scientists often use to distinguish supertasters and characterize taste sensitivity in studies. Personally, I am able to taste thiourea, PROP, and sodium benzoate—though I didn't have a strong reaction to any of them—but not PTC. Locate a reputable manufacturer of these kits, try them out for yourself at home, and draw your own conclusions about your taste preferences. This is more of an interesting and fun activity to do with your friends than something that has practical applications. Although, if you tend not to like bitter food and drink, perhaps you'll have a better clue as to why after taking a test like this.

CULTURE

Although some of the studies I referenced earlier focused on how genetics influence taste in different communities, there is also evidence that the culture we live in affects our perception of and sensitivity to taste, separate from genetics. However, the research around culture and taste is still in relatively early stages—the connection seems apparent, but the how and why of it all is still fuzzy. I'll highlight a few studies I found interesting when researching for this book.

Our cultures are intertwined with social, geographical, economic, environmental, and other factors, all of which influence (1) what type of food is around and (2) what our caregivers and other community members encourage us to eat. Yes, there are certain tastes—sweet, salty—that our primitive brains inherently prefer, but according to biopsychologist Julie Mennella, "You learn to like what you eat."[51] Mennella believes that this often starts before we are even born. Her work suggests that taste molecules find us first in the womb and then via breast milk. What our mothers are eating—which is presumably linked to what is available and what they enjoy—imprints on us. As we move through the world, we continue to gather taste experiences that are inherently shaped by the people and food around us, and that influences our aesthetic judgments of the things we eat and drink. In other words, if pineapple is all around us and everyone we know is eating pineapple and loving it, there's a good chance we're going to love it, too.

Different cultures also value different aspects of food, something that is likely taught—consciously or unconsciously—to children through various food traditions. Think about it: almost every culture has a delicacy that another culture generally finds revolting—or even taboo. I live in the United States, where many people grew up eating peanut butter and jelly sandwiches. Elsewhere in the world, PB&J makes no sense and may sound quite unappetizing, often because there is no tradition of peanut butter or because there is no tradition of combining sweet and salty together in such a fashion.

A 2018 article in the journal *Chemical Senses* compared the taste perception and sensitivity of two distinct food cultures: Thai and Japanese.[52] Thai cuisine is known for its use of hot chiles and how it blends three or even all five of the basic tastes in a single dish or meal. In contrast, Japanese cuisine rarely uses hot chiles, rarely allows different-tasting dishes to touch on a single plate, and often uses naturally umami ingredients, such as kombu.

The studies showed that Thai tasters had a stronger preference for heat than Japanese tasters, and Thai tasters had a higher threshold for taste recognition than Japanese tasters, meaning Japanese tasters could identify the five basic tastes at lower concentrations than Thai tasters. Interestingly, 20 percent of the Thai participants could not identify umami at all—even at the highest concentration tested—but all Japanese participants could identify all tastes within the bounds of the study.

Because the study controlled for other factors, researchers were comfortable saying that the differences were due to cultural or ethnic factors, but they stopped short of drawing definitive conclusions about how and why the relationship exists. Perhaps the results can be accounted for by differences in learned values, differences in food preparation and presentation, or even the preference for chile heat (and then there is the question of why there is the preference for chile heat in the first place)—but the point is that there were measurable distinctions between the two groups in terms of preference and sensitivity.

Coffee culture varies widely around the world, and even within cultures in the same country. In the United States, for example, the craft coffee industry tends to prize coffee that is complex (meaning you can taste multiple things at once) and that has noticeable acidity that is perceived to be balanced with the other basic tastes. In order to achieve this, lighter roasted beans are used and special attention is paid to the grind size of the beans, the temperature of the water, the ratio of beans to water, and the contact time of the beans and water in an attempt to extract flavor from coffee in such a way that highlights this balance. The presence of acidity in this coffee is often a turnoff to people who have mostly experienced the mainstream coffee culture that exists in the United States, which prizes darker roasted coffee with very low acidity and distinct roast characteristics, such as bitterness. I'd also go so far as to say that filtered coffee preparations—which remove fine sediment and oils from the brew, producing a so-called light body—tend to be preferred in professional coffee circles over preparations that leave those elements in.

People in other parts of the world prepare their coffee very differently. Different roast profiles and brewing methods are preferred, which result in coffee with different characteristics than are popular in the coffee culture that I, for example, move around in. For example, traditional Turkish coffee is brewed using extremely fine grounds in a (usually) copper pot designed specifically for the purpose. The way the coffee is brewed produces an intense, heavy-bodied coffee with a characteristic foam. Other coffee cultures primarily consume their coffee with milk or other additives. The list goes on.

Why You Can (and Should) Develop Your Sense of Taste

Some studies suggest that taste preferences are learned through social practice and that the related judgments and behaviors become habitual to the point that most of us perform them unconsciously.[53] This idea has stuck with me as I've written this book, likely because it confirms my own experience.

Most of us don't often have to think about our sense of taste beyond our immediate taste preferences and judgments ("this food is delicious" or "I really don't like this drink"). We often don't have reason to reflect on how our tastes have or haven't changed over the years—or how we got them in the first place. Aside from occasional congestion from colds and flus that temporarily decreases our ability to taste, our gustatory system is usually there for us. Until the COVID-19 pandemic, there had been very few reported cases of long-term damage to this system, aside from the decreased sensitivity that comes with age or through smoking.

I never thought about my palate until I started drinking coffee, evaluating extraction in pursuit of the perfect cup, and finding joy in discovering new flavor notes in my brew. But I quickly realized two important lessons: (1) my palate was limited by my own experience and (2) I could change my palate by intentionally gathering new points of reference.

It seems fairly obvious that we can intentionally train (or retrain) our palates. Although there are very few studies on the effect of sensory training on taste acuity, the ones that exist seem to suggest that training does increase your ability to perceive and recognize tastes, but exposure and habituation alone can increase your recognition capabilities—no complicated training required.[54] With training, though, it appears you can actually increase your *sensitivity* to tastes, meaning you can train yourself to detect tastes at lower concentrations. You already have the tools to do this with the basic taste exercises in this chapter. Create solutions of higher and lower concentration to test your ability to detect changes to intensity, and to see how low your threshold can go.

You can also reduce your intake of salty and sweet foods to increase your sensitivity to these tastes. Our taste buds can develop something of a tolerance to salty and sweet tastes, requiring higher doses to reach what researchers call the "bliss point," or optimal level of pleasantness.[55] For example, salt preference can be malleable, and we can learn to appreciate lower levels of salt. Anecdotally, I experienced this when I reduced my intake of processed foods—which tend to have high levels of salt. After making my own tomato sauce for a year, a sudden return to my favorite jarred variety was shockingly salty—almost unpalatable.

Another factor is repeated exposure.[56] Studies suggest that the more you are exposed to a taste, the more you tolerate it. This seems notably true for bitter tastes, and out in the world, this perhaps explains why so many of us enjoy quite bitter beverages, such as coffee and beer. That being said, if you are particularly sensitive to a taste that you do not enjoy, it may not be easy to overcome an aversion. I myself am particularly sensitive to the acidity of vinegars and other ferments, which I find quite annoying, as it limits my experience of many cuisines. Every once in a while, I try them again to see if anything has changed. As of this writing, unfortunately, nothing has.

CHAPTER 3

Coffee and Flavor

W E'VE COVERED TASTE IN THE TECHNICAL SENSE, but we all know that the act of partaking of food and drink imparts other sensations beyond the basic tastes. Our four other senses (smell, touch, sight, and hearing) also contribute. The sum of these sensory inputs is what we call *flavor*. This is the magical, mysterious part. When it comes to coffee, flavor—as you'll recall—is quality. And flavor is what brings us joy and wonder when we sip our cups. Flavor is what makes coffee taste like coffee—but also cocoa or fruit. How is that possible? Honestly, I'm not entirely sure and neither, apparently, is anyone else. But I promise that taking a close look at each component of flavor will make your morning cup seem even more remarkable and help you savor it on a deeper level.

In this chapter, we focus on smell (olfaction) and touch (somatosensation), as well as chemesthesis, sometimes called our trigeminal sense, which is related to our sense of touch. By the end, we'll have reviewed the primary sensory inputs that contribute to coffee flavor.

At base, flavor is the combination of sensory inputs that enable us to distinguish one item from another when we put them in our mouths. An apple may impart sweet and sour, but these qualities combined with its floral aroma, crisp texture, and more are what allow us to identify "Honeycrisp apple" and not, for example, "Bosc pear."

Flavor is not stagnant. As we saw in the previous chapter, coffee is a prime example of how flavor can change as we consume. Or as the writers of the excellent book *Chemesthesis* put it, flavor is "not a 'snapshot' in time, but more of a movie that unfolds while we eat."[1] Let's never forget to enjoy the show!

Our Sense of Smell and Coffee

Recall that our sense of smell is called olfaction. Like our sense of taste, our sense of smell helps us detect and identify chemicals in our environment, which from an evolutionary perspective has kept our species alive. Historically, our sense of smell has been discounted as not as important as our other senses. But one in fifty genes in humans is devoted to the sense of smell, and as we'll see, it plays an important role in many aspects of our lives—not least of all because our lives are often driven by flavor.[2]

Mammals tend to have well-developed olfaction systems, particularly when it comes to discriminating different smells. We humans can discriminate—that is, detect differences between—at least one trillion odor stimuli. That means we can discriminate more odors than colors (2.3 to 7.5 million) and sound tones (340,000).[3] People used to think that humans' sense of smell was inferior to that of other mammals, such as dogs and mice, since we have relatively few olfactory receptors in comparison. New research has shown that we have quite an advanced olfaction system and outperform many mammals, including dogs, with our *sensitivity* to tested odor stimuli—which are called odorants—and are on par with or only slightly worse at discriminating tested odorants.[4]

HOW DOES OUR SENSE OF SMELL WORK?

Our bodies detect smells in a similar way to how they detect the basic tastes of sweet, bitter, and umami: the lock and key principle. Odorants (keys) bind to olfactory receptors (locks) in sensory neurons, which are part of what's called the olfactory epithelium in the nose. The receptors activate (unlock) and the neurons transmit the information to the brain, which then results in our sensory perception of smell. Processing odor is a sophisticated procedure that involves a relatively large part of the brain, especially compared to other mammals. The sensory neurons transmit information directly to the olfactory bulb and orbifrontal cortex (part of the frontal lobe), as well as to the limbic system (which you'll recall is the so-called primitive brain). Our brain power makes up for the fact that our olfactory receptors are sparse compared to other mammals (we have about six million, and dogs have about three hundred million, for example).[5]

What we may be able to describe as a distinct smell—coffee, for example—is actually a combination of odorants simultaneously activating their corresponding receptors to produce what neuroscientist Gordon M. Shepherd calls "smell images" in the brain. In other words, the brain processes odor spatially, and each odor molecule triggers a unique spatial pattern. The brain reads many sensory inputs as spatial patterns—the most familiar being the pattern that results in what we call visual images—and odor is no different, although it's a bit harder to conceptualize. In fact, the brain creates smell images very similarly to how it creates visual images. The brain can then recognize an odor's unique spatial pattern and interpret it, much like how we recognize a face. Scientists can physically map out neural activity that creates these patterns, meaning we can actually *see* the smell images ourselves. Keep in mind, it's not the odor receptors in the nose that do this; they send the signal to the olfactory bulb in the brain, where the smell image is created.[6]

As with our sense of taste, our sense of smell helps us avoid danger (we are generally repulsed by the stench of rot, for example). And although modern life does not often require us to consciously do so, humans *can* use their sense of smell in the way that other mammals do: to find genetically dissimilar sexual partners (you've heard of pheromones, right?), to detect information about other people and animals (what they eat, if they are related to us, if we know them, and so on), and to track food via a scent trail.[7]

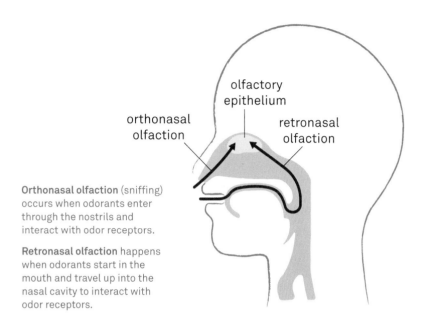

olfactory epithelium

orthonasal olfaction

retronasal olfaction

Orthonasal olfaction (sniffing) occurs when odorants enter through the nostrils and interact with odor receptors.

Retronasal olfaction happens when odorants start in the mouth and travel up into the nasal cavity to interact with odor receptors.

Olfaction also plays a major role—a dominant role, really—in flavor perception, including in coffee.[8] Remember, there are only a handful of basic tastes that our taste buds detect, but we can detect thousands upon thousands of odorants, often at minuscule concentrations. As we'll see, taste and odor molecules combine, in a sense, to create seemingly infinite flavors.

Recall that we smell in two different ways—orthonasally and retronasally—and that those two types of smelling allow us to experience coffee in different ways. The first, orthonasal olfaction, happens when we sniff something, such as freshly ground beans (fragrance) and freshly brewed coffee (aroma). When odor molecules from those grounds or that cup of coffee enter the nasal passage through our nostrils, they stimulate the olfactory receptors and we recognize that characteristic coffee smell.[9]

Orthonasal olfaction is likely what you think of when you think of your sense of smell; it detects what's going on around us. Humans are pretty good at this—think of the last time you knew someone in the neighborhood was grilling outside though you couldn't see them, or that it was about to rain because you smelled petrichor in the air,* but the physical structure of our olfaction system is not as optimized for this type of smelling as it is in other animals, which is a big reason scientists used to believe that our sense of smell was inferior by comparison. For example, a dog's olfaction system is designed for it to be constantly sniffing the environment, pulling in odiferous clues about what's happening now and what has already happened. There is a reason they are trained to sniff out drugs, dead bodies, and low blood sugar.

We, on the other hand, are optimized for retronasal olfaction. Retronasal olfaction plays the biggest role when it comes to flavor—and this is where the human olfactory system really shines. Retronasal olfaction originates inside the mouth when we chew or swallow something and then exhale through the nose. When we swallow coffee, odor molecules are released in the mouth and travel through the back of our throats up into our noses, where they are decoded by receptors. Retronasal olfaction is such an integral part of flavor creation and eating that we usually aren't aware of it—we think we are tasting ("I love how this tastes!"), and it seems to be happening only in our mouths, not our noses. In reality, our brains are simultaneously decoding disparate taste and tactile information from the mouth and smell information from the nose to create a detailed story that "reads" to us as a single, cohesive perception. That's what flavor is. And it's hard to overstate the critical role that retronasal

---

* Petrichor is the name of the characteristic earthy smell that happens before it rains. It's a mix of volatile compounds—from plant oils, microorganisms, and more—that gets released into the air when soil dampens. A compound called geosmin, which is a byproduct of bacterial activities in soil, plays a big role, and humans are extremely sensitive to it. Geosmin can be found in coffee, contributing an earthy or beet-like odor. This earthiness is often considered a defect in the industry, but according to Le Nez du Café (described in the next section), it is characteristic of certain coffees that are dry processed on soil.

Basic Tastes or Retronasal Olfaction?

Use this exercise to discover for yourself the outsized role retronasal olfaction plays when it comes to flavor.

What you'll need

- measuring spoons
- granulated white sugar
- ground cinnamon

Mix together 1 teaspoon of sugar and 1 teaspoon of cinnamon. Plug your nose and taste the mixture. What do you taste? Release your nose and exhale through your nose. What do you taste now? This exercise should illustrate the pivotal role that retronasal olfaction plays in flavor perception.

Tip

- You can also try a blinded version of this exercise by choosing a type of chewy candy that comes in different flavors, such as jelly beans. Close your eyes and select a piece from the bag. With your eyes still closed, plug your nose and eat half the candy. What do you taste? Can you guess what flavor you are eating? Unplug your nose and exhale. Can you guess the flavor now? Open your eyes and see if you are right.

olfaction plays in all of this. Without odorants, we'd detect only the basic tastes: bitter, sour, sweet, salty, and umami. What we think of as flavor derives largely from our sense of smell.

ODORANTS IN COFFEE

We learned in the last section that odorants are chemical compounds that interact with specific odor receptors. We also learned that multiple individual odorants may be responsible for a single smell, or sensory quality, that we can name: freshly cut grass, wet dog, chocolate chip cookie, coffee. Scientists believe there are close to one thousand different odorants in roasted coffee, which is a big reason for its alluring complexity.[10] As we've seen, odorants behave like a symphony throughout the coffee tasting experience, shifting in intensity and character from the fragrance of dried grounds to the aroma of brewed coffee to the brewed beverage's flavor to the lingering aftertaste.

So, what are these odorants and where do they come from?

Some odorants are present in green (unroasted) coffee and others develop during the roasting process. According to the SCA, scientists classify coffee odorants by their chemical family, and it's a long list: hydrocarbons, alcohols, aldehydes, ketones, acids and anhydrides, esters, lactones, phenols, furans and pyrans, thiophenes, pyrroles, oxazoles, thiazoles, pyridines, pyrazines, miscellaneous nitrogen-containing compounds, and miscellaneous sulfur-containing compounds. More than 140 compounds are in the furans and pyrans family alone, which are created via Maillard reactions during roasting.[11]

You might think the odorants within these families would have similar sensory qualities, but it isn't as cut and dried as that. Instead, the SCA recommends thinking about coffee odorants as fitting into two broad categories: those that contribute to "characteristic" coffee aroma/flavor—what makes us say "that's coffee, by golly!"—and those that contribute to "a distinctive character of the cup"[12]—what makes us say "this coffee tastes like a blueberry muffin!"

Scientists believe that so-called potent odorants—odorants that are intense even at very small concentrations—that are common across different types of coffee (no matter the variety, processing, roasting, etc.) are responsible for coffee's characteristic sensory qualities. These odorants, the "basic ingredients," if you will, might be present in different concentrations and with various other compounds in different coffees, but they are a through line; that's why scientists believe they are responsible for coffee's, well, coffeeness.[13] Some research suggests that there are as many as thirty-eight potent odorants in coffee, and strangely, they tend to not smell great on their own: descriptors such as meaty, catty, roasty, and earthy abound. Other associated descriptors—caramel-like, spicy—sound better. Nevertheless, taken together, they create the pleasant, alluring odor we know as coffee. Still, different coffees can smell wildly different. There are hundreds of different compounds that contribute to the unique character of individual coffees. The SCA says to think of these as the "spices and condiments that add complexity, depth, and diversity to the basic ingredients." Some of these compounds have known effects; for example, the compound ethyl 3-methylbutanoate is known to produce a blueberry quality.[14] But it's likely that not every odor compound in coffee has been identified, and even if we can tie isolated compounds to certain sensory qualities, what happens when nature and roasting mix them together in different combinations and different ratios still cannot be predicted beyond broad strokes, if at all.

Coffee professionals often train their noses with an aroma kit called Le Nez du Café, which contains references for thirty-six key coffee aromas, grouped into ten categories: earthy, vegetable, dry/vegetal, woody, spicy, floral, fruity, animal, toasty, and chemical. Le Nez du Café is created in France by highly skilled craftspeople in much the same way that perfume is made. Each reference is a vial of liquid that has been precisely dosed to replicate an aroma. Often, the reference contains the chemical associated with the aroma, such as 4-ethylguaiacol, which is responsible for a clove-like characteristic in coffee (and wine). This kit is quite expensive, and therefore impractical for casual tasters. Although it is used in SCA sensory training courses, students don't usually purchase the kit themselves; they use the one their educator supplies. They repeatedly smell the references to lock the aromas and names into their memory bank until they can identify all of them during blinded testing. The idea is that they will then be able to identify and name the aromas when they are present in coffee. We will cover some similar aromas with different (more accessible) references in chapter 4.

There are some indications that smell can influence texture—one study found that the odor of vanilla increased the perception of creaminess in pudding.[15] Although I could not find studies specific to coffee, other research suggests that specific aroma compounds can influence our perception of the basic tastes. One showed that certain aroma compounds in brown sugar could increase the perceived sweetness of a sugar solution (without increasing the true sweetness of the solution).[16] This kind of thing might be the key to why coffee can taste sweet, even though its level of sweet tastants is below a human's detection threshold. Coffee has many aromas that are associated with fruity sweetness and caramel sweetness, for example.

Our Sense of Touch and Coffee

Our sense of touch is called somatosensation. The somatosensory system responds to three main types of physical stimulus via corresponding somatosensory receptors: pain (nociceptors), temperature (warm or cool thermoreceptors), and taction (mechanoreceptors). Taction includes several familiar stimuli, including touch, vibration, pressure, stretching, and more. The somatosensory system also helps us recognize where the parts of our body are and what they are doing, such as if our hand is behind our back or above our head, as well as what's required of our muscles at any given time.[17] As we'll see, our sense of touch plays a key—though often overlooked—role when it comes to flavor perception

SMELL, ODOR, AROMA, FRAGRANCE . . . OH MY!

You may have noticed at this point that the terms related to smelling—that is, perceiving a sensory quality through the olfactory system—are somewhat confusing. This is because laypeople use terms one way in everyday speech, while scientists may use these same terms to refer to something specific—and coffee professionals have added further levels of distinction for the language of their industry.

As mentioned, scientists tend to use the word *odor* to refer to any sensory quality that results from an odorant interacting with the olfactory system. Coffee people have two different terms they use for odor, depending on when it happens during the coffee experience: *fragrance* for the odor of freshly ground dry coffee and *aroma* for the odor of brewed coffee. Both refer to orthonasal olfaction. (Likewise, the World Coffee Research *Sensory Lexicon* uses the term *aroma* to refer to sensory attributes that are experienced orthonasally.) In the coffee industry, once olfaction is happening retronasally, the odorants are either contributing to *flavor* or considered *aftertaste*.

In this book, I try to use the term *smell* to refer only to the sense we call smell or the verb associated with the action—so I don't use it to refer to odor, even though we do that in everyday language.

There's one more term I'm going to throw into the mix: *aromatics*. The term *aromatics*—as in "the aromatics of this coffee"—is used by seemingly everyone to refer generally to the combination of odorants that contribute to the smell-related sensory qualities of a cup of coffee, no matter when it takes place in the experience or whether it happens orthonasally or retronasally.

in general. And although you may have never consciously considered how coffee feels when you drink it, I bet it's played a role more than once in how much you enjoyed a cup.

HOW DOES OUR SENSE OF TOUCH WORK?

Unlike our senses of taste and smell, our sense of touch is primarily a physical sense: it responds to physical stimuli as opposed to chemical stimuli (usually, as we'll see). Like our other senses, touch uses neural receptors to detect stimuli and send that information to the brain. It starts with receptors associated with the trigeminal nerve, the fifth cranial nerve. The information is then transmitted first to the brain stem, where vital functions are controlled. This makes sense—if you feel pain, for example, it needs to be dealt with immediately. From there, signals make their way to the thalamus and then a part of the cerebral cortex that is associated with somatosensation.[18]

Although most of us probably associate our sense of touch primarily with our skin, there are somatosensory receptors in almost every part of the body—think about the pain you feel in your tummy and esophagus when acid reflux strikes. Our mouths are full of somatosensory receptors, too, and these are the ones we'll focus on as we explore the role of touch in the experience of coffee. In fact, our mouths are about as sensitive to touch as our fingertips, and our tongues are more sensitive to temperature than any other part of our bodies.[19]

Our mouths are about as sensitive to touch as our fingertips, and our tongues are more sensitive to temperature than any other part of our bodies.

Mouthfeel is the general term for the somatosensory inputs that are gathered in the oral cavity. In other words, it's the physical and tactile sensations we feel in our mouths when we eat or drink something.[20] The neural network in our mouths lets us know if something is crunchy or squishy, piping hot or tepid, thick and sticky or thin and watery, hard as a rock or soft, and more. As mentioned, the trigeminal nerve plays a large role in our perception of mouthfeel. It's the sensory nerve of the face, large parts of the scalp, mouth, and teeth. On the motor side of things, it also controls your chewing and tongue. The movement of your tongue, along with nerve endings in your teeth, helps you determine the size, shape, and weight of something in your mouth—and also if it is painful or painless, hot or cold, crunchy or chewy, rough or smooth, and so on.[21] For the curious: a different cranial nerve—the facial nerve—is responsible for the sense of taste and the muscles that create facial expressions.[22]

Mouthfeel is often directly related to whether we find things pleasant or unpleasant, sometimes completely independently of the flavor of the item. Part of this is personal preference. I, for example, am completely repulsed by the texture of Jell-O, though the flavor is fine, and I enjoy the texture of bananas, though the flavor isn't my favorite.

However, our judgment about food or drink is also often linked with whether mouthfeel confirms or refutes the expectations set by past experience and other sensory inputs—sight, smell, etc.—before we put things into our mouths. For example, if we see a potato chip that has been crispy in the past and appears crispy in the moment, we'll likely be turned off when the chip turns out to be soft in our mouths—even though the other aspects of flavor are exactly the same.[23] This can be not just preference but a line of defense—just like our sense of taste and aroma, mouthfeel helps us determine whether something is safe to eat or not. When things that are usually hard are soft and things that are usually soft are hard, it's often a sign that the food is old, and possibly on the road to decay and danger. But mouthfeel also plays a role independent of expectation. Mouthfeel is what tells us our coffee is too hot to safely drink, for example.

CHEMESTHESIS (CHEMICAL IRRITATION)

Earlier I said that our sense of touch is "primarily a physical sense" and "usually" responds to physical stimulus. The somatosensory system can also respond to chemical stimuli, and when this happens it's called chemesthesis.[24] Sometimes, chemesthesis is simply referred to as "chemical irritation" because the result is often irritating: the *burning* caused by capsaicin in chiles, the sharp *cooling* caused by menthol in mint, the *pungency* caused by piperine in peppercorns, the *tingling* caused by carbonation in soda, the *warming* caused by gingerols in ginger. However, in the right balance, these "irritations" can contribute to our enjoyment of food and drink.

The compounds that cause chemesthesis often come from plant oils and extracts, and these compounds might protect a plant in the wild— from grazing animals, for example.[25]

Chemesthesis can seem like it's part of taste, but technically speaking, it's not. The chemicals that provoke chemesthesis do not interact with taste receptors; they interact with touch receptors. Some researchers think of chemesthesis as "a sensory subquality" of touch,[26] or a property of all three of the primary modalities of somatosensation (pain, temperature, taction). A chemical such as capsaicin interacts with temperature receptors, which is why we may perceive a room-temperature habanero as "hot" on our tongue, though it has nothing to do physical temperature. Chemesthesis can also trigger involuntary responses— coughing, salivating, sneezing—which are the body's attempt to rid itself of these irritants.

While chemical substances often interact with the sensory receptors of the trigeminal nerve, they can also interact with receptors and/or ion channels in epithelial cells (your skin is a type of epithelial cell), which means chemesthesis can happen all over your body, not just in your mouth and nose.[27] (You may have noticed this when, um, voiding after a spicy meal.)

The most common tactile sensation in coffee is *astringency*, the tongue-drying sensation. This sensation is also common in red wine, and it's caused by tannins, a compound found in many plants. Coffee contains tannins, too, although it doesn't appear that the mechanism behind astringency in coffee has been studied much. Tannins are generally thought to contribute to coffee's astringency, as well as some acids, such as quinic acid and chlorogenic acid.[28]

It has been well established that astringency occurs when compounds, such as tannins, bind with proteins in saliva, causing them to separate out and create a residue in the mouth. Proteins are what cause saliva to feel slippery, so the binding action decreases that slippery feeling. This combined with the residue creates the drying sensation we know as astringency.[29]

However, there is some scientific debate about the mechanism that detects astringency—and remember, the mechanism is what scientists need to explain to definitively categorize the sensation. For example, astringency used to be considered a basic taste, but that has since been disproved, as taste receptors are not activated. The trigeminal nerve is involved, but details remain elusive. I have found research that refers to astringency as chemesthesis (meaning, it interacts with chemical receptors). But I've also found research that says it's not clear whether astringency is the result of an interaction with chemical receptors or other tactile receptors.[30]

The important thing, though, is to realize that astringency in coffee—whatever it is—falls under the umbrella of touch, or mouthfeel. People tend to conflate astringency with bitterness, and although both may be present in coffee at the same time, they are distinct sensory perceptions. Still, astringency is an important component of a coffee's mouthfeel, so it's well worth training yourself to detect it. Astringency is a distinctly drying, puckering, tightening, or tingling sensation felt on the surface and/or edges of the tongue. You may also feel it in in your cheeks.

Astringency or Bitterness?

Use this exercise to train yourself to discriminate between astringency (touch) and bitterness (taste).

What you'll need

- digital scale (0.1 gram precision)
- alum
- 1 liter filtered or spring water (no additives), plus more for tasting plain
- 0.05% bitter solution (page 29)
- three equal-size drinking glasses

Create a 0.05% alum solution by dissolving 0.5 grams of alum in 1 liter of water, stirring or shaking until the alum is completely dissolved.

Pour the alum solution into the first glass, plain water into the second glass, and the bitter solution into the third glass. Taste each and compare the sensations you feel on your tongue and around your mouth.

Tips

- Alum can usually be found with the spices or herbs at the grocery store. It's used for pickling, so it may be placed near other pickling paraphernalia. If you can't find it, you can also identify astringency by eating an underripe banana. Try to focus on the drying sensation it produces in your mouth. Keep in mind that the intensity of astringency and where you feel it may be unique to you.

- Store the solutions in the refrigerator and use within a couple of days. Let them come to room temperature before tasting.

- The alum solution is the reference for the "mouth drying" attribute in the *Sensory Lexicon*. See chapter 4 for more on these attributes.

Mouthfeel contributes to our ability to distinguish and identify flavor. It can actually influence our perception of the other senses that contribute to flavor—and vice versa. For example, studies have found that viscosity increases the detection threshold (that is, it decreases the intensity) of sour, sweet, and bitter, while it increases the intensity of umami. Temperature also affects our ability to taste. Very hot temperatures impede our ability to taste. Research finds that we best detect sucrose (sweet) and other tastants at 72 to 91°F. Likewise, you can taste freshly brewed hot coffee better after it has a moment to cool.[31] In fact, the SCA outlines protocols related to temperature for when professional coffee tasters evaluate coffee. The first taste should not happen until the coffee reaches 160°F. Certain aspects of coffee (acidity, body, and balance) are evaluated between 160 and 140°F, and other aspects (sweetness, uniformity, cleanliness) are not evaluated until the brew "approaches room temperature," or below 100°F. Professional tasters are not supposed to taste coffee below 70°F.[32]

MOUTHFEEL AND COFFEE

A coffee's mouthfeel contributes to not only our overall perception of its flavor but also our enjoyment of it. You can even use it to help you decide what kind of coffee preparation you prefer and how to adjust your brewing method to your liking. The main components of mouthfeel in coffee are temperature, astringency, thickness, and texture. Temperature and astringency may already be top of mind for you when you drink coffee. We tend to have our preferences about the preferred temperature of coffee—when it's cold outside, we tend to want it hot, and when it's hot outside, we increasingly want it cold.

The level of a coffee's astringency likely also contributes to your enjoyment of coffee, even if you didn't know it was called astringency until you read this book. Unlike in red wine, where astringency is often a desired quality, astringency in coffee is generally considered an unpleasant characteristic, as it can easily dominate the cup.[33] According to the SCA, astringency is associated with coffee that is underripe or underroasted, both of which may have larger concentrations of chlorogenic acids, which we have learned contribute to astringency in coffee.[34] In the United States, astringency also tends to be associated with poorly extracted coffee. Chlorogenic acids are relatively large, which means it takes some doing for water to extract them. But in some brewing methods, such as pour over, water can sometimes channel through the coffee bed, causing it to bypass some grounds and spend too much time with others. The latter provides an opportunity for water to extract the chlorogenic acids, increasing astringency.[35]

Together, thickness and texture are what coffee professionals call *body*. This is the definition that the SCA gives in the *Sensory Cupping Handbook*.[36] In my experience, coffee people often use the terms *body* and *mouthfeel* interchangeably—you may have noticed this out in the world, too. But I'm going to go with the SCA on this one: Body is a characterization of only the tactile qualities of coffee, and it is a mere component of mouthfeel. Mouthfeel (for coffee specifically) includes temperature, astringency, thickness, and texture.

To complicate matters, the terms *thickness* and *texture* are nebulous. My understanding is that *texture* is the broadest term that describes tactile sensory qualities, and *thickness* is a subcategory, one that is associated with the coffee's "weight" (another euphemism that the coffee industry uses) or "viscosity" (a term related to a liquid's flow rate that science uses). But thickness and texture are often thought of separately in the coffee world. The simplest description I can come up with is this: thickness describes how close to water coffee feels in the mouth. The closer to water that coffee feels in the mouth, the "thinner" or "lighter" it is. The more that coffee feels like water plus something else, the "thicker" or "heavier" it is. Texture, on the other hand, describes all the other tactile sensations of drinking coffee.

Heavy and Light Body

Use this exercise to help you distinguish between light body and heavy body in beverages, including coffee.

What you'll need

- skim (fat-free) milk
- 1% milk
- whole milk
- filtered or spring water (no additives)
- four equal-size glasses

Pour equal amounts of skim milk, 1% milk, whole milk, and water into the glasses. Sip from each, focusing on the weight of the liquid in your mouth. Press your tongue through the liquid to help you get a sense of its thickness. Rinse your mouth with water between each sample. It may also help to compare the milk samples to the water. Can you tell the difference between them? Which feels heaviest? Lightest?

These milks all have different levels of butterfat in them, while the rest of the components should be largely the same. These percentages vary by country, but in the United States, skim milk has 0 to 0.5 percent, 1% milk has 1 percent, and whole milk has 3.25 percent. Fat is a lipid and lipids contribute directly to body.

Tips

- If you'd like to do this blinded, simply label the cups on the bottom and ask a friend to arrange them for you so you don't know which is which.
- For a more extreme comparison, throw half-and-half (10.5 to 18 percent butterfat) into the mix. Note: 1% milk and half-and-half are used as references for the oily mouthfeel attribute in the *Sensory Lexicon*.
- For vegan readers, try this exercise with canned coconut milk. Shake the can very well to distribute the coconut cream, then distribute the coconut milk evenly between two measuring cups. Set one cup aside; this is your full-fat reference. Dilute the second cup with an equal amount of water (so 1 part coconut milk, 1 part water); this is your medium-fat reference. Pour half of this mixture into a third measuring cup. Dilute this mixture with an equal amount of water (so 1 part mixture, 1 part water); this is your low-fat reference.

The biggest challenge, which extends beyond the coffee world, is that texture is abjectly difficult to describe, so we reach for words and end up speaking in a kind of metaphor. Senses tend to be like this, and it's hard enough when you can *see* the thing in question—how would you describe the color blue to someone?—let alone when you can't. Language is an imperfect medium, and in the end we tend to mix up terms, including those that have scientific specificity. On the facing page, I have adapted and renamed a table of expressions used to describe liquid foods from an academic paper called "Texture Is a Sensory Property" to focus it on coffee mouthfeel terms and offer some concrete definitions.[37] In the Notes row, I have tried my best to provide context where needed and shore up the discrepancies between the science terms and the coffee terms. There is currently no exhaustive lexicon of common coffee mouthfeel terms,[38] so keep in mind that these definitions are based on my own experience hearing and using these terms in the world. Perhaps we'll get a codified lexicon one day! In the meantime, I hope this table helps you describe your coffee more accurately.

Coffee's body (thickness and texture) is caused by insoluble solids—that is, compounds that cannot be dissolved by water—that are suspended in the brew. One type of these compounds is called polysaccharides (carbohydrate molecules such as cellulose, hemicellulose, arabinogalactan, and pectin), which are too large to dissolve. Instead, they "uncoil" and remain suspended in the coffee. Some bits of plant material are so large we can see them in the brew—we call these fines, or sediment when they settle. These are very fine particles of the beans, a by-product of grinding. Another big contributor to body is lipids (triglycerides, terpenes, tocopherols, and sterols). In lay terms, coffee oil is an example of a lipid. Lipids are hydrophobic, which means they can't dissolve in water. But they can become emulsified—think of a salad dressing that needs a good amount of shaking or whisking for the oil to combine fully with the acid and other parts. With the help of other compounds, coffee oils can become stabilized in coffee just like the oil in salad dressing. This is very apparent in

EXPRESSIONS OF MOUTHFEEL FOR COFFEE

SCA / Coffee terms	Mouthfeel				
	Body			Astringency	Temperature
	Thickness/ weight	Texture			
Scientific category	Body, viscosity	Feel on soft tissue surfaces	Coating of oral cavity	Chemical effect	Temperature
Typical coffee attributes	• thick/heavy • thin/light/ tea-like/ delicate	• smooth • rough/gritty/ sandy • creamy • juicy • round	• oily/buttery • mouth-coating • lingering • clean	• astringent • drying • grippy • powdery • chalky	• hot • cold
Notes	Science distinguishes between viscosity and body. It's blurrier in coffee. In my experience, the terms *thick* and *thin* are used as criticisms, while *heavy* and *light* are used to describe coffees that conform to expectations. But they all relate to the same thing: a coffee's thickness.	In my experience, *creamy* is used to describe a round, smooth, velvety feeling, and *juicy* is used to describe a feeling of increased salivation. These are on par with how science uses these terms, but these are much more subtle textures in coffee than, say, in dairy products or fruit juice. *Round* is an impression that you can feel the coffee all around the tongue/mouth simultaneously.	In my experience, *oily*, *mouth-coating*, and *lingering* go hand in hand. Oily coffees literally contain oils that tend to leave residue behind, so feelings of mouth-coating and lingering contribute to aftertaste as well. In my experience, *clean* is used to describe the opposite of oily: an absence of mouth-coating.	These terms are often used to describe aftertaste, too. This makes sense, as the chemical effect of astringency lingers. New research suggests that there can be different qualities of astringency, so that's why I put all these terms here. I'm not sure everyone would associate powdery with astringency, for example, but I do.	Thank goodness: one straight-forward category!

espresso crema, but drip coffee can have suspended oil, too, though it may not be as incorporated—have you ever seen a shiny oil slick floating on top of your coffee? Lipids contribute to texture that is said to be smooth or oily.[39]

The upshot is this: the more suspended stuff there is in coffee, the more our mouths can detect it—and the less like water it feels.

To some degree, body is influenced by the variety, processing, and roasting of coffee. For example, robusta coffee (*C. canephora*) tends to be denser with fewer lipids than arabica coffee (*C. arabica*), so robusta's body can feel heavier and rougher. Natural processed beans—in which the coffee cherry is left on the bean as it dries after harvesting—tend to have heavier bodies than washed, possibly because of the influence processing has on polysaccharides.[40] And roasting degrades coffee material and forces more oil from the bean, which means that longer, darker roasts can also result in a heavier body than shorter, lighter roasts.[41]

But arguably, brewing method plays the biggest role when it comes to body. That is because some brewing methods allow insoluble compounds into the final cup, while others hold them back, out of the cup. For many manual coffee methods, this is primarily dependent on the type of filter that is used. A French press, for example, has a relatively open metal filter that allows many suspended compounds through into the brew, while something like a V60 or Chemex uses a paper filter, which captures many of those same compounds. The result is that French press coffee tends to have a heavier body than paper-filtered coffee. Decoction methods—which involve boiling coffee and water together to extract flavor, such as those made with an ibrik/cezve—tend to produce coffee with lots of suspended particles, which contribute to a characteristic heavy, gritty texture. On the other hand, espresso methods use pressure to help emulsify lipids, which results in not only crema but also a heavy, oily body.

When you are tasting coffee and evaluating mouthfeel, keep in mind the potato chip example (see page 63): our impression of mouthfeel

> There is no platonic ideal when it comes to body, and context is often key.

often has a lot to do with expectation. If you purchase an espresso, which is supposed to be characteristically heavy and oily, you'll likely be disappointed with a thin, watery shot—it's a sign that it wasn't prepared to expectation. Likewise, if you order coffee made with an ibrik/cezve and fault it when it does not taste like a Chemex, I'd argue that's on you, buddy, not the coffee. In other words, there is no platonic ideal when it comes to body, and context is often key.

Of course, preference plays a role—and you can choose preparation methods that align with your preference, once you know them. There is simply a lot of variability when it comes to body. In my circles at least, coffee professionals tend to prize so-called clean coffee (those with few fines and oils), which means noses sometimes get turned up at French press coffee, with its "inferior" thickness and texture. It's not inferior; it's just different. Don't let anyone tell you otherwise.

One complicating factor is that body can be a sign of under- and overextracted coffee—that is, coffee that has been prepared at the extremes of the spectrum. Underextracted coffee tends to be watery (because there wasn't enough time for water to extract compounds) and overextracted coffee tends to feel thick (because there was too much time for water to extract compounds). But body is only one of many signs of faulty extraction. Underextracted coffee also tends to have faint aroma and flavor and may be too sour. Overextracted coffee tends to be overpoweringly bitter and astringent in addition to feeling thick. In other words, you must consider the whole, not just individual parts, when making a judgment.

Exploring Body

Use this exercise to apply what you learned with Heavy and Light Body (page 69) directly to coffee.

What you'll need

- ground coffee of choice
- French press
- paper-filter coffee device (such as V60 or Chemex)
- filtered or spring water (no additives)

Prepare coffee in a French press and with a paper-filter method. Try to time it so they are ready at the same time, or use an insulated thermos to keep one hot so you can taste them at the same temperature. Alternatively, buy these two types of coffees in a café. Taste each and compare their body. Compare each to water. What do you notice? Describe the thickness and texture using the terms from the table on page 71.

Tip

- The more types of coffee you drink—side by side, if you can—the better you'll be at distinguishing body. If you have the opportunity to travel, seek out different methods of preparation that might not be available where you live and make a conscious effort to note the body of the coffee.

Bringing It All Together: Flavor and Coffee

We've explored the senses that contribute to flavor individually, but how does our perception of flavor happen? At base, the brain simultaneously synthesizes sensory inputs—taste, smell, touch—to produce a singular complex impression in which the components cannot easily be teased from the whole. That whole is what we recognize as flavor. As described by neuroscientist Gordon M. Shepherd, "the brain actively creates the sensation of flavor" by generating patterns from sensory inputs, which can then be associated with specific meaning to us.[42] The meaning of flavor—nutritious, dangerous, pleasant, unpleasant—can be stored and recalled quickly, as well as manipulated.

As we've seen, each of our senses starts with some kind of receptor that relays information to the brain. The pathways to the brain are different, but they all meet up in one place: the orbitofrontal cortex—part of the prefrontal cortex that is just above our eye sockets (aka "orbits"). According to Shepherd, this potentially means that this is where sensory inputs are combined, the site of flavor recognition. The cells in this region are also connected to the parts of the brain that are involved with emotion, flexible learning, memory, and decisions about rewards. All of these are necessary processes when it comes to responding to flavor: Do we like it? Is it good or bad for us? Have we had this before? Did it result in an unpleasant outcome? Does it remind us of anything we've eaten before? Should we keep eating?[43] My understanding is that flavor exists to be responded to.

One of the most interesting things about flavor is that despite our intellectual understanding of its myriad components, it is a unique, singular impression—it's too simple to say it is the sum of taste plus smell plus touch. All these senses interact with each other, are informed by each other, and in some cases transform each other to create the perception we call flavor. This is called multisensory integration. If you read Shepherd's book *Neurogastronomy*—and I hope that you do—you'll see there are many examples that illustrate how flavor is more than the sum of its parts, but I'll mention just a few concepts here.

The first is costimulation, when two sensations, such as taste and retronasal olfaction, are experienced together. If you completed the exercise on page 57, you experienced this for yourself. When costimulation happens, it activates a larger portion of the brain than the sum area of each stimulus experienced individually. Sometimes, the sensations "fuse" together (aka sensory fusion), and we think we can, for example, smell a taste ("This coffee smells sweet"), which is not physiologically possible. In some cases, it's not just that the two stimuli are being detected at the same time; some cells actually *respond* to both stimuli at the same time. For example, some taste cells also respond to texture and temperature (mouthfeel).[44]

Sometimes, sensory modalities influence each other—we've touched on this briefly in other parts of the book. For example, viscosity (our sense of touch) is affected by the basic tastes: "sweetness enhances it, sourness lessens it, bitterness has no effect."[45]

And sometimes, different sensory stimuli enhance each other. This happens when two or more stimuli are perceived together and result in a fundamentally different perception than if each stimulus was experienced individually. Intramodal enhancement means this happens between two like stimuli (such as two of the basic tastes) and crossmodal enhancement means this happens between stimuli of different senses (such as taste and smell). For example, research has shown that when two tastants that are individually below the threshold for human perception are mixed and experienced at once, humans can suddenly detect both. The same thing happens between certain tastes and smells, although they must "complement" each other.[46] As alluded to earlier, this is related to one of the theories floating around that attempts to explain why we all claim we can taste sweetness in coffee when all potential

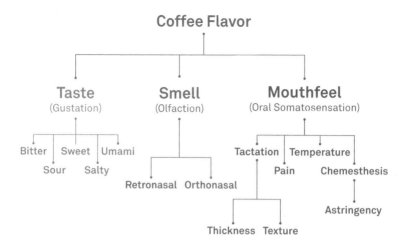

A representation of the primary taste, smell, and mouthfeel (touch) inputs that contribute to coffee flavor.

sweet tastants in coffee are below the human threshold for detection. Perhaps tastants and odorants are enhancing each other.

Shepherd coined the term "human brain flavor system" to describe the myriad parts and processes of the brain that result in flavor.[47] He encourages us to think of this system in two stages. The first is all the sensory systems—olfactory, gustatory, somatosensory—that receive sensory input and combine it into flavor. Combined, these patterns create what Shepherd thinks of as an "'internal brain image' of a flavor object."[48] The second is all the other parts of the brain that respond to flavor, "the action systems that draw on the full capacity of the human brain systems that generate and control behavior."[49]

Remember, from a biological perspective, flavor is a tidy packet of information—some hardwired and some learned—that tells our brain how to respond to the things we put in our mouths. The parts of our brain that engage in detecting, processing, and synthesizing flavor are vast, even when compared to other mammals, which implies it has played a critical role in our survival as a species. This aspect of our biology—the sheer amount of processing power the brain offers up for flavor—is, indeed, uniquely human. And perhaps most important for this book, our ability to *articulate* and *appreciate* flavor is uniquely human as well. To understand that a bit more, we should take a look at how flavor, emotion, and memory are interconnected.

FLAVOR, EMOTION, AND MEMORY

In the last section, I briefly mentioned that all roads of sensory input lead to the orbitofrontal cortex and that cells in this part of the brain are also linked to the limbic areas that deal with emotion, memory, flexible learning, and decisions about rewards. Biologically, this all boils down to motivation: to get what our bodies need, the brain must create a desire for food and drink. Emotionally, we interpret motivation, or lack thereof, as liking or disliking something. As mentioned earlier, the more scientific term for this is hedonic value, how pleasant or unpleasant we perceive something to be. So, at least in part, our emotions play a role in getting us to consume the nutrients we need to survive.

Interestingly, research has shown that our hedonic reactions to the basic tastes are hardwired from birth—sweetness creates pleasant reactions and bitterness creates unpleasant reactions and so on.[50] But flavor seems like so much more than that. We all have experienced the emotion-eliciting power of food and drink. It can make us smile. It can make us recoil in disgust. It can surprise us. It can also trigger memories, which are linked to emotion.

For example, have you ever smelled something that triggered a memory of a specific time or place? Perhaps you couldn't even name the aroma, but a vivid scene from days gone by flashed in your mind's eye: a day spent at Coney Island, bath time as a child, the forest behind your parents' house. This phenomenon is not a fluke. Aroma and memory in particular are closely linked—and it has to do with the anatomy we've discussed before. Recall that aroma is first processed by our olfactory bulb, which is a part of our forebrain. The olfactory system is the only sensory system that sends information directly to the forebrain. The information is then sent quickly to the limbic system, specifically the amygdala and hippocampus, which are responsible for memories and emotions.[51] Scientists believe that this more direct route makes aroma more deeply intertwined with memory. All the other senses go to the thalamus, the relay station deep in the center of the brain, for processing first; aroma bypasses it.[52]

Usually, a smell triggers an emotion first, then the memory follows (or sometimes it doesn't and you're left with just the emotion). The memories tend to be quite specific. For example, when I was trying out Le Nez du Café while researching for this book, one of the scents struck me as quite familiar—it reminded me of my horseback riding lessons in middle school and how my friends and I used to climb the hay bales and peer down to the arena from above. I hadn't thought about doing that in years. The aroma turned out to be straw.[53]

As we'll see in chapter 4, memories and emotions will play a key role as you set out to develop your palate. We will try to create aroma and flavor experiences (memories) so that you have a better chance of recalling them later. And you can use your personal memories to suss out clues as you try to identify sensory attributes in coffee.

WHAT INFLUENCES COFFEE FLAVOR?

There is still much to learn about the taste, aroma, and mouthfeel compounds that influence coffee flavor. Some say there are over a thousand compounds that contribute to coffee flavor. What we've talked about so far is just a tiny peek into the complexity of the coffee bean.

Although coffee's sensory attributes have been studied for more than one hundred years and many compounds (though not all) have been identified, there isn't a ton of research that comprehensively links *specific* compounds to *specific* perceived sensory qualities in coffee. Besides that, most research that does exist focuses on one type of coffee—a specific variety, processing technique, or origin. So, there is no comprehensive view or detailed list of chemicals and corresponding flavor attributes that I can reproduce here.[54] And even if there were, we have just learned how multisensory integration—individual sensory attributes that add up to more than the sum of their parts—is at the heart of flavor. We have very little grasp of how coffee compounds combine to create the flavors we find in the cup.[55]

That being said, we know that coffee's flavor compounds are impacted by a variety of factors, including genetics, origin and processing, roasting, and brewing and consumption. Let's take a high-level look at the factors that affect coffee flavor.

GENETICS

The chemical makeup of a particular variety of coffee predisposes it to certain sensory characteristics. The exact chemical makeup of a coffee bean depends, first, on its species. The two most common species of coffee are arabica (*C. arabica*) and robusta (*C. canephora*). For example, the typical chemical makeup of green arabica coffee (the kind that is most frequently used in specialty coffee) is:

- Polysaccharides (50.0 to 55.0 percent)
- Lipids (12.0 to 18.0 percent)
- Proteins (11.0 to 13.0 percent)
- Oligosaccharides (6.8 to 8.0 percent)
- Chlorogenic acids (5.5 to 8.0 percent)
- Minerals (3.0 to 4.2 percent)
- Aliphatic acids (1.5 to 2.0 percent)
- Trigonelline (1.0 to 1.2 percent)
- Caffeine (0.9 to 1.2 percent) [56]

The other common coffee species, robusta, has a different chemical makeup, one that many specialty coffee professionals (at least in the West) have historically viewed as less desirable, with harsh, bitter, burnt, and rubbery attributes.* Chemically speaking, robusta has more caffeine (which may contribute to its more bitter taste), fewer lipids, and more chlorogenic acids (which may also contribute to its bitterness, as well as astringency).

Next, different varieties of coffee have different genetic makeups. Within specialty coffee there are dozens of arabica varieties, with new hybrids being developed as we speak. You have likely seen the names of varieties on your coffee bags: bourbon, typica, caturra, K7, maragogipe, SL32—the list goes on. Think of the mix of compounds in these varieties as the raw material—it is the starting point for the tastants, odorants, etc., that will eventually interact with our sensory systems. The potential of this raw material is shaped by how and where the bean is cultivated, how it's processed, how it's roasted, and how it's brewed. But genetics are where it all begins. If the potential for quality (read: flavor!) is not already encoded in the genetics, you can't make up for it at any later stage. You can, however, destroy quality (read: flavor!) at any or all of the later stages.[57] You can also work to unlock the best qualities at each stage. Because so many factors influence coffee flavor, it's hard to make even generalizations about varieties and coffee flavor. But as you'll see in the next chapter, I do share some commonly accepted beliefs about flavor and variety.

---

* This view is starting to change. A pro-robusta movement within specialty coffee argues that robusta has the capacity to be as high-quality as arabica when it is grown and processed with the same level of care (which it often isn't).

ORIGIN AND PROCESSING

Where and how the coffee is grown, harvested, and processed can help green beans reach their highest sensory potential—or not. It all starts with how the coffee is grown; complexity develops as the coffee cherry— the fruit around the seeds we call coffee beans—develops.[58] Research has shown that ripe fruit has lower concentrations of phenolic compounds (which means less astringency) and higher concentrations of volatile compounds (which means more aroma) than immature fruit; thus coffee must be picked at peak maturity.

Environmental and agricultural factors—geographic origin, climate, elevation, temperature, shading, fertilizers, and more—can also impact the coffee's flavor potential. In this way, coffee is like other agricultural products. Consider the wine industry, where it is relatively common knowledge that terroir of grape affects the flavor. These elements are so well studied in wine that master wine tasters can tell what region grapes were grown in just by smelling and tasting the wine. We're not quite there yet with coffee.

Processing, or how the fruit is removed from the coffee bean and how the bean is dried, has a big impact on flavor. For one thing, if this process is botched, it results in taints or defects in the cup. But in addition, the processing method producers choose to use can impart distinct flavor characteristics. There are two primary types of processing, and each affects coffee flavor in different ways.

In very general terms, wet processing (also called washed process) means the fruit is removed from the coffee bean (the seed) before the coffee bean is dried. A machine removes the outer skin and pulp, then the beans often go through a fermentation process before the rest of the fruit is removed with water and the beans are dried. Dry processing (also called natural process) means the beans are dried with the whole fruit on before it is removed. (There is also an in-between process where only part of the fruit is left on as the bean dries; this is called honey process, among other names.)

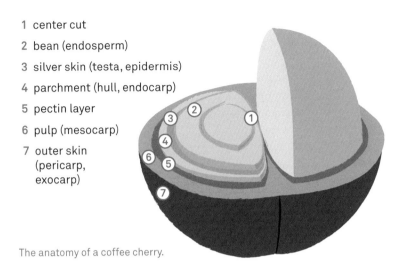

1 center cut
2 bean (endosperm)
3 silver skin (testa, epidermis)
4 parchment (hull, endocarp)
5 pectin layer
6 pulp (mesocarp)
7 outer skin
  (pericarp,
  exocarp)

The anatomy of a coffee cherry.

Which process producers use often depends on where they are in the world. For example, localities with little access to water use dry processing methods. Similarly, it can be challenging to naturally process in countries with high humidity, as the moisture in the air can lead to long dry times and spoilage.

The process of removing the mucilage (pectin) layer contributes flavor compounds. If coffee goes through a fermentation stage, the enzymes and yeast involved with breaking down parts of the coffee cherry are thought to produce additional flavor compounds[59] (though fermentation gone awry can produce chemical notes and other off-flavors). Some producers have been experimenting with various yeast strains and lactic acid bacteria during the fermentation process to encourage pleasant flavors, but this has not been scientifically studied in-depth.[60]

Natural process coffee dries with the fruit on, and it's thought that chemical reactions occur between the fruit and the bean as it dries, which accounts for the distinct fruity flavor notes of carefully processed natural coffee.[61] Sometimes naturals are criticized for being "boring," perhaps because most natural coffees have similar fruit-forward flavor notes (often of dried fruit; page 108). But on the other hand, natural coffees tend to be surprising and bold for people who've never tried them before. Many coffee professionals were inspired to get into coffee after drinking their first natural, often an Ethiopian natural, which can taste exactly like a blueberry.

Wet process coffees tend to let the compounds inherent in the bean itself shine. They are often described as "clean."[62] Research shows they tend to have higher acidity, lighter body, and more aroma than dry process coffees.[63] Dry process coffees often have a distinct quality; they tend to be sweet and smooth with heavier body. And although science hasn't pinned down all the reasons why, I'm betting your tongue is already capable of distinguishing a natural coffee from a washed coffee.

ROASTING

The way a coffee is roasted makes the beans' highest sensory potential available to us or diminishes it. Lots of chemical reactions happen during the roasting process to alter or transform flavor compounds in coffee. And thank goodness. If you were to crush up raw coffee beans and extract them, you'd get a grassy, astringent beverage. Roasting transforms the mix of compounds into something enjoyable and makes the bean itself more soluble—so our brewing water can extract flavor compounds.[64] In fact, the two hundred volatile compounds estimated to be in green coffee transform into more than one thousand volatile compounds after roasting.[65]

While trigonelline and caffeine, for example, reach the other side of the roaster virtually unscathed, sugars, amino acids, polysaccharides, and chlorogenic acids decrease significantly and lipids and organic acids slightly increase.[66] Many compounds are changed through thermal reactions, including Maillard reactions, the same reactions that lead to delightful sears on vegetables and meats during cooking. The molecular products of Maillard reactions (called "melanoidins") are largely, to quote one scientific article, "ill-known structures."[67] What we do know is that these reactions produce lots of carbon dioxide *and* the array of volatile compounds that contribute to coffee's characteristic aroma (and thus flavor) and brown color.[68]

The time and temperature of a roasting profile affects the coffee's flavor in the cup. But keep this in mind: roasting can't magically impart qualities that weren't in the bean to begin with. The most skilled roaster cannot take low-quality coffee and turn it into high-quality coffee with roasting alone. However, a roaster can obliterate flavor potential.

Generally speaking, coffees roasted to lower temperatures for shorter amounts of time (often called "light" and "medium" roasted coffee) emphasize the natural characteristics of the bean. They have complex aromas and flavor (meaning you can smell and taste many notes at the same time). They can range in flavor from fruity and floral to nutty and chocolatey. Coffees roasted to higher temperatures for a longer period of time (often called "dark" roasted coffee) tend to emphasize the flavors produced by the extremes of the roasting process itself, or "burnt/acrid, ashy/sooty, sour, pungent, coffee, and roasted characteristics."[69] These roasted characteristics tend to mask the flavors associated with the bean itself.

If you want to develop your palate and explore the wide range of available coffee flavor notes, you won't really be able to do that by drinking only dark roasted coffee. Companies that roast "traditionally" tend to roast darkly. That really popular coffee company? Its "blonde" roast is brunette at best when compared to coffee roasted by companies that use modern roasting techniques that preserve the characteristics of the bean. The type of coffee you like is, of course, personal preference. But if you want to taste all that coffee has to offer, you'll need to explore coffee across the spectrum of roasting profiles.

Different countries have different coffee preferences. In general, France and Italy tend to produce traditionally roasted coffee. Countries that have been developing a coffee culture around modern roasting techniques include the United States, the United Kingdom, Australia, Japan, and many Scandinavian countries—but this is just the tip of the iceberg.

BREWING AND CONSUMPTION

How roasted beans are ground, extracted, and consumed has a huge effect on the end flavor we perceive in a cup of coffee, even though the whole process takes only a few minutes. We have touched on this a little bit throughout the book, but I'll summarize a few high-level points here.

First, let's take a step back and talk about what we are actually doing when we brew coffee: we are combining water and roasted coffee grounds together in order to transfer flavor compounds from the coffee (a solid) into the water (a liquid). This is what we call extraction. Extraction happens in three stages. First, the coffee ground absorbs the water; this is important, as evenly wetted coffee grounds extract more evenly. Often, coffee brewers wet the bed first to allow this absorption to take place. Gases are displaced, which makes the brew bed bubble during certain brew methods, like pour over. This is called the bloom. Some espresso machines have pre-infusion capabilities, which is the equivalent of the bloom. Second, soluble flavor compounds are transferred from the beans to the water. (Water acts as a solvent, so soluble compounds are transferred into the water,[70] whereas insoluble compounds become suspended in the water.) Last, the water and coffee grounds are separated from each other. In the end, you are left with a beverage that contains water infused with soluble compounds, oil (insoluble compounds), and fine coffee matter (also insoluble). All three contribute to the flavor profile of coffee.

Recall from the first chapter that different volatile aroma compounds—which play an outsized role when it comes to flavor—are released at different stages of the coffee experience. Similarly, compounds in coffee beans are extracted and subjected to chemical reactions caused by water and heat in different ways and at different rates. Some compounds are more soluble, and they extract first. Other compounds are less soluble, and they extract at a slower rate. A cup's sensory attributes are ultimately influenced by (1) the type of compounds that are extracted, (2) the chemical reactions that transform compounds into different compounds, and (3) the amount of each compound present in the cup.

Keep in mind that science has not definitively explained how all of this works, and many generally accepted observations have not necessarily been substantiated by science. That being said, percent extraction seems to correlate with broad sensory attributes.

Percent extraction, or PE (also called extraction yield, or EY), is the way extraction is scientifically measured. It is the ratio between the amount (mass) of the coffee you started with (your dose) and the amount (mass) of the coffee material that makes it into the brew. Research has suggested that, in general, an extraction between 18 and 22 percent will result in a pleasant-tasting cup. From a sensory standpoint, coffee with less than an 18 percent extraction ("low extraction" or "underextraction") can taste sour and sweet, and coffee with more than a 22 percent extraction ("high extraction" or "overextraction") can taste bitter and astringent.[71]

However, these objective numbers do not always correlate with or predict the multitude of sensory attributes that characterize a cup, many of which we will explore in chapter 4. And two coffees with the same percent extraction can taste wildly different. Sensory attributes, as you'll recall, can be measured only through sensory evaluation, which uses us humans as instruments. But the goal, of course, is to find a pleasing balance of sensory qualities—and that is usually described by coffee professionals as "well extracted" or "evenly extracted" coffee.

If you've read my first book, you know that there are things you can do to manipulate extraction and find your perfect balance. There are six main factors that affect how and when compounds extract, and the first three in the following list are interrelated. The upshot: a change in any of these factors will affect the final chemical composition of the brew and thus its sensory qualities.[72]

- **Temperature.** Hot water impacts extraction in two ways: it speeds up chemical reactions and it increases the solubility of certain compounds. The ideal temperature for hot brewing is generally agreed to be between 195 and 205°F. But cold brewing is also growing in popularity. It takes much longer to complete the extraction process (hours compared to minutes) when cold brewing, and the compounds extract differently. The same coffee that is hot brewed and cold brewed will have a different chemical composition, and thus a different sensory profile. It's also generally accepted that too-hot water extracts overly bitter and astringent compounds, reducing quality.[73] Too low a temperature can result in underextraction (if coffee is not in contact with water long enough).

- **Particle size.** It is easier for water to extract solubles when the surface area of the coffee beans is increased. You can't really extract coffee from whole beans; you must grind it and increase the surface area. That means that the smaller the grind size (particle size), the easier it is for extraction to take place. In general, brew methods that use very fine grind sizes require less time to brew, and vice versa. Coffee professionals emphasize how important it is to have the most even grind size possible. Even the best burr grinders still result in a range of particle sizes. And each size has its own brew time. It is generally accepted that limiting this range results in a higher-quality cup. A too-coarse particle size can be a cause of underextraction and a too-fine particle size can be a cause of overextraction.

- **Contact time.** This is how long coffee is in contact with water. As we just learned, contact time is inextricably linked with temperature and particle size. In my experience, it is generally accepted that, in practice, certain compounds are extracted at the beginning of the process and other compounds are extracted later. I included an exercise in my first book that demonstrated this. The idea is that compounds that are acidic and sweet extract first and compounds that are overly bitter and astringent extract later. With certain methods, quick brew times result in low percent extraction, which we know tends to be acidic and sweet, and long brew times result in high percent extraction, which we know tends to be bitter and astringent. Both outcomes suggest an imbalance of specific compounds associated with those basic tastes. But according to the SCA, research shows that "there is only very basic evidence of specific types of compounds in the coffee extract being reliably dependent on time."[74] In other words, what's actually happening on a chemical level is probably more complex than a simple factor of time.

- **Water quality.** It's long been known that off-flavored water will result in off-flavored coffee. But the chemistry of water also plays a role. The compounds in water—particularly calcium, magnesium, and potassium—affect extraction and must be present to get good results. You may already know that water that has no minerals (distilled water) does not extract well and results in poor-tasting coffee. Likewise, very hard water, with lots of minerals, may also result in less-than-ideal brews. Christopher Hendon is one of the leading researchers looking at how water chemistry affects coffee. *Water for Coffee*, the book he cowrote with barista Maxwell Colonna-Dashwood, explores the role of water chemistry on coffee flavor.

- **Coffee-to-water ratio.** This is the measure of dry coffee mass to water volume used. We know that the ratio greatly impacts the strength—or concentration—of the final cup. Strong coffee has a high concentration of coffee material in the brew, and weak coffee has a low concentration. Strength, as we mentioned in chapter 3, is correlated with body. Strong coffee tends to have a thicker body, and weak coffee tends to have a thinner body.

- **Extraction pressure.** In this context, pressure is the driving force that pushes water through a bed of coffee. The more pressure you use to force water through coffee, the more extraction happens, often in a short period of time. Pressure can also change the physical properties of the beverage. With espresso, for example, the pressure emulsifies coffee oils into the liquid, creating the distinctive crema on top of a shot.

As we touched on earlier, the type of brewing method you use also has a huge impact on flavor as it relates to mouthfeel. Most brewing methods can be grouped into one of three categories: decoction, infusion, and pressure.

- **Decoction methods.** These methods require the coffee and water to be in continuous contact for a certain length of time, often at high temperatures. They tend to extract more quickly than other methods, but the methods that require the use of boiling water with the coffee in direct contact with high heat—or those with extended brew times—can result in the extraction of undesirable flavors and the loss of aromatics, which equates to flavor loss. At the same time, strength increases the longer you brew.[75] Examples of decoction methods include boiled coffee, coffee made with an ibrik/cezve, percolator coffee, and vacuum coffee.

- **Infusion methods.** These methods involve hot or cold water flowing through a loose bed of coffee grounds, which results in a shorter contact time and the introduction of fresh water at intervals, before being filtered. Fun fact: the term *infusion* comes from the Latin verb *infundo*, which means "to pour over." So, there you go: the more common term for these methods is *pour over*. In general, these methods are milder in comparison to decoction methods, with increased acidity and flavor.[76] Examples include drip/filter coffee (manual methods, such as pour over, and automatic drip machines).

- **Pressure methods:** These methods require water to flow through a compacted bed of coffee grounds (often called a coffee cake), with the help of pressure and heat. The most familiar pressure method is espresso, but plunger methods (such as the French press and AeroPress) and moka pots are also considered pressure methods. Pressure methods tend to have heavier bodies than other methods. And as we've discussed, the very high pressure of the espresso method gives the resulting shot a very distinctive thick, syrupy body and the crema on top. It also produces a strong (concentrated) beverage with intense aromas and flavors. In fact, because the pressure amplifies sensory qualities, there is nowhere for off-flavors inherent in the bean to hide. They are put on full display in espresso, which is one reason the perfect espresso shot is hard to achieve. The pressure component of espresso also seems to extract compounds differently, as the sensory qualities of the same coffee brewed with an espresso machine and via a drip method will be quite different. Additionally, espresso is meant to be enjoyed right away, as its name suggests (in Italian, the word *espresso* implies that it is made "on the instant, on an explicit order," or "extemporaneously"). And for good reason: when espresso sits out or is not enjoyed right away, compounds quickly start to change, which most notably results in the degradation of the crema and increased acidity.[77]

Within these categories, the methods themselves can result in distinct sensory qualities—and the same coffee brewed on different devices will have different sensory qualities.[78] It is logical to conclude that this is because each method results in a different combination of the six factors listed on page 88. But there are other factors at play as well. As mentioned earlier, the type of filter used (if any) has a big influence on the final cup, as paper filters remove most insoluble compounds, such as fines and oils, from the brew, and metal filters (or no filters) let them pass through to the final cup. This has a great impact on body, but those insolubles also bring other sensory compounds to the party. For a detailed explanation of different brewing methods, see the chapter called "Technology IV: Beverage Preparation: Brewing Trends for the New Millennium," in *Coffee: Recent Developments.*

HOW WE EXPERIENCE COFFEE

As we've learned, sipping a cup of coffee is a multisensory experience, and there are a couple of things I want to emphasize at this point. First, there is no single flavor that is "coffee." True, it's unlikely that if you sipped a cup of coffee while blindfolded, you'd mistake it for anything else, but it contains hundreds of taste and aroma molecules—many of which science hasn't even identified yet—that result in a complex, layered experience. Especially with modern processing and roasting techniques that are geared toward preserving the characteristics of the bean, there are myriad flavor notes just waiting to be identified in your cup.

That being said—and here comes the second thing—when you begin tasting coffee thoughtfully, it may be difficult for you to describe your brew as anything other than "pleasant coffee" or "unpleasant coffee." You may not actually taste individual flavor notes. That's okay. The thing I call your palate—your sensory receptor to brain connection—is something that needs to be trained and practiced, just like any other skill.

And finally, you may not experience coffee exactly the same way someone else does. You and a friend may try the same coffee, and one of you may enjoy it while the other does not. That's okay, too. Part of what's fascinating about coffee flavor is just how many factors can influence our perception of how coffee tastes. Let's take a step back and look at all the factors that contribute to a person's coffee sensory experience.

- **The coffee's chemical and physical properties (product).** These are the compounds in coffee that can be measured and analyzed, such as the taste and aroma molecules present in the bean, as well as the compounds that cause chemesthesis, temperature, texture, and color. These properties are rooted in the genetics of the bean variety, which predisposes it to certain sensory characteristics. These characteristics can be shaped by how the coffee is grown, processed, roasted, and brewed.

- **Your consumption of the coffee (behavior).** People drink coffee differently, and this affects how a person perceives the sensory properties just outlined. This includes how much you sip, how you breathe, how you move the coffee in your mouth, how you swallow, and more.

- **Your neurological and physiological makeup (brain/body).** Our genetics to some degree determine the physical characteristics of our sensory receptors, how they communicate information to the brain, and how the brain perceives the information. For example, some of us experience bitter and sweet with greater intensity than others. Some people may not sense certain aromas (this is called anosmia). This complex system of sensory communication and perception boils down to two things: how our neurological system is wired and how our body parts function (also called physiology).

- **Your psychology and sociology (life experience).** Your past experiences, culture, mood, and more can all affect the way you experience coffee. Certain aromas may trigger memories that influence your perception of flavor. Your level of exposure to a certain flavor can affect your ability to taste it. It's been shown that we can grow accustomed to tastes, like bitter, and that we can develop our ability to detect and identify tastes and aromas with practice.[79]

At the end of the day, what this means is that two people can experience the same cup of coffee in different ways. Given this, how on earth can we ever know what each person is experiencing—let alone how to communicate it? Well, you'll find out in the next chapter.

CHAPTER 4

Developing a Coffee Tongue

Language and Palate Development

A T THIS POINT YOU HAVE A BASIC UNDERSTANDING of how your brain creates flavor, the current state of science as it applies to coffee flavor, and where, to the degree that it can be known, coffee flavor comes from. Now for the fun part: palate development! As I've mentioned throughout this book, anyone can develop their palate—that is, increase their ability to discern and identify the sensory attributes of their food and drink. The first step is simply to be more mindful when you consume: slow down and pay attention to the eating and drinking experience. What does the coffee smell like? Can you identify any basic tastes? What does the flavor remind you of? How does the coffee feel in your mouth? How does its flavor and aroma change as you drink it?

Now that's all well and good, but if you can't accurately describe what you're experiencing, you won't be able to effectively articulate what it is you've identified. And this is key. You need two things to develop your palate: sensory experiences and the vocabulary to describe them.

In this chapter, we explore language's role in palate development— and why I think language is the biggest hurdle we consumers face when it comes to identifying the coffee we like to drink. We'll look at the tools the specialty coffee industry has developed to help solve the problem of language in the professional and scientific communities, and then we'll use those same tools to help ourselves gain the experiences and vocabulary needed to identify sensory attributes in the coffee we consume at home and at coffee shops.

Rather than explore all sensory attributes that have been identified in coffee, I present you with six broad categories, which will give you a good understanding of the basic flavor attributes coffee offers. Each attribute has an exercise—something to taste and/or smell—to help you lock in the sensory memory so you can draw upon it when you are sipping brews in the real world. Together with the basic tastes (bitter, sour, sweet, salty, umami) and other attributes (astringency, oily body) you've already explored, you will have dozens of sensory experiences locked into your brain by the end of this book.

Language: An Imperfect Medium

I am a writer and a book editor, so my entire professional life is organized around the principle that language is an imperfect medium. I am reminded every day that we humans are not mind readers. Whatever is going on in our heads cannot be directly beamed into someone else's head. We must *represent* it with language—symbols, signs, and/or sounds—and our representation must then be *interpreted* by another party. In other words, a pure idea must be translated, in a sense, twice by imperfect means. There is plenty of room for error. First, language offers a finite set of symbols, signs, and sounds to represent infinite feelings and ideas—I'm sure you've experienced a time when you simply couldn't find a single word or set of words to describe something the way you wanted to. Second, language has all manner of gray area, connotations, shades of meaning that can be interpreted different ways by different people, depending on context and life experience.

In the writing side of my life, this is exciting. Language is like clay that we can shape for desired effect. Language can be magical—sometimes the shape can be interpreted not only the way you intend but in unique ways that somehow simultaneously ring true. A reader can find something in your language that you didn't consciously put there, yet it can resonate with you deeply, feel even more truthful than the thing you intended. The imperfection provides the opportunity for magic.

On the editing side of things, I can see how language can be easily misinterpreted—especially when all you have to go on are the written symbols, without the benefit of tone, facial expressions, body language, and touch. A single word or punctuation mark on the page transforms the meaning of a sentence or increases the likelihood of reader confusion. My job is often to "optimize" language, but there is no one right way to do that, as it is so dependent upon the author and their target audience. And then there is that pesky fact that you will eventually hit a wall: language is simply imperfect.

None of this is more fully realized than in the language we use to describe our sensory perceptions, an idea I have touched on a few times already in this book. Describing a complex feeling or sensation is difficult under any circumstances. It's made more difficult when people can physiologically experience something in fundamentally different ways, as is very much the case with our sense of taste. It is made even more difficult when we don't share a common vocabulary or a common experience to attach to that vocabulary.

This, I believe, is one of the main roadblocks when we coffee lovers enter a coffee shop and attempt to interact with the language of flavor we find there. The language is all over the place. How should we interpret a "toasted marshmallow" flavor note? What, exactly, should we expect to find in our cup of coffee? There is no dictionary of sorts to help us—or the coffee professionals—understand it.

Or, is there? (There is.)

The World Coffee Research *Sensory Lexicon* is a product of a collaboration between sensory scientists and the SCA to produce a standardized language and reference list of the common sensory qualities present in coffee. From what I can tell, scientists researching coffee have largely adopted this lexicon, and the SCA promotes its use as its "trade language" in the training and research of producers, graders, sellers, roasters, and other coffee professionals. The SCA's comprehensive *Sensory Cupping Handbook*, which I have used as an authoritative touchstone throughout this book, emphasizes the importance of the lexicon's use in the industry—and promotes communication with this language between scientists and those in the coffee industry; indeed, it is the main purpose of the handbook.

A standardized language (vocabulary) that is directly tied to shared experience is crucial when it comes to scientific research and unbiased evaluation—but also, I'd argue, any kind of effective discourse between consumers and the industry. However, as of this writing, the lexicon is not always used by consumer-facing coffee professionals (baristas) or in the consumer-facing language we encounter every day in coffee shops and other coffee retailers. This is precisely why everything in this section is seeded in the lexicon itself and uses its language.[1] Let's adopt it as our language, too. I want us to meet the coffee industry in the middle, so we are more successful in our communication with each other.

Tools of the Trade: World Coffee Research *Sensory Lexicon* and the Coffee Taster's Flavor Wheel

World Coffee Research first released its *Sensory Lexicon* in 2016, after more than one hundred hours spent evaluating 105 coffees from thirteen different countries. As of this writing, the lexicon includes 110 sensory attributes that have been identified by scientists to exist in coffee.[2] The term *attribute* is used to refer to a sensory quality—basic taste, aroma, flavor, or mouthfeel—found in coffee. These attributes are descriptive, quantifiable, and replicable. They are *descriptive* because the lexicon provides a neutral description that does not indicate whether an attribute is "good" or "bad"; it just is. The attributes are *quantifiable* because each one also has an intensity score on a 15-point scale—does it taste a lot like the attribute or a little? The intensity score means that if you are trained to know what "4" means, you can compare attributes in coffee with a certain level of precision (for instance, "This coffee has a more intense raspberry note than that one"). Finally, each attribute is tied to what is called a *sensory reference*, something specific you can smell or taste that represents the attribute. The reference is what allows people across the world to not only share the same sensory experience but name it in the same way—which makes the attribute *replicable*. The sensory reference is very important because, as I've mentioned, words alone have their limits. As the SCA says, "The only way to truly communicate [a flavor] experience is through a shared sensory experience."[3]

Let's take a look at what an attribute entry looks like in the lexicon, as I will be referring to these attributes throughout this chapter. The following is the entry for the blueberry attribute.

Blueberry

The slightly dark, fruity, sweet, slightly sour, musty, dusty, floral aromatic associated with blueberry.

REFERENCE	INTENSITY	PREPARATION
Oregon Fruit Products Blueberries in Light Syrup (canned)	Aroma: 6.5	Put 1 teaspoon of syrup from canned blueberries in a medium snifter. Cover.
	Flavor: 6.0	Serve blueberries in a 1-ounce cup. Cover with a plastic lid.

Source: World Coffee Research *Sensory Lexicon*, 2017

As you can see, the attribute is named (blueberry) and described ("the slightly dark, fruity, sweet, slightly sour, musty, dusty, floral aromatic associated with blueberry"). The sensory reference (Oregon Fruit Products blueberries in light syrup) and its preparation are clearly stated. There are also intensity scores (6.5 for aroma and 6.0 for flavor), which we're not going to worry about for the purposes of this book. To use the lexicon, you prepare the reference as indicated and then taste it (in the case of a flavor attribute) or smell it (in the case of an aroma attribute). Because the lexicon is designed to eliminate bias and ensure that everyone who uses it has as close to identical an experience as possible, even the size and type of serving vessel is indicated. Generally, you cover the prepared reference with a lid until you are ready to taste or smell, so as not to let the aromatics dissipate, which could affect your experience with the attribute.

The attributes from the lexicon have also been organized into the Coffee Taster's Flavor Wheel (see page 170), which is a tool intended to make the lexicon "meaningful and accessible to the coffee community."[4] Many food and beverage industries use flavor wheels, as they are highly effective at organizing and displaying information in an accessible way.

The coffee industry has had other versions of the flavor wheel, but the current one—published by the SCA in 2016—was revised with the lexicon as its basis. Additional research was done to help scientists categorize attributes by their relationship, which makes the wheel easier to use. Broad categories (roasted, spices, nutty/cocoa, sweet, floral, fruity, sour/fermented, green/vegetative, and other) are found at the center of the circle. Under those umbrellas, attributes get more specific as they reach the outer edges of the circle—fruity to berry to blueberry, for example. Additionally, the wheel visually displays these relationships with meaningful colors. For example, research has found that we associate red hues with certain types of fruit. The basic fruity category is red, and the more specific attributes transition to shades of pink and other colors (such as blue in the case of blueberry), depending on our associations with that fruit—remember this, as it will come in handy later.

Now, 110 attributes are way too many to cover in this book—and too overwhelming for those of us who are just starting our tasting journeys. Instead, we are going to focus on exploring the basics, the inner circle of the wheel, which will provide a solid foundation for those of you who want to continue to develop your palate on your own. In the following section, I have selected those attributes that, in my experience, are the most common and represent either one of the major flavor profiles that coffee offers or some other attribute I want you to be aware of. Your mission, should you choose to accept, is to collect the sensory references, prepare them, taste them, and create a sensory memory to carry off into the coffee world. You will provide yourself with the experience, pair it with the vocabulary, and then seek out the attribute in the coffee you drink.

In addition to the major coffee attributes, I throw in a few challenges and recommendations for additional exploring. For example, I may suggest you compare certain attributes or include more attributes in your tasting. Lastly, I provide some context to carry with you as you start to consciously taste coffees in the real world. Remember, the lexicon itself is value neutral. It is a tool that simply says "these attributes exist in coffee," not "this attribute is associated with defect" or "this attribute is highly prized." Where it is possible, I offer some guidance for the types of coffees you might wish to seek out to find each attribute, including the flavor notes that might point toward such an attribute. But remember: in coffee, there are no flavor guarantees. The best way to discover attributes is to taste widely and taste often. Give yourself the opportunity to come across them, and you will!

If you'd like to drill deeper than this introduction to flavor attributes, please refer to the *Sensory Lexicon* itself, which is available online free to everyone.[5] Without further ado, let's get started!

The Broad Aroma and Flavor Attributes of Coffee

Before you begin tasting sensory references and locking attributes into your mind, remember this: the vast majority of the time, attributes in coffee are *subtle*. Tasting isolated references in this way is much more intense than you will find in coffee, where the attribute is found not only in lower concentration but also among a mix of many other aromas, tastes, and mouthfeel attributes. The lexicon also distinguishes between "aroma" and "flavor" attributes. Aroma attributes are those that you sniff orthonasally. Flavor attributes are those that you put in your mouth. Sometimes, the same sensory reference is used for both actions, and sometimes it's one or the other. In the following exercises, I follow the lexicon's lead.

Although World Coffee Research attempted to identify accessible ingredients for the attributes' references—and you may have some in your pantry already—gathering all the references for these exercises can be a bit daunting, so I recommend doing these exercises with friends so you can share. Most of the time, you will have some leftovers. I have tried to include recommendations for what to do with less familiar ingredients.

In terms of preparation, I have also followed the lexicon's lead, though in many cases I offer more detailed instructions than the lexicon provides (I am a recipe editor by trade, after all!). In some cases, I have adapted the lexicon's instructions or made them more precise so that the instructions are easier to follow at home. The whole point of the lexicon is to provide uniform instructions to ensure we are all having identical sensory experiences, but sometimes the lexicon's instructions are vague, incomplete, or challenging to accomplish in the kitchen. In these cases, I have used my best judgment for clarifying things, and I have noted when my directions substantially diverge from the lexicon's original.

You'll notice that the lexicon recommends snifters for smelling and 1-ounce cups for tasting. If you do not have a snifter, a small wine glass will do. If you don't have a 1-ounce cup, use one of similar size, such as a shot glass (which tends to hold between 1 and 1.5 ounces). If you are comparing references, make sure you use equal-size cups for serving. The lexicon also recommends you cover the references with lids until you are ready to smell or taste them. This keeps aromatics in the cup. I find that coasters, mason jar lids, and lids from round food containers (yogurt, cottage cheese, and so on) work well for this.

We have already explored some of the attributes from the lexicon via exercises: bitter (see page 29), sour (see page 33), sweet (see page 37), salty (see page 39), mouth drying (see page 66), and oily (see page 69). The first four are listed under "Taste Basics" in the lexicon and the last two are mouthfeel attributes, but some show up in other places as well, as you'll see.

FRUITY

Fruity

Description: A sweet, floral, aromatic blend of a variety of ripe fruits.
Reference: Juicy Juice 100% Juice, kiwi-strawberry flavor

Fruity is often the first attribute coffee drinkers recognize when their brew tastes like "more than just coffee." A general fresh fruity character, while delicate, can be distinctively present in coffee, especially those that are roasted to emphasize the character of the bean (as opposed to roast character). This makes sense: coffee beans are the seeds of a fruit, the coffee cherry.

Indeed, one of the most likely candidates in which to find that fruity attribute is naturally processed coffee or semiwashed (honey) processed coffee, in which coffee is dried with all or part of the fruit, respectively, after harvesting. Research has shown that natural processing of arabica coffee results in a greater concentration of known fruity odorants compared to coffees without the fruit attribute.[6] That isn't to say washed coffee can't be fruity; it can. But if you are seeking out this flavor attribute to experience and lock into memory, you might want to try a natural coffee first.

Fruity is the umbrella attribute for all fruity attributes. The lexicon breaks the general fruity category into four subcategories: berry, dried fruit (see page 108), other fruit, and citrus fruit. Each of these are broken down further for a total of eighteen specific fruit attributes. Parsing between some of them—such as raspberry and strawberry—as they appear in coffee can be difficult without practice, but detecting a general fruity quality is well within reach. In some instances, I find certain specific attributes, such as apple and the citrus fruits, to be linked with distinct qualities of acidity, which we explore on page 110.

Fruity

Use this exercise to familiarize yourself with the fruity attribute, as both an aroma and a flavor.

What you'll need

- 1 box/bottle kiwi-strawberry Juicy Juice
- fresh water
- medium snifter or wine glass
- 1-ounce cup or shot glass
- lids

Aroma: Mix ¼ cup of kiwi-strawberry juice and ¼ cup of water in the snifter, then cover to keep the aromatics in. When ready, lift the lid to smell. What does the aroma remind you of? Describe it as best you can and/or connect it to a memory.

Flavor: Pour full-strength kiwi-strawberry juice into the cup and cover to keep the aromatics in. When ready, lift the lid and taste. What does the flavor remind you of? Describe it as best you can and/or connect it to a memory.

One interesting phenomenon is that fruit flavors and aromas often taste or smell artificial in coffee, closer to candy than the actual fruit. Some naturally occurring compounds in roasted coffee are not found in the real fruit they are associated with, but they are the compounds the food industry uses to artificially flavor candy. For example, furfuryl acetate is not found in real bananas, but it is used to create banana-like artificial flavor—and it is naturally occurring in coffee. A similar artificial aroma or flavor can occur when naturally occurring fruit compounds show up in coffee—because they show up in relative isolation. For example, isoamyl acetate is part of a real banana's characteristic flavor, and it's also found in roasted coffee. But in a banana, it shows up alongside many other compounds, creating the complex flavor we know as banana. Coffee does not have all those compounds, so the resulting aroma or flavor may suggest a banana but it doesn't replicate all the complexity of the real thing.[7]

ETHIOPIAN NATURALS: YOUR TICKET TO FLAVOR TOWN

One exception to my "difficult to parse" qualification might be the blueberry note that is characteristic of Ethiopian naturals. Sometimes, this flavor presents so spectacularly that coffee folks refer to them as "flavor bombs." Multiple times in this book I have tempered your expectations, emphasizing that flavor attributes are often subtle in coffee. In this case, the blueberry flavor can be so present, you might think it has been artificially flavored. Ethiopian naturals are often spark coffees—they show us how exciting coffee can be!

If you'd like to prime your palate for the blueberry attribute—"the slightly dark, fruity, sweet, lightly sour, musty, dusty, floral aromatic associated with blueberry"—the lexicon reference is Oregon Fruit Products brand canned blueberries in light syrup. Put 1 teaspoon in a medium snifter or wine glass for smelling, and put some in a 1-ounce cup for tasting.

When trying to seek out this note, look for light to medium roasted coffees—particularly those with natural or semiwashed (honey) process—with flavor notes that correspond to the lexicon attributes, fresh fruit, fruit jams, berries, or food products made with fruit, such as fruit candies, beverages, desserts, and more.

Dried Fruit

Description: An aromatic impression of dark fruit that is sweet and slightly brown and is associated with dried plum.
Reference: Sunsweet Amaz!n prune juice

Although I am recommending that you need not worry about distinguishing between all eighteen specific fruit attributes on the flavor wheel, I do think it's worth learning to recognize a dried fruit attribute and to distinguish between fresh and dried fruit characteristics.

When trying to find this attribute in coffee, find a naturally processed coffee. Remember, naturally processed coffee is dried after harvest with the coffee cherry on, so it makes sense that a dried fruit quality might infuse into the bean. If you have a chance to try cascara—dried coffee cherries you can brew like tea—you'll be able to get a good idea of what dried fruit tastes like, too. Drinking cascara helped me identify dried fruit attributes in coffee even though the attribute may express a bit differently. For example, the lexicon includes prune and raisin attributes under the general dried fruit category. Distinguishing between prune and raisin attributes in coffee is difficult, but being able to identify a general dried fruit characteristic is within reach.

When trying to seek out this note, look for light to medium roasted coffees with flavor notes that correspond to the lexicon attributes (dried fruit, raisin, prune), any other dried fruit, or food products made with dried fruit, such as fig cookies and trail mix.

Dried Fruit (general)

Use this exercise to familiarize yourself with the dried fruit attribute, as both an aroma and a flavor.

What you'll need

- Sunsweet Amaz!n prune juice
- fresh water
- medium snifter or wine glass
- lid

Aroma + Flavor: Mix ¼ cup of prune juice with ¼ cup of water in the snifter, then cover to keep the aromatics in. When ready, lift the lid to smell and taste. What does the aroma remind you of? The flavor? How are they similar? Different? Describe them as best you can and/or connect them to a memory.

Tips

- If you don't want to purchase a whole bottle of prune juice but have raisins or prunes (dried plums) on hand, either or both will give you a general idea of the dried fruit attribute. Chop ½ cup of raisins or prunes and combine them with ¾ cup of water in a microwave-safe bowl. Microwave on high for 2 minutes, then strain the liquid. Transfer 1 tablespoon of the liquid to a snifter or wine glass to sniff, and pour the rest into a 1-ounce cup to taste.

- If you really want some practice with this attribute, it's relatively easy to set up a blinded test for yourself (see page 148) with the prune juice, homemade raisin liquid, and homemade prune liquid. Let all liquids come to room temperature before tasting. Can you distinguish between these three aromas and flavors?

Citric Acid

Description: A mild, clean, sour aromatic with slight citrus notes accompanied by astringency.
Reference: Citric acid

Malic Acid

Description: A sour, sharp, somewhat fruity aromatic accompanied by astringency.
Reference: Malic acid

Acetic Acid

Description: A sour, astringent, slightly pungent aromatic associated with vinegar.
Reference: Acetic acid

As we've learned, acidity is an important characteristic in specialty/craft coffee. The term *acidity* is associated with the sour basic taste, and if you've been following the exercises, you know that we made a 0.05% citric acid solution, which is the reference for the sour attribute, earlier in the book. It's also the reference for citric acid, and I recommend that you compare the citric acid attribute to two other acid attributes in the lexicon: malic and acetic.

Recall that there are lots of different acids. Many of them possess a sour quality, but they have additional qualities that give them a unique character. The three in this section—citric, malic, and acetic—are

> Citric acid is present in green coffee beans, and the roasting process does not amplify it; it slowly degrades it.

common in our everyday lives and associated with familiar items: lemons, apples, and white vinegar, respectively. Comparing and contrasting them will give you not only an appreciation for the subtle differences between acids (the recommended solutions are about the same in intensity of flavor) but also a head start in identifying these references in your coffee.

In my experience, these different acids play a key role in identifying the various fruit attributes in coffee. Citric acid plays a critical role in the citrus fruit attributes; indeed, the lemon attribute's reference is diluted lemon juice, which will give you an idea of citric acid if you don't have access to food-grade citric acid itself. But the term *citric* also shows up in the descriptions for the citrus fruit, grapefruit, orange, and lime attributes. These attributes can be thought of as a combination of a citric acid quality and additional qualities. Furthermore, citric acid is often responsible for what coffee people call "brightness," "zest," or "zing" in both washed and natural coffees. Citric acid is present in green coffee beans, and the roasting process does not amplify it; it slowly degrades it. For example, a medium roasted coffee may have about half as much citric acid as its green counterpart.[8] This explains why citric acid can contribute to a pleasant acidity but be overpowering and unpleasant at high concentrations, such as in underdeveloped coffee beans.

Likewise, malic acid is often associated with apples, but it's also the main acid in many other fruits that appear as attributes in the lexicon, including blackberry and blueberry (under the "berry" attribute) and cherry, grape, peach, and pear (under the "other fruit" attribute). Malic acid is a component of these notes in coffee, and research has shown that coffees that seem "fruitier" tend to have higher concentrations of malic acid.[9] Malic acid is somewhat similar to citric acid, so learning how they differ through comparison is an informative (and fun!) exercise.

Most of us have acetic acid (white vinegar) in our homes, but you may not have realized that it plays a key role in coffee quality. Some acetic acid develops during fermentation stages when coffee is processed, but most acetic acid develops during roasting as carbohydrates break down, which can lead to an increase of twenty-five times acetic acid's original levels. Because acetic acid is formed from carbohydrates, green coffee beans with more sugar tend to have higher levels of acetic acid after roasting. Acetic acid is most present in light to medium coffees, as it starts to break down again if roasting continues beyond that point. Acetic acid is not as strong of an acid as citric and malic acids, but acetic acid is key to overall perceived acidity in coffee, as well as to aroma—human noses are very sensitive to it. In low concentrations, acetic acid "imparts a pleasant clean, sweet-like characteristic," but in high concentrations, it gives off a fermented quality that is generally considered an off-flavor.[10]

Most light and medium roasted coffees have an element of acidity, as it is considered part of a balanced cup in many coffee cultures. If you are seeking an acidity-forward coffee, look for flavor notes such as "bright," "sparkling," and similar euphemisms, as well as those associated with food and beverages with known sour/acidic qualities, such as lemonade, candies, and fruit.

The lexicon also includes the references butyric acid (associated with fermented dairy products, like Parmigiano-Reggiano) and isovaleric acid (associated with foot sweat and aged cheeses like Romano). These acids are associated with a cheesy, fermented quality that is generally considered a defect by professional cuppers. These attributes are also rare, even at a professional cupping table, so it's highly unlikely that you'd come across them as a consumer. The acid references aren't as easy to come by either, but if you really want to level up, get some Parmesan and Romano and compare their scents and tastes.

It's more likely that you'd come across the fermented attribute ("the pungent, sweet, slightly sour, sometimes yeasty, alcohol-like aromatic characteristic of fermented fruits or sugar or over-proofed dough"). As mentioned, fermented qualities are frequently considered defects, but some cuppers like them and they are expected from certain coffees, so it's possible that a roaster likes them, too. The lexicon reference for the fermented attribute (aroma) is Guinness Extra Stout beer, and it instructs to fill a 2-ounce jar one-third full of the beer for every three participants, lidding it to keep the aromatics in. It can be served at room temperature.

Most light and medium roasted coffees have an element of acidity, as it is considered part of a balanced cup in many coffee cultures.

Citric, Malic, and Acetic Acids

Use this exercise to familiarize yourself with three acid attributes—citric, malic, and acetic—by comparing them. Note that malic acid does not have an aroma component, while the other two do.

What you'll need

- 0.05% citric acid solution (page 33)
- food-grade malic acid
- 5% acidity distilled white vinegar
- fresh water
- three 1-ounce cups or shot glasses
- lids

Citric acid (Aroma + Flavor): Pour the citric acid solution into the first cup, then cover to keep the aromatics in. When ready, lift the lid to smell and taste. What does the aroma remind you of? The flavor? How are they similar? Different? Describe them as best you can and/or connect them to a memory.

Malic acid (Flavor): Create a 0.05% malic acid solution by dissolving 0.5 grams of malic acid in 1 liter of water, stirring or shaking until the malic acid is completely dissolved. Pour into the second cup, then cover to keep the aromatics in. When ready, lift the lid to taste. What does the flavor remind you of? Describe it as best you can and/or connect it to a memory.

Acetic acid (Aroma + Flavor): Create a 1% acetic acid solution by combining 20 grams of white vinegar and 80 grams of water. Pour into the third cup, then cover to keep the aromatics in. When ready, lift the lid to smell and taste. What does the aroma remind you of? The flavor? How are they similar? Different? Describe them as best you can and/or connect them to a memory.

Tips

- I recommend preparing the citric and malic acid solutions in 1-liter water bottles, so you can store them and use over a couple of days. This is a great exercise to do as a blinded tasting (see page 142).

- Malic acid and citric acid can be purchased online or at well-stocked pharmacies or supplement stores (powdered or capsule malic acid) or grocery stores (food-grade citric acid). The leftover citric acid has tons of uses, including in candy making, cooking, cleaning, and bath bomb making.

- If you don't have access to citric and malic acids, use lemon juice (citric) and applesauce (malic) in place of them. If you dilute one part fresh lemon juice in four parts water, you now have the flavor and aroma reference for the lemon attribute (under "citrus fruit" on the flavor wheel). Gerber 2nd Foods apple puree is the flavor reference for the apple attribute (under "other fruit" on the flavor wheel). Although lemon and apple have additional qualities in addition to their acidity, you should still be able to get a sense of how the acidities differ when you compare the two attributes.

FLORAL

Floral

Description: A sweet, light, slightly fragrant aromatic associated with fresh flowers.
Reference: Welch's 100% white grape juice

Distinguishing floral notes is a challenge for beginners and may more rightly be the objective of more experienced tasters, but they play a critical role in contributing to other attributes like specific fruits, spices, and nuts, which is why I want you to give it a shot. The lexicon also lists four specific attributes under the general floral category—rose, jasmine, chamomile, and black tea—but I recommend starting with the basic floral attribute first. If you are interested in sharpening your floral detection skills, it can be expensive to gather the references listed in the lexicon. An alternative is to seek out rose and jasmine at your local nursery and smell and sample some high-quality rose tea, jasmine tea, chamomile tea, and black tea. It may also be informative to compare the floral attribute to the fruity (see page 105) and dried fruit (see page 108) attributes to help you distinguish the difference.

Floral notes are considered delicate, and as mentioned earlier, the easiest place to spot them might be at the fragrance stage, right after you grind whole beans. They are associated with esters, which are volatile, often fragrant, compounds derived from carboxylic acids. Research has shown that floral attributes, along with fruity, sweet, spice, and sour acid, are most prized by cuppers and green coffee buyers—and have the biggest impact on coffees' quality scores.[11]

Floral notes tend to be overwhelmed by roast characteristics, so light and medium roasted coffees are more likely to express floral notes than darker roasted coffees. The gesha variety of coffee—made famous by the

Floral

Use this exercise to familiarize yourself with the floral attribute, as both an aroma and a flavor.

What you'll need

- Welch's 100% white grape juice
- fresh water
- medium snifter or wine glass
- 1-ounce cup or shot glass
- lids

Aroma: Mix together ¼ cup of grape juice and ¼ cup of water. Pour half of the mixture into the snifter, then cover to keep the aromatics in. When ready, lift the lid to smell. What does the aroma remind you of? Describe it as best you can and/or connect it to a memory.

Flavor: Pour the remaining mixture into the cup, then cover to keep the aromatics in. When ready, lift the lid to taste. What does the flavor remind you of? How does it compare to the aroma? Describe it as best you can and/or connect it to a memory.

Peterson family at Hacienda La Esmeralda in Panama—is said to have a distinct jasmine quality. If you want to seek out a floral quality in coffee, you may want to start there. Just keep in mind that there is no guarantee; floral qualities can be elusive, and you may find it on the nose more easily than in the mouth. Otherwise, seek out coffee with flavor notes associated with the lexicon attributes and other flowers, such as hibiscus, honeysuckle, and coffee blossom (which is very similar to jasmine, by the way).

NUTTY/COCOA

Nutty

Description: A slightly sweet, brown, woody, oily, musty, astringent, and bitter aromatic commonly associated with nuts, seeds, beans, and grains.
Reference: Diamond sliced almonds, Diamond shelled walnuts

Research has found that the nutty attribute is associated with light roasted whole coffee beans and light to medium roasted ground and brewed coffee.[12] Chemically speaking, the nutty attribute is often associated with pyrazines, which are primarily formed in the early stage of roasting and tend to degrade and become obscured by other compounds as roasting continues.[13]

In my experience, nutty and cocoa (see page 120) attributes are often found together in coffee (and they are often lumped together when coffee professionals evaluate coffee). If a person is transitioning from drinking coffee that emphasizes roast characteristics to coffee that emphasizes bean characteristics, I often recommend coffee with nutty/cocoa attributes. These "brown" flavors are often perceived as robust, round, full, and comforting, which are qualities people tend to appreciate about roast characteristics. However, the nutty/cocoa attributes are often accompanied by a sweet attribute in light to medium roasted coffee

Nutty

Use this exercise to familiarize yourself with the nutty attribute as a flavor.

What you'll need

- Diamond sliced almonds
- Diamond shelled walnuts
- blender
- bowl
- 1-ounce cup or shot glass
- lid

Flavor: Puree an equal amount of the almonds and the walnuts in a blender on high speed for 45 seconds. Transfer to a bowl. Serve in the cup, then cover to keep the aromatics in. When ready, lift the lid to taste. What does the flavor remind you of? Describe it as best you can and/or connect it to a memory.

Tip

- If you don't have a blender, try to chop equal amounts of almonds and walnuts together as finely as possible, then mix together thoroughly.

instead of a roasted/burnt attribute in dark roasted coffees, making the overall profile less robust.

The lexicon breaks the general nutty attribute into three specific attributes: almond, hazelnut, and peanut. The peanut reference doubles as the medium roasted reference (see page 128), but it's easier to pick out a general nutty attribute in coffee than to distinguish between specific nut notes.

When trying to seek out this note, look for light to medium roasted coffees with flavor notes that correspond to the lexicon attributes, any other nut, or food products made with nuts, such as praline.

Cocoa

Description: A brown, sweet, dusty, musty, often bitter aromatic associated with cocoa beans, powdered cocoa, and chocolate bars.
Reference: Hershey's cocoa powder (natural, unsweetened)

Research has found that the cocoa attribute is associated with light roasted whole coffee beans and light to medium roasted ground and brewed coffee—and that the cocoa attribute tends to decrease in intensity as roast level increases. Cocoa can sometimes be easier to perceive when smelling whole beans rather than ground (although research has generally found the opposite, that attributes are easier to perceive when smelling ground coffee).[14]

There are two other specific chocolate references in the lexicon: chocolate and dark chocolate. These are similar to cocoa, although dark chocolate is characterized by increased bitterness and astringency.

When trying to seek out this note, look for light to medium roasted coffees with flavor notes that correspond to the lexicon attributes (cocoa, chocolate, dark chocolate), cocoa or chocolate products (candy bars, sauces, etc.), and food products made with chocolate, such as ice cream, cakes, cookies, and other desserts.

Cocoa

Use this exercise to familiarize yourself with the cocoa attribute, as both an aroma and a flavor.

What you'll need

- Hershey's cocoa powder (natural, unsweetened)
- fresh water
- medium snifter or wine glass
- 1-ounce cup or shot glass
- lids

Aroma: Combine ¼ teaspoon of cocoa powder and 100 grams of water. Pour half of the mixture into the snifter, then cover to keep the aromatics in. When ready, lift the lid to smell. What does the aroma remind you of? Describe it as best you can and/or connect it to a memory.

Flavor: Pour the remaining mixture into the cup, then cover to keep the aromatics in. When ready, lift the lid to taste. What does the flavor remind you of? How does it compare to the aroma? Describe it as best you can and/or connect it to a memory.

Tip

- The three cocoa-related attributes (cocoa, chocolate, dark chocolate) are good candidates for exercising your palate through comparison tasting:
    - Prepare the cocoa reference as described here.
    - Prepare the chocolate reference. For aroma, place 1 teaspoon of chopped Nestlé Toll House semisweet chocolate morsels in a snifter, then cover.[15] For flavor, place another 1 teaspoon of the chocolate in a cup, then cover.
    - Prepare the dark chocolate reference. For aroma, chop a piece of a Lindt Excellence 90% chocolate bar and place 1 teaspoon in a snifter, then cover. (Save the rest for a snack.) For flavor, serve a ½-inch square of the chocolate in a cup (chop it up to make it less visually distinguishable), then cover.
    - Smell and taste each side by side and compare their qualities. What distinguishes them for you?

GREEN/VEGETATIVE

Green

Description: An aromatic characteristic of fresh, plant-based material. Attributes may include leafy, viney, unripe, grassy, and peapod.
Reference: Parsley water

Green/vegetative attributes are always present in green coffee and can show up in the final cup, although roasting tends to diminish their presence and so are more likely to be found in light roasted coffee.[16] The lexicon divides the green/vegetative attribute into four subcategories: olive oil, raw (see page 126), beany, and green/vegetative (again), which is further divided into seven specific attributes: underripe, peapod, fresh, dark green, vegetative, hay-like, and herb-like.

We humans are very sensitive to some of the compounds responsible for green attributes—such as 2-Isopropyl-3-methoxypyrazine, the compound associated with the earthy, fresh, green peapod attribute. We could detect just a few drops in an Olympic size swimming pool of water.[17]

Some coffees are expected to have a green, vegetal, herbaceous note. For example, Southeast Asian coffees, such as those from Sumatra, are known to have a characteristic green earthy note that some liken to green bell pepper.* This particular flavor can be polarizing, and it may even be considered a defect if it presented in coffee from other origins. Unless a coffee is known for its green character, an overwhelmingly green/vegetative note would likely be considered an off-flavor by most coffee professionals at a cupping table. But if the green note shows up in

~~~~~

* This green character is often attributed to the unique wet-hull process (called Giling Basah) that is common in Indonesia. It is different from the washed (wet) processing that you are likely more familiar with.

Green

Use this exercise to familiarize yourself with the green attribute, as both an aroma and a flavor.

What you'll need

- digital scale (0.1 gram precision)
- knife
- 1 bunch fresh flat-leaf parsley (rinsed)
- fresh water
- strainer
- medium snifter or wine glass
- 1-ounce cup or shot glass
- lids

Aroma: Chop 25 grams of parsley. Place in a small bowl with 300 grams of water, cover, and let sit for 15 minutes. Strain out the parsley and discard. Transfer 1 tablespoon of the remaining parsley water to the snifter, then cover to keep the aromatics in. When ready, lift the lid to smell. What does the aroma remind you of? Describe it as best you can and/or connect it to a memory.

Flavor: Transfer 2 teaspoons of the parsley water to the cup, then cover to keep the aromatics in. When ready, lift the lid to taste. What does the flavor remind you of? How does it compare to the aroma? Describe it as best you can and/or connect it to a memory.

Tips

- There are usually two types of parsley available at the store: flat-leaf (Italian) and curly. World Coffee Research does not specify which one to use, so I am assuming they mean flat-leaf, which has a stronger taste.

- To up your game, compare the green attribute to the herb-like attribute ("The aromatic commonly associated with green herbs that may be characterized as sweet, slightly pungent, and slightly bitter. May or may not include green or brown notes."); it's easy to do a blinded tasting (see page 142) with this one. You'll need some McCormick dried herbs: bay leaf (crushed with your fingers), ground thyme, and basil leaves. Combine 0.5 grams of each herb in a mortar and pestle (or spice grinder) and grind together until fine and combined. Combine the herb mixture with 100 grams of water in a bowl. Transfer 5 grams of the herb water to a snifter, then add 200 grams of water. This is your aroma reference. Combine another 5 grams of the herb water with another 200 grams of water, then serve some in a cup. This is your flavor reference. Smell and taste, then compare to the parsley water.

- It can be difficult to get the bay leaf to crush to a powder without an electric spice grinder. If this is the case for you, do the best you can, prepare as directed, and then strain the liquid to remove the larger chunks of bay leaf.

the background or in a pleasant supporting role among other attributes, that might be acceptable, depending on preference.

By the time coffee gets to us consumers, the most common cause of a green note in coffee is probably underdevelopment—that is, coffee that has been roasted in a way that falls short of unlocking its full potential. I included this attribute because light roasted coffee is becoming increasingly common and sometimes you run into an underdeveloped coffee (I did once while I was working on this book), which is considered a roast defect. A green attribute combined with an intensely sour attribute and/or astringent attribute is usually a sign of underdeveloped coffee.

To find coffee with a green note that isn't a roast defect, seek out Indonesian coffees, such as those from Sumatra and Sulawesi. Look for flavor notes that correspond to the lexicon attributes, as well as related ones, such as "herbaceous" and "dried basil."

DEFECT FLAVOR: THE POTATO DEFECT

Reference: Raw potatoes or the cut base of a head of romaine lettuce

Defect flavors are, in general, rare for consumers to experience because the coffee professionals all along the supply chain are trained to detect off-flavors. Defects disqualify coffee from being considered specialty coffee, so it's unlikely that your local specialty roaster is dealing with defective coffee.

However, there is one defect that does occasionally make its way to us consumers: the potato defect. It affects only coffee that is grown around the Great Lakes in Africa. The potato defect—so called because its sensory effect is reminiscent of raw potato—is caused by the antestia, a bug that lives in East Africa. As of this writing, there is still some debate about how the bug actually causes the defect, but there are two likely ways. One, the bug feeds on the plant, leaving it vulnerable to bacteria that produce the foul-smelling pyrazine that causes the defect. And two, the damage left by the bug may cause the coffee plant itself to produce the pyrazine in response to stress.[18]

The problem is that beans infected by the bacteria don't look different from uninfected beans. It really can't be detected until coffee is roasted, which is how it makes its way into the supply chain. Technically, any coffee from the Great Lakes region—which includes Ethiopia, Kenya, Burundi, Rwanda, the DRC, Tanzania, and Uganda—is at risk of the potato defect. In my experience, it's most common in coffees from Burundi and Rwanda.

Although processes have been put into place to reduce the instances of potato defect—and please don't let it put you off from trying coffees from the affected countries—it's still common enough that I recommend using your sniffer before brewing coffee. After grinding a dose of Burundi or Rwanda coffee, smell the grounds: the potato defect is so potent that you should be able to tell that something is off right away. It smells just like raw potato. I've found that another good reference is the stem end of a head of romaine lettuce. Next time you are slicing romaine stems from the head's base, take a good sniff of the cut part. Now you have the potato defect aroma locked into memory.

The defect affects individual beans, not whole bags. You may have only one bad bean in the entire bag. One bean will ruin your brew, but don't throw away the whole bag. Just smell as you go and dump any doses with the defect. If you don't catch it and you end up drinking the coffee, it won't make you sick. But I guarantee you'll be able to tell that something is off—it will not taste as good as other brews from the bag!

RAW + ROASTED + BURNT

Raw

Description: An aromatic associated with uncooked products.
Reference: Fisher whole natural almonds

Roasted

Description: Dark brown impression characteristic of products cooked to a high temperature by dry heat. Does not include bitter or burnt notes.
Reference: Raw blanched peanuts

Burnt

Description: The dark brown impression of an overcooked or overroasted product that can be sharp, bitter, and sour.
Reference: Raw blanched peanuts

Though this may seem obvious, research has corroborated that roasted (and burnt) attributes are associated with dark roasted coffee beans and medium to dark roasted ground and brewed coffee—and that the intensity of these attributes increases with the level of roast.[19] Roasting—specifically the Maillard reactions and other chemical reactions—creates the compounds that give us roasted attributes. And if the roasting continues, the compounds responsible for burnt attributes are produced. We tend to be sensitive to these compounds, and the more there are in the coffee, the more likely it is that they will supplant or overwhelm more delicate, subtle characteristics in the cup.

The compound 2-furfurylthiol has long been considered an important player in coffee aroma and flavor, as it contributes significantly to roasted attributes in coffee. In fact, one of the first in-depth studies of coffee aroma, in the 1920s, identified this compound as "exhal[ing] a pleasant note indicative of coffee."[20] This compound is what is used as the roasted coffee reference in Le Nez du Café. Modern research has shown that during the roasting process, 2-furfurylthiol increases as roasting continues for some coffee varieties, while for others it increases during the light to medium-dark stages and then slightly decreases at the dark roasted stage.[21] Phenols are associated with burnt notes.[22] Burnt attributes are generally considered undesirable—a roasting defect—in the coffee community.

Raw, roasted, and burnt attributes live on a spectrum, and I think it's interesting and informative to compare them to one another. The more familiar you are with the flavors, the easier it will be to identify the different intensities of roast characteristics in your brew. Even when coffee is roasted to emphasize bean characteristics, roast characteristics still play a role in the overall flavor of coffee—and you may even learn to detect when a characteristic is unintended, such as when a raw attribute crops up in underdeveloped coffee or a burnt attribute shows itself in an overdeveloped cup.

The more familiar you are with the raw, roasted, and burnt attributes, the easier it will be to identify the different intensities of roast characteristics in your brew.

Raw + Roasted + Burnt

Use this exercise to familiarize yourself with qualities associated with roast level by comparing five flavor attributes: raw, light roasted, medium roasted, dark roasted, and overroasted/burnt.

What you'll need

- rimmed baking sheet
- parchment paper
- raw blanched peanuts
- Fisher whole natural almonds
- five 1-ounce cups or shot glasses
- lids

Preheat the oven to 425°F. Line the baking sheet with the parchment paper, then spread the peanuts evenly across the sheet, making sure the nuts aren't touching each other (if they touch each other, they may steam instead of roast). Place the baking sheet in the oven and roast for the time indicated to achieve each reference.

Raw (Flavor): Put unroasted almonds in a cup, then cover to keep the aromatics in.

Light roasted (Flavor): Roast the peanuts for 7 minutes, then remove about one-quarter of the nuts from the pan. The nuts should show no change in color. Transfer them to a cup, then cover.

Medium roasted (Flavor): Return the pan to the oven and roast for 3 more minutes (10 minutes total), or until the nuts are medium brown. Remove about a third of the remaining nuts from the pan, transfer them to a cup, and cover.

Dark roasted (Flavor): Return the pan to the oven and roast for 5 more minutes (15 minutes total), or until the nuts are dark brown. Remove half of the remaining nuts from the pan, transfer them to a cup, and cover.

Overroasted/Burnt (Flavor): Return the pan to the oven and roast for 5 more minutes (20 minutes total), or until the nuts are burnt. Remove from the oven, transfer to a cup, and cover.

Taste the almonds and each type of peanut, covering between tastings to keep the aromatics in. How are they similar and different? What do the flavors remind you of? Describe each as best you can and/or connect it to a memory. This is a great opportunity to test yourself with a blinded tasting (see page 142).

Tips

- Note that the raw attribute ("an aromatic associated with uncooked products") is under the green/vegetative general category, but it's a good point of comparison to the roasted attributes.
- The lexicon's reference is almonds (not peanuts) for raw, but if you don't want to buy two types of nuts, you can probably get the idea of raw by eating the raw, unroasted peanuts.

ROAST CHARACTERISTICS AND COLOR

I've been using the common terms *light roasted*, *medium roasted*, and *dark roasted* in this book to refer to the level of coffee roasting because that is the language that lots of my research used, but I want to emphasize that these terms are an oversimplification. Roast level is a complex matrix of heat and time, and although coffee beans do tend to turn darker brown the hotter and/or longer they are roasted, physical color is not an ideal indicator of flavor characteristics. Two types of beans may be an identical "medium brown" color, but one could have intense roast characteristics and the other may not. Indeed, the scientists behind the lexicon are quick to point out that the roast attributes listed there are related to "the intensity of roast character." They write that "it is common for panelists to [detect] some flavor attributes that seem to relate to color, with a direct measure of intensity as they would with color, but this may not be correct. . . . There is not a linear relationship of light to dark roast. One cannot simply add more brown notes and get a darker roast flavor because the flavor actually changes to different types of notes."[23] Because color-related roast terms are overly simple, many craft roasters do not even list them on their bags of coffee.

The Problem with Flavor Notes

Flavor notes are the descriptions that roasters and coffee shops use to describe the sensory attributes of coffee. It's the main way they have to set the expectations of consumers so they know what kind of coffee they are getting. Unfortunately, the coffee industry has not yet done a great job in setting our expectations around the limitations of flavor notes.

Many people have had the experience of purchasing coffee with delicious-sounding flavor notes—hibiscus, pink lemonade, effervescent—only to taste none of them. They immediately think they've done something wrong—that they've brewed or tasted it incorrectly. This may not be the case, and there are a few reasons for it.

First, as we've discussed, flavor attributes tend to be pretty subtle and often require a measure of palate development—or at least the ability to taste consciously and thoughtfully. Hopefully, this book helps you overcome that challenge.

Second, those flavor notes may have been decided by the roaster on a specific day, in a specific place, with a specific kind of water, and a specific brew method, the cupping method (see page 137). The cupping method dictates a specific roast level and preparation method, neither of which may match how the coffee is ultimately roasted and prepared for consumers. Think back to the "What Influences Coffee Flavor?" section (page 79). Because coffee by nature is complex—and so many factors can affect its flavor—it's possible you (or a barista) might not be able to replicate the exact flavor notes when it's time to brew. If you spend any time brewing coffee at home, you likely already know that tweaks to your preparation method can change flavor outcomes. And that it's not uncommon for coffee's flavor to change slightly from the beginning to the end of the week, even without preparation changes. That doesn't mean the coffee is "bad" or brewed incorrectly. It might just taste a little different.

In my experience, however, coffee does not usually change *fundamentally*; a bright fruity coffee likely wouldn't turn into a dark chocolate one, but a distinct blackberry note at the cupping table might materialize as a general berry or fruity note many months later when the coffee is brewed in the shop. Or a delicate floral note could be lost entirely. Or one characteristic may become more pronounced than another. Remember, you can't create flavor in a bean if the potential is not already there to begin with—but you can destroy flavor and obscure it.

Last, always remember that there is no guarantee that the person who is writing flavor notes is a certified Q grader—a top sensory professional in coffee—and/or using the standardized vocabulary of the lexicon. They also may not have any marketing training, meaning they aren't well versed in communicating product information effectively to consumers. Honestly, sometimes it doesn't even seem like the flavor notes are intended for consumers but rather are there to impress or interest other coffee professionals.

Some roasters and coffee shops recognize these issues with flavor notes and are actively trying to more effectively communicate with their audience of consumers, often by simplifying flavor note language so that it resonates with common, likely shared, and replicable flavor experiences. But many others are guilty of the opposite: extremely specific descriptions and flowery, meaningless marketing language that obfuscate common, replicable experiences and create confusion.

So, what are you to do when you encounter such language? I recommend you interpret it broadly and try to break up overly specific attributes into parts using the language of the lexicon and flavor wheel, since they've done a lot of the hard work for us. Because the primary characteristics of coffee don't fundamentally change, most of the time you can set your own flavor expectations well enough. Of course, this means guesswork is still involved, but now you have the tools you need to make informed assumptions.

Let's take a look at the flavor notes I mentioned earlier—hibiscus, pink lemonade, effervescent—which happen to be on the bag of coffee I'm drinking as I type. Notice, first, that none of these attributes are part of the lexicon or flavor wheel. To the average coffee consumer, they are at once specific and nebulous. Here's how I interpret them:

Hibiscus: A flower, the specific flavor of which many people would not be able to describe off the top of their head. This is overly complicated marketing language that is trying to suggest an "exotic" quality, I guess. I would expect a general **floral** note.

Pink lemonade: Lemonade = sweet + fruit, perhaps a citrus fruit. A citrus fruit suggests a sour component. Now for "pink." Most pink lemonade is simply dyed and has no discernable difference from regular lemonade, so they probably chose "pink lemonade" because it sounds appetizing and nothing more. It's possible this is trying to imply another fruit quality, such as strawberry, but that doesn't affect my general assessment. I'll expect to find **sweet**, **fruity**, and **sour** notes in this coffee.

Effervescent: The coffee is not carbonated, so it cannot be literally effervescent. This is likely an attempt to sound appealing and fancy, but it's probably also attempting to describe acidity, since the word *effervescent* is often associated with crisp, fresh, bright beverages and those euphemisms are also used to describe acidity. So, this coffee likely has pronounced acidity, which means a **sour** characteristic, probably **citric acid**, based on the other flavor notes.

Overall: This coffee likely balances **tropical fruit–like acidity** with **sweet**, **fruity**, **floral notes**.

The problem with specific flavor notes is that not all people share that flavor experience, which makes the note exclusionary. It implies that consumers are not on the same level as the coffee roaster ("I know what hibiscus tastes like; too bad if you don't"), which smacks of pretention. And because these specific notes are not in the lexicon, there really isn't a way for consumers to "get on the roaster's level" because there are no descriptions or references available to calibrate the palate. Until the industry as a whole decides to use standardized language with consumers, we will have to do our best to interpret overly specific flavor notes.

In general, in my experience, flavor notes are best interpreted broadly. Very specific notes are almost always disappointing. Instead, try to break a note down into broad categories based on the specific note: roasted, spices (which I did not cover here), nutty, cocoa/chocolate, sweet, floral, fruity, sour/fermented, and green/vegetal. So, if you see the flavor note "s'more," don't expect to taste the campfire treat. Instead, expect to taste a broad sweetness, with chocolate and roasted qualities. If you see "green apple," expect a broad fruitiness with some level of acidity.

CHAPTER 5

Practical Tips for Tasting Coffee

I N THE PREVIOUS CHAPTER, YOU STARTED BUILDING your brain's reference library, stuffing it full of coffee-related sensory attributes and committing their names to memory. This, of course, is all in the hope that you will find these attributes in your daily brew and be able to articulate them in the moment. This is called sensory literacy. To develop sensory literacy, you must taste coffees—a lot of different coffees. Preferably, side by side, if you can. Tasting individual coffees in isolation is fine, but their subtle sensory differences become clearer—sometimes startlingly so—when you taste two or three at the same time.

Now, this poses challenges. As we've seen, preparation can greatly impact a coffee's sensory attributes, those attributes evolve over time, and small differences—such as temperature—affect the way we taste. To present coffees on a level playing field and reduce our biases as much as possible, we need a way to taste coffee that has been prepared the same way at the same time at the same temperature. We also need a method that isn't so onerous that we never want to do it.

Lucky for us, coffee professionals have already figured out a quick, easy, systematic way to taste multiple coffees at once—it's called cupping. In this chapter, you'll learn how to set up a cupping so that you can easily taste different coffees at the same time. You will also find tips on testing yourself with a specific kind of cupping exercise called triangulation, setting up a blinded tasting, and tasting mindfully.

How to Set Up a Cupping

Technically speaking, cupping is a tool that coffee professionals use for the specific purpose of evaluating green (unroasted) coffee. The SCA has developed a detailed protocol, which you can view online.[1] This protocol is quite involved and rigid because cupping is a sensory tool used to evaluate and describe the sensory attributes of coffee with limited bias, something that's a challenge when the human palate is your instrument of measure.

In order for the results of the cupping to be quick and accurate, everything from the coffee's roast and grind size to the brewing temperature and tasting method is streamlined and controlled. Cuppers use the SCA Cupping Form to assess specific categories: roast level, fragrance/aroma, flavor, acidity, body, balance, aftertaste, uniformity, sweetness, cleanliness, overall, and defects.[2] The SCA is very clear about the intended purpose of cupping in its handbook: "Though sometimes demonstration 'cuppings' are done for educational or promotional purposes, this is not cupping *per se*; cupping proper exists within the green coffee trade as an evaluation and quality assessment tool."[3]

So, we aren't going to worry about the complicated cupping form—much of it does not apply to us because we are drinking coffee that has already gone through the rigorous cupping assessment. The outcome of this assessment is a score on a 100-point scale. The specialty coffee we drink must score more than 80 points, so there is no reason for us to assess the quality of the coffee in the way that professional cuppers do.

That being said, we can still use the preparation method as an outline—it's really the simplest way to taste multiple coffees at once—and we are still going to call it "cupping," despite what the SCA says. Instead of evaluating coffee, we will use cupping as a way to explore a coffee's flavor and develop our sensory literacy. We can do this with two kinds of tastings: discriminative tasting (deciding whether there is difference between samples) and descriptive tasting (articulating the difference between samples). If you already know how to cup, you'll quickly realize that I'm paring things down. For example, a professional cupper would have five samples of each type of coffee on the table (to check for uniformity across the samples), which is unnecessary for tasters like us. I recommend you cup two to three different coffees at a time to explore their differences.

~~~

Cupping uses a very basic brewing process—you set out equal-size cups, pour equal amounts of different coffee grounds into each, and then fill the cups with hot water. The coffee steeps, much like tea, for a set amount of time, then you skim out the grounds using spoons. In this way, samples can be prepared almost simultaneously, and you don't need to worry about keepings things warm or about inconsistencies in the brewing method. You then taste the coffee using a spoon. The spoon—each taster has their own—allows multiple people to taste the coffee at once while keeping things sanitary. What follows is a pared-down version of the SCA cupping process. As you'll see, I generally recommend that you try to be as uniform as possible to achieve the most consistent samples.

WHAT YOU'LL NEED

- **Fresh filtered water.** It should not smell of chlorine or other odors. Do not use distilled or softened water.

- **A burr grinder.** This will ensure your grounds are as evenly chopped as possible. If you do not own one, have your coffee ground at a local coffee shop. You're looking for a size that is "slightly coarser than for drip."

- **A way to heat water and measure its temperature.** I use an electric kettle with a built-in thermometer. If you don't have this, use a food thermometer, or use the water immediately after taking it off boil.

- **Digital scale.** This should be accurate to 0.1 grams. I recommend you weigh everything (including the water) in grams because it's the simplest and fastest way to prepare the cupping.

- **Timer.** You can, of course, use your phone!

- **Spoons.** You'll need a spoon for skimming out grounds, plus a spoon for each taster for sipping coffee. There are special cupping spoons, but no need to invest in them. Use soup spoons if you have them, but any spoon will do in a pinch.

- **Small, shallow, wide-mouth cups.** Professionals use special cupping bowls, but you don't need to invest in those. Just use coffee cups or small bowls that hold between 7 and 9 fluid ounces (which is 207 to 266 grams). You need one cup for each coffee you are tasting. Make sure they are all the same size, shape, and color—you should not be able to tell them apart by looking.

- **Cups of any size.** One is for spent coffee grounds. The others (one per taster to keep things as sanitary as possible) will be filled with water for rinsing your spoons.

THE METHOD

1. **Figure out how much water your cups hold.** Figuring out the capacity of the cup means you won't have to worry about measuring water when you brew. Place one of your identical cups on the scale set to grams, zero it (hit the "tare" button), pour water to the very top, and write down that measurement. If the only glasses you have are too large, weigh out 207 to 266 grams and make a fill-line mark (with masking tape) on each cup so you know how much water to add later. That way you don't have to fumble with the scale during brewing.

2. **Figure out your dose.** You should use 8.25 grams of coffee per 150 grams of water. Remember, 1 milliliter of water is the same as 1 gram of water, so it's easy to weigh everything out. For example, if your cup will comfortably hold 220 milliliters of water, that's the equivalent of 220 grams, so you'd start with 12 grams of coffee. I recommend writing down your dose for future use. Now that you've completed the first two steps, you can skip directly to the third step next time.

3. **Prepare your setup.** Set out as many shallow wide-mouth cups as you have coffee samples. Arrange them in a row on a table or counter so that you can easily work from left to right, stepping to the side to taste the next one. Place your other cups behind the row. Fill all but one with water. Set out one spoon and give another spoon to each taster. Place the timer within easy reach. Once you're ready to brew, things go quickly, so this preparation step is key.

4. **Grind the beans and note the fragrance.** Weigh out your beans, adding a little extra since some grinders tend to "eat" beans. Remember, the grind size should be slightly coarser than you'd use for drip (around a medium coarseness). If using different beans, flush out the grinder between each type of bean—just throw a few of the next type in there, grind, and discard. This will reduce the risk of cross contamination. Weigh the coffee again after grinding (removing extra as needed to get the desired weight), and place each dose of grounds in a separate cup. While the water heats (step 5), smell each coffee and note its fragrance (see page 15).

5. **Heat your water to 195 to 205°F.** Keep in mind that once the coffee is ground, you don't want it sitting around for too long before you brew, as precious aromatics quickly dissipate. The SCA recommends no longer than 15 minutes.

6. **Pour water into each cup and note the aroma.** Set a timer for 4 minutes and, working from left to right and as quickly as you can, immediately pour the water into each cup, filling it to the brim or to the fill line you marked (the coffee grounds float, so the coffee grounds are what reach the fill line). As you wait for 4 minutes to elapse, note the aroma (see page 17) of each sample.

7. **Break and remove the grounds.** When the timer sounds, starting on the left with the first cup you poured, use your personal spoon to "break the crust" by stirring the coffee a few times. (If you are the one breaking, you can note the aroma again. Professionals say it's most potent after the break, but it's also not strictly necessary for us to do.) Then use the same spoon and the one on the table to skim off the grounds and transfer them to the empty cup. Try to skim just the grounds and foam but not the coffee. Skimming might be tricky at first, but you'll get better with practice. Start at the top of the cup with both spoons and curve them along the edge of the cup like parentheses, collecting grounds as you go. It's easier to learn by watching.[4] Rinse the spoons in the cup of clean water before moving on to the next sample to avoid cross contamination. At a professional cupping, a different person usually breaks and removes the grounds from each cup, so it's done all at once, but you can instead designate one person to do it.

8. **Taste the coffee.** Once the samples have reached the target temperature (see the tips on page 153), work from left to right and start with the first cup you poured. Using your personal spoon, take a small amount of coffee from the surface, then taste (see the Tasting Method section on page 151). Rinse your spoon in your cup of clean water, and move to the next sample to the right. Now there's an open spot at the table for the next taster to follow you. Repeat this process with the remaining samples until everyone has tasted all samples.

If you don't want to go through the process of cupping, you can of course order two different coffees (or share with a friend) at a coffee shop and compare them. They'll likely be ready around the same time. The following are some pairings you may find informative. You can also use these for triangulation (see page 148) ideas to test your palate. Depending on where you live and the coffee shops around you, you may be able to ask the barista for help finding these coffees on the menu. But remember, not all shops prioritize the same things and not all baristas receive sensory training.

- Natural coffee and washed coffee
- Fruity profile and cocoa/nutty profile
- High-acidity coffee and low-acidity coffee
- Traditional roast and modern roast (or dark roasted and light roasted)
- African coffee and South American coffee
- Blend and single origin
- Espresso and filter (drip) coffee, made from the same beans

I've found that the problem with doing side-by-side taste testings at home is simply the time it takes. It's hard to keep one coffee hot while brewing the second, but you can probably achieve it with high-quality insulated thermoses and some patience.

How to Set Up a Blinded Tasting

Several of the sensory reference exercises in this book suggest that you taste things blinded, or without knowing which sample you are tasting. Triangulation (see page 148) in particular must be done blinded, and professional cuppers always cup blinded. When you are starting out,

I think it's worthwhile to taste known coffees because you are trying to build up associations, so not every cupping you do must be blinded. But when it comes to taking it to the next level or testing your palate, blinding the cuppings becomes essential.

Tasting blinded is important because it's common to form biases from known information. There are three categories for bias and error when it comes to tasting: physiological (when something physically diminishes our abilities, such as a cold), neurological (when our brain causes us to perceive something "incorrectly"), and psychological (when our expectations color our experience). Blinded tastings are designed to reduce psychological bias and error, sometimes called expectation bias.

Professional tasters are not immune from psychological bias; in fact, they may be more susceptible to it because their knowledge base is so great. They may "associate certain sensory attributes to other factors such as origin, variety, processing method, roast level, etc."[5] Then, on a conscious or subconscious level, they either search for those attributes when tasting or "find" them there, confirming the expectation. For example, if a taster knows they are tasting a naturally processed coffee, they may expect it to taste fruity and score it higher in the fruity category. Indeed, the SCA recommends that each "cupper should know the minimum amount of information as is practical when cupping a coffee."[6]

So how do you accomplish this? In an ideal setup, you'd ask a friend to choose coffees for you and/or prepare the cupping, so you'd have no idea which coffees you were tasting and/or what order you were tasting them in. This is not always feasible, especially when you are trying my recommended pairings in this book—you will necessarily know, at least, what samples are on the table. The following are some options you can try to help eliminate bias during cupping when the group of samples on the table are known. In both methods, identical cups must be used, and in an even more ideal scenario, the cups would be opaque and/or black so that you cannot see the contents.

DON'T ALWAYS GO IN BLINDED

Though blinded tasting reduces bias, flavor explorers can often learn a lot with full knowledge of which coffees they taste while cupping. Comparing coffees can make their differences more apparent on a neurological level. I mentioned neurological biases earlier, and this is one example. Studies have shown that when professional tasters are cupping left to right, a defective coffee can make the next sample in the lineup seem higher quality than it may objectively be. Cuppers tend to score them higher than they would if there was no defective coffee in the mix.[7] The influence that a cup of coffee can have on the next one is called the carry-over effect.[8]

If you are a professional who is attempting to objectively evaluate coffee, you want to limit the carry-over effect as much as possible. But I argue that for home tasters, comparison tasting helps us solidify our understanding of different flavor profiles. The carry-over effect, I think, can help highlight differences between two disparate coffees and help you describe that difference. In isolation, a coffee with a fruity profile may seem only slightly different from a basic coffee flavor. But when you sip a fruity coffee and then sip a chocolate coffee, the difference can be remarkable. In science terms, this is called "release from suppression." If you taste something that is intense in a certain category, such as fruitiness, your palate adapts to that flavor and stops sensing it as acutely. I'm sure you've experiences this with smells—if you're baking cookies, after a while, you might stop being aware of the delicious smell. But if someone new walks into the room, they might remark on how delicious the cookies smell. Likewise with coffee: when you taste another sample, the quality you adapted to is muted in the new sample, and contrasting flavors will seem elevated.[9] It may not help as much with similar coffees, but there are workarounds.

When preparing a tasting of known coffees, be sure to order the coffees from the lightest roast/most delicate/most subtle to the darkest roast/least delicate/least subtle, then start tasting on the light/delicate side.

Otherwise, you may overwhelm your palate with bold flavors, and the subtle flavors will be harder to detect and appreciate. This is also recommended in wine pairings, where you taste from lightest white to boldest red.

One easy, fun tasting is to prepare coffees that run the gamut of roasting techniques. As a generalization, I mean "light roast" to "dark roast," but that terminology is often tricky. Many craft roasters don't use these terms at all, and big specialty brands might say "light roast" but it's more roasted than anything you'd get from your local craft roaster.

If you are having trouble sourcing coffees, your local roaster or barista may be able to help you select them. Just tell them what you're trying to do: taste different roasting styles. Here, I have provided at least one suggestion for each category. It's tricky to give specific recommendations because coffees I have access to might not be available everywhere. Also, coffee is a seasonal product. Single-origin coffees usually aren't available year-round, but they tend to have more varied flavor attributes than blends, which offer consistent product year-round.

- **The lightest roasted coffee you can find.** Try a Scandinavian roaster, if you can. They have a modern roasting tradition that tends to skew quite light. Two Scandinavian roasters I enjoy are Coffee Collective (Denmark) and Morgon (Sweden), but of course, there are many to choose from.
- **A light roasted coffee.** Try Ethiopia Mordecofe or Rwanda Huye Mountain, both of which are usually available for at least half a year from Stumptown Coffee Roasters.[10]
- **A medium roasted coffee.** Try Holler Mountain or Homestead from Stumptown.
- **Starbucks blonde roast, such as Veranda Blend.**
- **Starbucks medium roast, such as Pike Place.**
- **Starbucks dark roast, such as Caffè Verona.**

DOUBLE BLINDED TASTING

This method involves two people, and neither know which coffee is being tasted. The setup is a bit complicated, and at a cupping, the method would need to be accomplished during the 4-minute brew window. You would prepare the cupping as outlined on page 137, knowing which samples are on the table, but while the coffee brews, you randomize the samples in such a way that neither of you know the order. You need to be able to mark the cups *and* remove the marks during the 4-minute brew time. I recommend colored dry-erase markers and a phone with a camera to record what's happening.

STEP 1
Person A marks each cup with a different color.

STEP 2
Person A writes down which samples correspond to which colors, then shuffles the cups.

STEP 3
Person B marks each cup a second time, using new colors.

STEP 4
Person B takes a photo of the setup, removes the first set of marks, and then shuffles again.

Here are the steps—in this scenario, person A sets up the initial cupping with person B out of the room. At the beginning of the randomization, only person A knows the order. For the purposes of this example, let's say there are three different coffees and they start in this order: Ethiopia, Panama, and Brazil.

1. With person B out of the room, person A marks each coffee with a different color marker. In this case, person A marks Ethiopia **red**, Panama **blue**, and Brazil **green**. (If you're doing a triangulation [see page 148] and two of the cups are the same, you'd still mark each with a different color.)

2. Person A writes down which samples correspond to which colors, then shuffles the order of the cups. Let's say the new order is Panama (**blue**), Ethiopia (**red**), and Brazil (**green**). Person A exchanges places with person B but does not show person B the paper.

3. Person B is now alone in the room with the cups: they see the order—**blue**, **red**, **green**—but do not know which coffee is which. Person B adds a second mark to each sample, using different colors. In this case, person B marks **orange** (**blue**), **purple** (**red**), and **black** (**green**).

4. Person B takes a photo of the setup to record the color pairings, then they wipe off the first marks (**blue**, **red**, and **green**) and shuffle the cups. Person A returns but is not shown the photo.

Now neither person A nor person B knows which coffee is which. When the timer sounds, the tasters can break the grounds and proceed with the cupping as normal. At the end of the cupping, person A and person B can reveal the information contained on the paper and in the photo and discover in which order they tasted the coffees.

BLINDED TASTING BY YOURSELF

If you are tasting by yourself, you can still set up a blinded tasting. Make sure you are using identical cups—you should not be able to distinguish any of them by looking. Label the bottom of each cup with the coffee you intend to brew in it, then add the grounds. Before you start evaluating fragrance, close your eyes and randomize the order of the cups. Then you can complete the rest of the cupping process (see page 137). After you're done tasting, you can peek under each cup to reveal the coffee.

SHH! DON'T INFLUENCE OTHERS' OPINIONS!

If you are attempting to conduct a blinded tasting with a group of friends, resist talking about your thoughts while the tasting is going on. Commentary from the tasters in the room can influence others' opinions, which is called social bias. This is especially difficult to overcome when the person providing the commentary is considered the most skillful taster by others (authority bias). Humans tend to want to follow the leader and fit in with groups.[11] So go ahead and write your thoughts down, but keep them to yourself until the tasting is over. In fact, everyone at the tasting should try to keep their poker face on—facial expressions, gestures, and other nonverbal communication can also influence others' opinions.

How to Triangulate Coffee

Triangulation is a type of sensory test that reveals whether a person can distinguish between two different coffees. In a triangulation, you seek to identify the different coffee from three samples. The three samples are called a triad; two are the same coffee and one is different. The goal is simply to pick out the different cup, not necessarily what the difference is. Triangulation is common in the professional coffee world, and Q graders must pass triangulation tests to get their certification. The World Cup Tasters Championship also employs triangulation tests. Other coffee professionals, such as roasters and baristas, may triangulate coffee as part of their sensory training and maintenance. You can use the same method to test your differentiation skills. It's also fun!

Because triangulation is concerned with difference, it's super important that the two like samples are actually the same. The SCA recommends batch brewing instead of cupping for triangulation so that the two like samples actually come from the same brew and thus are identical.[12] However, best practices also state that all other factors be controlled—including keeping temperature the same—which I've already mentioned can be difficult to achieve when brewing at home. Again, one alternative might be to conduct your tasting at a coffee shop that can serve you two different coffees at once, or else taking those coffees home in insulated thermoses and checking temperature with a thermometer.

All that being said, you can still achieve good results with the cupping method (see page 137). Simply follow the same steps, making sure that two samples are the same and one is different. When conducting a triangulation, however, it is even more important that you are being as careful as possible to eliminate unintentional difference, especially when grinding beans and measuring doses. Because the color of the brew can signal difference, it's crucial to use an opaque (ideally, black) set of cups and to make sure the tasting is blinded (see page 142).

Triangulation is an excellent way to test differentiation skills, especially when multiple tests are done in a row. This is because it's statistically unlikely for a person to get the right answer by chance multiple times in a row. For example, the probability that a person passes five out of six triangulations by chance is only 1.8 percent (about 2 in 100).[13] That means that if you can pass five out of six triangulations in a row, you likely are good at differentiating between two coffees!

TRIANGULATION TEST IDEAS

Triangulation tests can be easy or hard. For example, differentiating between a light roasted and dark roasted coffee might be easy (because the difference is large), while telling the difference between two different Kenyan coffees might be hard (because the difference is subtle, depending on the coffees). Beyond generalizations, I don't have any way to measure how difficult my recommended triangulation tests are, but you can have fun figuring it out. If you are testing with a group, it's reasonable to assume that easy tests will result in more correct answers and hard tests will result in fewer correct answers.

You can triangulate any or all of my suggestions from the "A More Casual Affair" box on page 142. You can also use triangulation to test your skills with the basic tastes and other attributes. And here are some more ideas. Have fun creating your own!

- **Standard coffee versus strong coffee:** Using the same coffee beans, brew two samples with a standard brew ratio and a third with a strong brew ratio (that is, use more beans but keep the water the same). For example, if you are typically cupping with 220 grams of water and 12 grams of coffee, up the third cup to 15 grams. The bigger the difference in ratio, the easier the triangulation will be; the smaller the difference, the harder. You can also do this with standard coffee and weak coffee (meaning, use fewer beans but keep the water the same).

- **Standard coffee versus added acidity:** Using the same coffee beans, brew all three samples in the same manner. (This test is perfect for batch brewing because you are dealing with only one type of coffee. Simply brew a batch of coffee and pour equal amounts into your three cups.) Add 5 grams of 0.05% citric acid solution (page 33) to one sample. The more you add, the easier it will be. You can do this test with all five of your basic taste references. By increasing and decreasing the amount of the reference you add, you can determine your detection threshold!

Remember the neurological biases I mentioned earlier, in which the position of a cup in a tasting can highlight difference? This affects triangulation tests, too. If the different cup is in the middle position, it is easier for us to taste the difference. To counteract this, professionals make sure to randomize the cupping order and do multiple tests. If you are really trying to test yourself, it might also be a good idea to balance your tests like the professionals do. That is, if the first test had two of coffee A and one of coffee B, then the next test would have two of coffee B and one of coffee A.[14]

Tasting Method and Tips

We all know how to taste the food we eat, but in this section, we'll explore how we can try to work with our physiology to give us the best shot at discerning and identifying flavor in coffee. This section will help you taste more consciously, whether you're sipping your daily brew, setting up a tasting among friends, or testing yourself with a blinded triangulation. It also provides advice for using the flavor wheel to help you identify flavors.

If you really want to get into it, I recommend taking notes as you taste any new coffee or challenge yourself with exercises and tests. Writing things down helps many people commit information to memory and strengthen recall, and also provides a handy record to look back on to refresh your memory. For those readers who like a programmatic approach, I have included a coffee tasting resource in the back of the book (see page 172). It's something you can use to guide your tasting and is available for download at jessicaeasto.com/coffee-tasting-resource.

TASTING METHOD

Before you get started tasting, reacquaint yourself with the order of the experience, which we went over in chapter 1. Recall that the coffee experience starts with your nose—the orthonasal olfaction we use to smell the dried coffee grounds (fragrance) and the brewed coffee (aroma).

Once the coffee is in our mouth, we experience flavor (basic tastes + mouthfeel + retronasal olfaction). But it's not over. The flavor we experience as we drink is often noticeably different from the flavor that remains (aftertaste) in our mouths once we swallow the coffee. There are a few techniques you can use while drinking the coffee that may help you detect flavor notes.

- **Slurping.** This is a hallmark technique of professional coffee tasters, and some are quite exuberant about it. It's easy to make fun of, but there is a reason they do this. To slurp, you quickly suck a small amount of coffee (from either a cupping spoon or cup) into your mouth, spraying it across your entire palate. This not only gives your entire tongue an opportunity to join the tasting party but also helps vaporize and push aromatic compounds that need to travel to the back of your throat and up into your nose. I think some people are hesitant to do this because they have seen others slurp loudly, but the effectiveness of the slurp is not measured by how loud you do it. You can slurp quietly, too, if you want.

- **Exhaling after swallowing.** Exhaling after swallowing continues the work that slurping started. It forces air from the oral cavity up into the nose and out your nostrils, providing an extended opportunity for your nose to detect the aromatics that contribute to flavor via retronasal olfaction. Take a very deep breath in before slurping, slurp, swallow, and slowly exhale through your nose. You can extend that flavor detection quite a bit to allow time from your brain to do its magical calculus and recall. When concentrating on aftertaste, I also like to take a deep breath in, swallow (so there is no coffee in my mouth), and slowly exhale through my nose.

- **Moving tongue through coffee.** For judging mouthfeel, it often helps to take another sip and focus only on that. Sip some coffee, hold it in your mouth, and press your tongue through it. Move your tongue slowly up and down and side to side, focusing on the tactile sensations detected by your tongue and cheeks. If you are having trouble separating feeling from flavor, plug your nose to eliminate the aromatic component.

In general, when tasting coffee to develop your palate, it may be beneficial to limit yourself to one or two small sips. Ida Steen, a sensory scientist at CoffeeMind and the author of *Sensory Foundation*, encourages coffee drinkers to "take small sips of coffee and keep each sip in the mouth for only a couple of seconds."[15] This is because your palate will be most sensitive to the first and second sips. She also recommends that you wait fifteen to sixty seconds between sips.

OTHER TIPS

- **Let your coffee cool slightly.** High temperatures make you less sensitive to flavor detection in general, so it's a good idea to let your coffee cool slightly before tasting it. You also don't want to burn your mouth. Steen recommends letting your coffee cool to about 130°F before tasting.[16] The SCA Cupping Protocol states that tasting should begin once the sample is cooled to 160°F, which is eight to ten minutes after filling the cups with hot water in a cupping situation. This is the best time to do your slurp because the aromatics are at maximum flight strength at this temperature. After that, the SCA recommends evaluating other factors at lower temperatures, down to room temperature, which it defines as 100°F, and stopping the tasting once the coffee has reached 70°F.[17] We might not have to worry about all that, but I do recommend tasting the same coffee multiple times as it cools— it's an interesting exercise. We have already learned that coffee's flavor changes as it cools, mostly because different compounds are active (or not active) at different temperatures. This exercise illustrates the evolving flavor of coffee.

- **Don't distract your senses.** Avoid wearing perfumes or other strong scents, and avoid smoking before tasting. Scents can get in the way of detecting delicate notes in coffee, and smoking tends to cloud both your palate and your nose (in both the short and long term).[18]

- **Avoid sensory fatigue.** Sensory fatigue happens when the sensory receptors in your mouth and nose become physically or chemically saturated, making them less effective at detecting what they're supposed to detect. This can happen when you taste lots of coffee. To avoid this, limit the number of different coffees you taste in one session to three to five. You can also take breaks from tasting and smelling to give your taste buds and olfactory receptors a break. Don't take a break by eating or drinking other flavorful things, though. The next tip explains why.

- **Avoid the carry-over effect.** Earlier I explained why I think tasting disparate coffees one right after the other can be beneficial in highlighting difference. Other times, especially when coffees are more similar, it may muddle things. This is most apparent if your first tasting sample is the first coffee you've had in a while. Science has found that tasters often find the flavor and aroma of first cups to be more intense. To avoid this, use palate cleansers and take some time between tasting samples. Popular palate cleansers include plain water, sparkling water, and unsalted crackers. Cleanse your palate between each sample that you taste. You should also avoid eating while tasting, as strong tastes and flavors can lead to adaptation and release from suppression (see page 144).

Understanding Mixture Suppression

Earlier in the book, I told you that machines cannot perceive flavor as well as humans. Part of the reason is that machines can't replicate how humans experience flavor. A scientific concept called mixture suppression illustrates this point well—and I think it also partially explains why it's so difficult to reliably predict flavor outcomes in coffee. Mixture suppression means that we perceive individual components more intensely when we taste them alone than when they are mixed together. Something about mixing them tones down the intensity of each. Try this yourself with any combination of the basic taste references you created in chapter 2.

What you'll need

- two basic taste references, such as the 1.0% sucrose solution (page 37) and the 0.05% citric acid solution (page 33)
- three identical small cups

Pour some of the sucrose solution into the first cup, some of the citric acid solution into the second cup, and equal parts of the sucrose and citric acid solutions into the third cup. Taste the pure sucrose solution and note its intensity, then taste the mixture of sucrose and citric acid, noting its intensity. Do the same for the citric acid solution, followed by the mixture.

Although the mixture contains an equal concentration (intensity) of sucrose as the pure sample, the mixture will likely taste less sweet. The same goes for the citric acid solution.

FINDING YOUR WORDS

Taking a triangulation test to see if you can differentiate between samples is one thing, but tasting to *describe* coffee is another ball of wax. When our intention is to describe, we must use our words, and most of this book is an attempt to help you build your vocabulary so you have the words when you need them. But finding the words in the moment? That's that hardest part.

I have created a coffee tasting resource (page 172) that helps guide you through tasting a sample. You may find that this helps you as you begin learning how to taste to describe. I recommend using the tasting resource together with the Coffee Taster's Flavor Wheel (page 170) to help you pinpoint vocabulary. This section will provide some guidance on how to do this.

- **First thought, best thought.** Before you get too into the weeds— or if you simply want to simplify things—take note of the first thought or association you have when you first take a sip of coffee. Remember, flavor (aroma in particular) is deeply connected to memory. Latching onto those sparks in the beginning can help us intellectualize what's happening later. This is one of my favorite things about being *alive*. I love walking through a smell and being immediately whisked away to the past. You'll remember the story I shared earlier about the coffee that reminded me of the stables where I used to ride horses in middle school. Eventually I realized it's because the coffee had similar pleasantly sweet, earthy, grainy qualities of hay, which was stored in one of the barns. If you have an association, write it down without thinking about it too much at first. Keep tasting and come back to it later, if needed.

- **Don't discount color associations.** Sometimes when you are tasting, you may find that an attribute is familiar but you can't quite put your finger on the word. Sometimes you might think, "It tastes red" or "This reminds me of green." These are often helpful clues. Our brains associate flavor and color, which is why the flavor wheel is in color. If something tastes "red" to you, start looking through the reddish sections of the wheel for attributes. If something tastes "dark" or "brown," you might start in with the attributes created during literal browning processes during roasting (roasted, nutty/cocoa, etc.), which by no coincidence are brownish on the wheel. Your memory might be sparked by something you find there.

- **Start at the center of the wheel and work out.** Remember, the center of the wheel holds the broadest attribute categories, and these are what we focused on in this book. It's tempting to want to be as specific as possible, but I find you have a better shot at being accurate if you start in the center and methodically work your way out. Ask yourself broad questions to help narrow things down: "Is this coffee sour or bitter?" "Does this coffee read as sweet? If so, does it remind me of anything, such as a flower or a fruit?" "Is it more fruity or more nutty/cocoa?" These are just a few examples. If you land on, say, the broad category of fruity, you can start to get more specific by looking at the next row of attributes—you may try to determine if the fruity attribute is a fresh fruit attribute, a dried fruit attribute, or a citrus attribute.

- **Build off basic attributes.** As we saw in chapter 4, many of the attributes listed in the lexicon and flavor wheel can be parsed into even simpler notes. For example, fruity's description is "a *sweet*, *floral*, aromatic blend of a variety of fruits" (emphasis mine). And we also know that fruity attributes often go hand in hand with sour/acid attributes. If you pinpoint something like fruity, you may be able to investigate other areas of the wheel by taking your cues from the attribute itself. If you start at fruity, you may investigate sour/acid to see if you're picking up on citric acid or malic acid. That might give you a clue as to the type of fruit attribute you're dealing with. It works the opposite way, too. If you can pinpoint both sour/acidic and sweet, you might decide to take a look at the fruity section to see if anything sparks your memory.

- **Keep in mind that coffee can have overlapping profiles.** A coffee can have more than one major characteristic, so you may need to go through the wheel more than one time.

- **Don't forget mouthfeel!** The mouthfeel attributes in the lexicon are not present on the flavor wheel. That's why I have given it its own section on my tasting resource.

〰〰

Coffee is one of the most complex beverages ever created, and though we learn more about it every day, a comprehensive understanding of its flavor is likely to elude us for the foreseeable future. But we can come to understand coffee on a deeper, more intuitive level by tasting it widely, thoughtfully, and consciously. I hope this book has helped you develop your palate and your language around coffee flavor, deepening your appreciation of your daily brew and making it easier to communicate with fellow coffee lovers. One of the most exciting things about coffee is that its flavor can present in the cup in seemingly infinite ways, providing endless opportunities to challenge our sensory systems, to slow down and savor, and to admire the complexity of nature and our own abilities, which evolved to meet it.

ACKNOWLEDGMENTS

Fiirst and foremost, a big thank you to my intrepid volunteers who helped workshop the exercises found in this book: Max Schleicher, Karly Zobrist, Dan Paul, M. Brett Gaffney-Paul, Eric Pallant, Sue Pallant, Eric Schuman, Andrew Russell, Morgan Krehbiel, and Connie Sintuvant. Your feedback was invaluable, and I'm sure readers of this book will thank you, too!

Thanks also to my informal tasters—my family—who were always game when I said, "Hey, close your eyes and taste this" and "Put this unknown substance in your mouth" and "Tell me what this smell reminds you of." Thank you, Andreas, for always being my sounding board, Resident Coffee Expert, and lab rat no. 1. It's safe to say I wouldn't be this into coffee without you by my side—one of the many joys you've brought to my life!

Thank you to my writing group buddies, Brenna Lemieux, Janelle Blasdel, Anca Szilagyi, and Michael Kent. You all put up with reading and commenting on the majority of this manuscript—often in unpolished form—and your discriminating eyes and thoughtful feedback are much appreciated.

Thank you to every DePaul University librarian who helped me hunt down esoteric sensory science articles, the SCA for allowing me to participate in its Sensory Summit and reprint the Coffee Taster's Flavor Wheel, World Coffee Research for letting me reproduce information from the *Sensory Lexicon*, and First Crack for letting me take its sensory foundation and sensory intermediate courses as research for this book. I'm also grateful to *Psyche* magazine (psyche.co) for commissioning me to write an article about enjoying coffee, which helped me organize the thoughts that became this book, and to the Vanderbilt University Coffee Equity Lab for inviting me to speak on a panel about equitable access to information and education in the coffee industry. I represented home coffee enthusiasts, and my conversation with Brian Gaffney, Veronica Grimm (of Glitter Cat Barista), and Julio Guevara (of Perfect Daily Grind) encouraged me to continue on with this project and believe in the validity of my outsider perspective, which can be a hard thing to do sometimes.

Thank you to Doug Seibold, my publisher, and David Schlesinger, Karen Wise, and Amanda Gibson, who helped me polish this book up. Any remaining errors are, regrettably, my own. And another thank you to Morgan Krehbiel, who designed the cover and interior of this book and created the illustrations. Your talent knows no bounds.

Finally, thank you to anyone and everyone who has ever read, purchased, recommended, or reviewed *Craft Coffee: A Manual*. You are all the best!

FURTHER READING

THE FOLLOWING RESOURCES HELPED ME IMMENSELY in my research and/or offer a deep dive into the concepts I could only touch on here. If you are interested in learning more about sensory perception, these resources are a great start!

Chemesthesis: Chemical Touch in Food and Eating by Shane T. McDonald, David A. Bolliet, and John E. Hayes (editors). A comprehensive survey of the current research and understanding of chemesthesis, the "chemical touch" aspect of somatosensation. Although it was written for an academic audience, I found most of the chapters quite accessible.

Coffee Sensory and Cupping Handbook by Mario Roberto Fernández-Alduenda and Peter Giuliano. The Specialty Coffee Association's comprehensive guide to cupping and the sensory science of coffee. It was written for coffee professionals and scientists, but consumers will find it interesting as well.

Mouthfeel: How Texture Makes Taste by Ole G. Mouritsen and Klavs Styrbæk. A really cool analysis of how our sense of touch works in the mouth. It's both a highly enjoyable read and a practical synthesis of the latest science in this area.

Neurogastronomy: How the Brain Creates Flavor and Why It Matters by Gordon M. Shepherd. A fascinating exploration into how and why we perceive flavor, written by the researcher who developed a new field of study: neurogastronomy. Shepherd passed away in June 2022, while I was at work on this manuscript.

Tasting and Smelling: Handbook of Perception and Cognition, Second Edition, by Gary K. Beauchamp and Linda Bartoshuk. A very good overview, written for an academic audience, of how our gustatory and olfaction systems work. It was published in 1997, so some of the details might be outdated, but it's still a worthy starting point for people who want to understand these two modes of perception.

The Coffee Sensorium (@thecoffeesensorium), the Instagram of Fabiana Carvalho, a neuroscientist of flavor and multisensory experience who specializes in specialty coffee (and chocolate). She does a ton of cool research and helps coffee professionals communicate coffee's sensory qualities to consumers.

The Scent of Desire: Discovering Our Enigmatic Sense of Smell by Rachel Herz. An exploration of our often underappreciated olfaction system.

Water for Coffee by Maxwell Colonna-Dashwood and Christopher H. Hendon. The best place to go if you want to understand how water chemistry affects your brew. This book is heavy on science, but it's presented in way that can be digested by a general audience.

World Coffee Research *Sensory Lexicon.* The industry resource for coffee attributes and their references. The most recent edition is available for free on the World Coffee Research website.

GLOSSARY

acidity: the perceived sourness of a cup of coffee

aftertaste (coffee tasting): the perception of flavor that lingers in your mouth after you have swallowed a sip of coffee; the last evaluation stage of coffee tasting

aroma (coffee tasting): the second evaluation stage of coffee tasting, when you smell freshly brewed coffee before you take a sip; see also: *fragrance*, *olfaction*

astringency: a drying sensation on the tongue; see also: *chemesthesis*

basic tastes: sweet, sour, bitter, salty, and umami; caused by tastants detected by taste receptors

blend: a coffee made up of at least two different beans (variety, origin, etc.); created by roasters to offer a consistent product year-round

blinded tasting: a tasting in which you don't know which coffees you are tasting

body: a characterization of the tactile qualities of coffee, particularly thickness and texture; see also: *mouthfeel*

chemesthesis: the result of our somatosensation system responding to chemical stimuli as opposed to physical stimuli; the burning sensation caused by capsaicin in chiles is an example

coffee sensory science: a branch of study that seeks to understand how humans perceive coffee with our senses: taste, smell, touch (mouthfeel), sight, and hearing

Coffee Taster's Flavor Wheel: a visual tool developed by the Specialty Coffee Association and World Coffee Research to help tasters identify flavor attributes in coffee

cupping: a method of brewing and tasting coffee for the express purpose of evaluating green coffee with limited bias

descriptive tasting: tasting with the goal of articulating the differences between coffee samples

discriminative tasting: tasting with the goal of deciding only whether there is a difference between coffee samples

dose: the amount of coffee grounds you use to brew a cup of coffee

dry processing: a coffee processing technique that involves letting the cherry dry on the coffee bean before it is removed; also called natural processing

extraction: the act of combining water and roasted coffee grounds together in order to transfer flavor compounds from the coffee (a solid) into the water (a liquid); may also refer to *percent extraction*, the measure of how much coffee material from the dose made it into the cup during brewing

flavor: in general, the combination of sensory inputs (particularly taste, smell, and mouthfeel) that allows us to identify what we are eating and drinking; in specific reference to coffee tasting, the third evaluation stage in which you sip the coffee

flavor notes: the words used to describe the flavor of coffee

fragrance: the first evaluation stage of coffee tasting in which you smell freshly ground beans; see also: *aroma, olfaction*

green coffee: unroasted coffee

gustation: our sense of taste

hedonic value: a description of how pleasant or unpleasant a sensory perception is

insoluble: incapable of being dissolved in liquid, particularly water

intensity: a description of the magnitude of a sensory perception

Le Nez du Café: a sensory tool that contains thirty-six aromas found in coffee; used by coffee professionals to train their noses

Maillard reactions: a group of chemical reactions between amino acids and reducing sugars; responsible for the browning stage of cooking and its flavors

mouthfeel: the general term for the somatosensory inputs that are gathered in the oral cavity, particularly temperature, astringency, thickness, and texture when it comes to coffee; see also: *body*

odor: the general term used to describe the sensory result of olfaction

odorants: the chemical compounds that interact with odor receptors

olfaction: our sense of smell; see also: *orthonasal olfaction, retronasal olfaction*

orthonasal olfaction: the sensory perception of odor that happens when you breathe in odorants through your nostrils into your nasal passage

overextraction: what happens when coffee grounds spend too much time with water, resulting in an unpleasantly bitter, astringent brew

palate: your sensory receptor to brain connection

physiology: how your body parts function

retronasal olfaction: the sensory perception of odor that happens when you exhale through your nose and odorants travel from your oral cavity up into your nasal passage

sensory attributes: the words we use to describe flavor and aroma characteristics when tasting coffee; see also: *sensory reference*

sensory literacy: the ability to identify and articulate flavor

sensory modality: another way to say "sense"; used interchangeably with senses

sensory reference: something specific you can smell or taste that represents a sensory attribute

single-origin coffee: coffee that comes from only one location; highlights the unique characteristics of the time and place in which the coffee was grown

soluble: capable of being dissolved in liquid, particularly water

somatosensation: our sense of touch

Specialty Coffee Association (SCA): the professional organization that represents and serves the specialty coffee industry worldwide

strength: a characteristic of body; a measure of how many total dissolved coffee solids (TDS) are in a cup of coffee

supertaster: a person who is genetically predisposed to experience taste with greater intensity than an average person

tastants: the chemical compounds that interact with taste receptors

threshold: a person's sensitivity to sensory stimuli; those with low thresholds can detect and identify tastes and smells at low concentrations while those with high thresholds require higher concentrations

triangulation: a type of discriminative tasting in which the taster attempts to identify the different sample from a group of three

underextraction: what happens when coffee grounds spend too little time with water, resulting in an unpleasantly sour brew

volatile compounds: compounds that are prone to vaporize, or change from a liquid or solid phase into a gas phase; odorants are volatile compounds that have odor

wet processing: a coffee processing technique that involves removing the cherry from the coffee bean before it is dried; also called washed processing

World Coffee Research *Sensory Lexicon*: a document produced by World Coffee Research that includes 110 sensory attributes that have been identified in coffee and their corresponding sensory references

THE COFFEE TASTER'S FLAVOR WHEEL

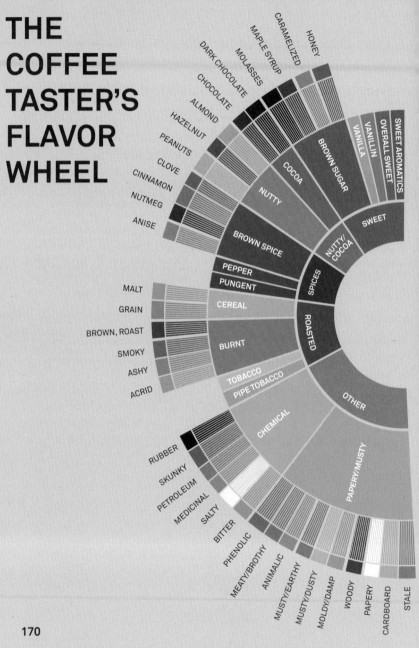

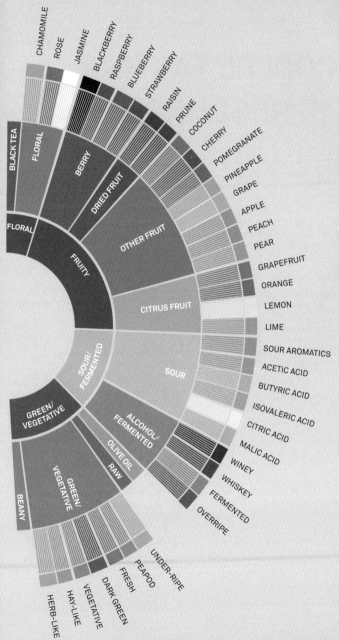

CHAMOMILE
ROSE
JASMINE
BLACKBERRY
RASPBERRY
BLUEBERRY
STRAWBERRY
RAISIN
PRUNE
COCONUT
CHERRY
POMEGRANATE
PINEAPPLE
GRAPE
APPLE
PEACH
PEAR
GRAPEFRUIT
ORANGE
LEMON
LIME
SOUR AROMATICS
ACETIC ACID
BUTYRIC ACID
ISOVALERIC ACID
CITRIC ACID
MALIC ACID
WINEY
WHISKEY
FERMENTED
OVERRIPE
UNDER-RIPE
PEAPOD
FRESH
VEGETATIVE
DARK GREEN
HAY-LIKE
HERB-LIKE

BLACK TEA
FLORAL
BERRY
DRIED FRUIT
FLORAL
OTHER FRUIT
FRUITY
CITRUS FRUIT
SOUR/FERMENTED
SOUR
GREEN/VEGETATIVE
ALCOHOL/FERMENTED
OLIVE OIL
RAW
GREEN/VEGETATIVE
BEANY

The Coffee Taster's Flavor Wheel by the SCA and WCR (©2016–2020) **171**

COFFEE TASTING RESOURCE

Coffee

Roaster: _____
Example: Onyx Coffee Lab

Elevation: _____
Example: 1,859 meters

Origin / Blend: _____
Example: Guatemala

Variety: _____
Example: Gesha

Producer: _____
Example: El Socorro

Roast Date: _____
Example: December 28, 2023

Location / Date: _____
Example: Home, Dayglow Coffee, etc.

Brew Method: _____
Example: Drip, French press, etc.

Initial Tasting Notes

Use this section to organize your thoughts after smelling and tasting coffee. Don't necessarily worry about the proper terms here. First memories, associations, etc. are all good starting points.

Fragrance	Aroma

Flavor	Aftertaste

Evaluate the following qualities of the coffee by adding a mark to each scale.

Basic Tastes

Sweet

Bitter

Sour

Umami

Mouthfeel

Weight

Thin ← → Thick

Astringency

Low ← → High

Temperature

Cold ← → Hot

Texture
☐ Smooth   ☐ Creamy
☐ Rough   ☐ Round
☐ Oily   ☐ Clean
☐ Mouthcoating/Lingering

Roast Characteristics

← →

| Underdeveloped/ Green/Raw | Bean Characteristics | Roasted Characteristics | Overdeveloped/ Burnt |

Flavor and Aroma Attributes

☐ Fruity   ☐ Fresh   ☐ Dried   Notes: _____
☐ Citric Acid   ☐ Malic Acid   ☐ Acetic Acid _____
☐ Floral   ☐ Nutty   ☐ Cocoa   _____
☐ Potato Defect   ☐ Fermented   _____

Final Tasting Notes

Hedonic Value / Do you like it? (1 to 10) _____

NOTES

INTRODUCTION

1   Mario Roberto Fernández-Alduenda and Peter Giuliano, *Coffee Sensory and Cupping Handbook* (Irvine, CA: Specialty Coffee Association, 2021), 8.

2   Fernández-Alduenda and Giuliano, *Cupping Handbook*, 9.

3   Fernández-Alduenda and Giuliano, *Cupping Handbook*, 20.

CHAPTER 1

1   Mario Roberto Fernández-Alduenda and Peter Giuliano, *Coffee Sensory and Cupping Handbook* (Irvine, CA: Specialty Coffee Association, 2021), 6.

2   Fernández-Alduenda and Giuliano, *Cupping Handbook*, 7.

3   Fernández-Alduenda and Giuliano, *Cupping Handbook*, 43.

4   Harry T. Lawless and Hildegarde Heymann, *Sensory Evaluation of Food* (New York: Springer, 2010).

5   Fernández-Alduenda and Giuliano, *Cupping Handbook*, 37.

6   Fernández-Alduenda and Giuliano, *Cupping Handbook*, 41.

7   K. Talavera, Y. Ninomiya, C. Winkel, T. Voets, and B. Nilius, "Influence of Temperature on Taste Perception," *Cellular and Molecular Life Sciences* 64, no. 4 (December 2006): 377–381, doi.org/10.1007/s00018-006-6384-0.

8   Fernández-Alduenda and Giuliano, *Cupping Handbook*, 37.

9   Fernández-Alduenda and Giuliano, *Cupping Handbook*, 37.

CHAPTER 2

1   Beverly J. Cowart, "Taste, Our Body's Gustatory Gatekeeper," Dana Foundation, April 1, 2005, dana.org/article/taste-our-bodys-gustatory-gatekeeper.

2   Bijal P. Trivedi, "Gustatory System"; Kumiko Ninomiya, "Science of Umami Taste: Adaptation to Gastronomic Culture," *Flavour* 4, no. 13 (January 2015), doi.org/10.1186/2044-7248-4-13.

3   Mario Roberto Fernández-Alduenda and Peter Giuliano, *Coffee Sensory and Cupping Handbook* (Irvine, CA: Specialty Coffee Association, 2021), 47–48; Yvonne Westermaier, "Taste Perception: Molecular Recognition of Food Molecules," *Chemical Education* 75, no. 6 (2021): 552–553, doi.org/10.2533/chimia.2021.552.

4   Gary K. Beauchamp and Linda Bartoshuk, *Tasting and Smelling* (San Diego: Academic Press, 1997), 30.

5   Cowart, "Taste."

6   Cowart, "Taste."

7   Appalaraju Jaggupilli, Ryan Howard, Jasbir D. Upadhyaya, Rajinder P. Bhullar, and Prashen Chelikani, "Bitter Taste Receptors: Novel Insights into the Biochemistry and Pharmacology," *International Journal of Biochemistry & Cell Biology* 77, part B (August 2016): 184–196, doi.org/10.1016/j.biocel.2016.03.005.

8   Laurianne Paravisini, Ashley Soldavini, Julie Peterson, Christopher T. Simons, and Devin G. Peterson, "Impact of Bitter Tastant Sub-Qualities on Retronasal Coffee Aroma Perception," *PLOS One* 14, no. 10 (2019), doi.org/10.1371/journal.pone.0223280.

9   Alina Shrourou, "Scientists Identify Receptor Responsible for Bitter Taste of Epsom Salt," News-Medical, April 8, 2019, www.news-medical.net/news/20190408/Scientists -identify-receptor-responsible-for-bitter-taste-ofc2a0Epsom-salt.aspx.

10   Sara Marquart, "Bitterness in Coffee: Always a Bitter Cup?" Virtual Sensory Summit, Specialty Coffee Association, 2020.

11   Marquart, "Bitterness in Coffee."

12   Marquart, "Bitterness in Coffee."

13   Paravisini et al., "Impact of Bitter Tastant Sub-Qualities."

14   Fernández-Alduenda and Giuliano, *Cupping Handbook*, 49.

15   Mackenzie E. Batali, Andrew R. Cotter, Scott C. Frost, William D. Ristenpart, and Jean-Xavier Guinard, "Titratable Acidity, Perceived Sourness, and Liking of Acidity in Drip Brewed Coffee," *ACS Food Science & Technology* 1, no. 4 (March 2021): 559–569, doi.org/10.1021/acsfoodscitech.0c00078.

16   Melania Melis and Iole Tomassini Barbarossa, "Taste Perception of Sweet, Sour, Salty, Bitter, and Umami and Changes Due to l-Arginine Supplementation, as a Function of Genetic Ability to Taste 6-n-Propylthiouracil," *Nutrients* 9, no. 6 (June 2017): 541, doi.org/10.3390/nu9060541.

17   Fernández-Alduenda and Giuliano, *Cupping Handbook*, 49.

18   Fernández-Alduenda and Giuliano, *Cupping Handbook*, 49.

19   Edith Ramos Da Conceicao Neta, Suzanne D. Johanningsmeier, and Roger F. McFeeters, "The Chemistry and Physiology of Sour Taste: A Review," *Journal of Food Science* 72, no. 2 (March 2007): R33–R38, doi.org/10.1111/j.1750-3841.2007.00282.x.

20   Roberto A. Buffo and Claudio Cardelli-Freire, "Coffee Flavour: An Overview," *Flavour and Fragrance Journal* 19, no. 2 (March 2004): 100, doi.org/10.1002/ffj.1325.

21   Batali et al., "Titratable Acidity."

22   "Acids and Bases," Biology Corner, accessed August 25, 2020, www.biologycorner.com /worksheets/acids_bases_coloring.html.

23   Batali et al., "Titratable Acidity."

24   Batali et al., "Titratable Acidity."

25   Fernández-Alduenda and Giuliano, *Cupping Handbook*, 49.

26   Melis and Barbarossa, "Taste Perception."

27   Cowart, "Taste."

28   Allen A. Lee and Chung Owyang, "Sugars, Sweet Taste Receptors, and Brain Responses," *Nutrients* 9, no. 7 (July 2017): 653, doi.org/10.3390/nu9070653.

29   Lee and Owyang, "Sugars."

30   Julie A. Mennella, Danielle R. Reed, Phoebe S. Mathew, Kristi M. Roberts, and Corrine J. Mansfield, "'A Spoonful of Sugar Helps the Medicine Go Down': Bitter Masking by Sucrose among Children and Adults," *Chemical Senses* 40, no. 1 (January 2015): 17–25, doi.org/10.1093/chemse/bju053.

31   Specialty Coffee Association, "Less Strong, More Sweet," *25 Magazine*, November 28, 2019, https://sca.coffee/sca-news/25-magazine/issue-11/less-strong-more-sweet.

32   Specialty Coffee Association, "Less Strong."

33   Fernández-Alduenda and Giuliano, *Cupping Handbook*, 50.

34   "How Is It That Coffee Still Tastes Sweet, Even Though in Scientific Literature We're Told All—Or Almost All—the Sugars Have Been Caramelised," Barista Hustle, November 16, 2018, www.baristahustle.com/knowledgebase/how-is-it-that-coffee -still-tastes-sweet.

35   Specialty Coffee Association, "The Coffee Science Foundation Announces New 'Sweetness in Coffee' Research with the Ohio State University," SCA.coffee, December 20, 2022, sca.coffee/sca-news/the-coffee-science-foundation-announces -new-sweetness-in-coffee-research.

36   Melis and Barbarossa, "Taste Perception."

37   "Taste and Flavor Roles of Sodium in Foods: A Unique Challenge to Reducing Sodium Intake," in *Strategies to Reduce Sodium Intake in the United States*, eds. Jane E. Henney, Christine L. Taylor, and Caitlin S. Boon (Washington, DC: The National Academies Press, 2010).

38   Jeremy M. Berg, John L. Tymoczko, and Lubert Stryer, "Taste Is a Combination of Senses that Function by Different Mechanisms," in *Biochemistry,* 5th ed. (New York: W. H. Freeman, 2020).

39   "Why Your Coffee Tastes Salty + How to Fix It," Angry Espresso, accessed August 25, 2022, www.angryespresso.com/post/why-your-coffee-tastes-salty-how-to-fix-it.

40   Melis and Barbarossa, "Taste Perception."

41   Nirupa Chaudhari, Elizabeth Pereira, and Stephen D. Roper, "Taste Receptors for Umami: The Case for Multiple Receptors," *American Journal of Clinical Nutrition* 90, no. 3 (September 2009): 738S–742S, doi.org/10.3945/ajcn.2009.27462H.

42   Chaudhari, Pereira, and Roper, "Taste Receptors for Umami."

43   "Umami: The 5th Taste Loved by a World Barista Champion: In 3 Videos," Perfect Daily Grind, July 1, 2016, perfectdailygrind.com/2016/07/umami-the-5th-taste -loved-by-a-world-barista-champion-in-3-videos.

44   Nicholas Archer, "Blame It on Mum and Dad: How Genes Influence What We Eat," The Conversation, September 28, 2015, theconversation.com/blame-it-on-mum -and-dad-how-genes-influence-what-we-eat-45244.

45 Archer, "Blame It."

46 Students of PSY 3031, "Supertasters," in *Introduction to Sensation & Perception*, University of Minnesota, pressbooks.umn.edu/sensationandperception.

47 L. C. Kaminski, S. A. Henderson, and A. Drewnowski, "Young Women's Food Preferences and Taste Responsiveness to 6-n-propylthiouracil (PROP)," *Physiology and Behavior* 68, no. 5 (March 2000): 691–697, doi.org/10.1016/S0031-9384(99)00240-1; Diane Catanzaro, Emily C. Chesbro, and Andrew J. Velkey, "Relationship Between Food Preferences and Prop Taster Status of College Students," *Appetite* 68 (September 2013): 124–131, doi.org/10.1016/j.appet.2013.04.025; Agnes Ly and Adam Drewnowski, "PROP (6-n-Propylthiouracil) Tasting and Sensory Responses to Caffeine, Sucrose, Neohesperidin Dihydrochalcone and Chocolate," *Chemical Senses* 26, no. 1 (January 2001): 41–47, doi.org/10.1093/chemse/26.1.41.

48 This exercise was adapted from taste expert Beth Kimmerle. You can see her demonstrate the exercise in *Wired*'s "Taste Support" video at youtu.be/MtMkU-1p7-0.

49 Catamo Eulalia, Navarini Luciano, Gasparini Paolo, and Robino Antonietta, "Are Taste Variations Associated with the Liking of Sweetened and Unsweetened Coffee?" *Physiology and Behavior* 244 (February 2022), doi.org/10.1016/j.physbeh.2021.113655.

50 Jie Li, Nadia A. Streletskaya, and Miguel I. Gómez, "Does Taste Sensitivity Matter? The Effect of Coffee Sensory Tasting Information and Taste Sensitivity on Consumer Preferences," *Food Quality and Preference* 71 (January 2019): 447–451, doi.org/10.1016/j.foodqual.2018.08.006; "Global Variation in Sensitivity to Bitter-Tasting Substances (PTC or PROP)," National Institute on Deafness and Other Communication Disorders, last updated June 7, 2010, https://www.nidcd.nih.gov/health/statistics/global-variation-sensitivity-bitter-tasting-substances-ptc-or-prop.

51 Nicola Temple and Laurel Ives, "Why Does the World Taste So Different?" *National Geographic*, last updated July 14, 2021, www.nationalgeographic.co.uk/travel/2018/07/why-does-the-world-taste-so-different.

52 Dunyaporn Trachootham, Shizuko Satoh-Kuriwada, Aroonwan Lam-ubol, Chadamas Promkam, Nattida Chotechuang, Takashi Sasano, and Noriaki Shoji, "Differences in Taste Perception and Spicy Preference: A Thai–Japanese Cross-Cultural Study," *Chemical Senses* 43, no. 1 (January 2018): 65–74, doi.org/10.1093/chemse/bjx071.

53 See, for example, Pierre Bourdieu, *The Logic of Practice,* trans. Richard Nice (Stanford, CA: Stanford University Press, 1990).

54 Karolin Höhl and Mechthild Busch-Stockfisch, "The Influence of Sensory Training on Taste Sensitivity," *Ernahrungs Umschau* 62, no. 12 (2015): 208–215, doi.org/10.4455/eu.2015.035.

55 "Taste and Flavor Roles."

56 "Can You Train Yourself to Like Foods You Hate?" BBC Food, accessed August 29, 2022, www.bbc.co.uk/food/articles/taste_flavour.

CHAPTER 3

1   Christopher R. Loss and Ali Bouzari, "On Food and Chemesthesis: Food Science and Culinary Perspectives," in *Chemesthesis: Chemical Touch in Food and Eating,* eds. Shane T. McDonald, David A. Bolliet, and John E. Hayes (Hoboken, NJ: Wiley-Blackwell, 2016), 250.

2   Ole G. Mouritsen and Klavs Styrbæk, *Mouthfeel: How Texture Makes Taste* (New York: Columbia University Press, 2017), 4.

3   C. Bushdid, M. O. Magnasco, L. B. Vosshall, and A. Keller, "Humans Can Discriminate More Than One Trillion Olfactory Stimuli," *Science* 343, no. 6177 (2014): 1370–1372, doi.org/10.1126/science.1249168.

4   Andrea Büttner, ed., *Springer Handbook of Odor* (New York: Springer, 2017).

5   Mouritsen and Styrbæk, *Mouthfeel,* 4; Peter Tyson, "Dogs' Dazzling Sense of Smell," PBS, October 3, 2012, www.pbs.org/wgbh/nova/article/dogs-sense-of-smell.

6   Gordon M. Shepherd, *Neurogastronomy: How the Brain Creates Flavor* (New York: Columbia University Press, 2012), specifically chapters 6, 7, and 8. I highly recommend this book for an overview of the full science, which I don't dare try to summarize here.

7   Büttner, *Handbook of Odor.*

8   Charles Spence, "Just How Much of What We Taste Derives from the Sense of Smell?" *Flavour* 4, no. 30 (2015), doi.org/10.1186/s13411-015-0040-2.

9   Meredith L. Blankenship, Maria Grigorova, Donald B. Katz, and Joost X. Maier, "Retronasal Odor Perception Requires Taste Cortex but Orthonasal Does Not," *Current Biology* 29, no. 1 (2019): 62–69, doi.org/10.1016/j.cub.2018.11.011.

10 Mario Roberto Fernández-Alduenda and Peter Giuliano, *Coffee Sensory and Cupping Handbook*, (Irvine, CA: Specialty Coffee Association, 2021), 43.

11 Fernández-Alduenda and Giuliano, *Cupping Handbook*, 43.

12 Fernández-Alduenda and Giuliano, *Cupping Handbook*, 43.

13 Fernández-Alduenda and Giuliano, *Cupping Handbook*, 43. *Uncommon* potent odorants are often associated with off-flavors and defects.

14 Fernández-Alduenda and Giuliano, *Cupping Handbook*, 43–45.

15 Mouritsen and Styrbæk, *Mouthfeel*, 22.

16 Jie Liu, Peng Wan, Caifeng Xie, and De-Wei Chen, "Key Aroma-Active Compounds in Brown Sugar and Their Influence on Sweetness," *Food Chemistry* 345 (2021), doi.org/10.1016/j.foodchem.2020.128826.

17 Mouritsen and Styrbæk, *Mouthfeel*, 5

18 Shepherd, *Neurogastronomy*, 131.

19 Fernández-Alduenda and Giuliano, *Cupping Handbook*, 52.

20 Christopher T. Simons, Amanda H. Klein, Earl Carstens, "Chemogenic Subqualities of Mouthfeel," *Chemical Senses* 44, no. 5 (2019): 281–288, doi.org/10.1093/chemse/bjz016.

21 Steven Pringle, "Types of Chemesthesis II: Cooling," in *Chemesthesis: Chemical Touch in Food and Eating* (Hoboken, NJ: Wiley-Blackwell, 2016); Mouritsen and Styrbæk, *Mouthfeel*, 5.

22 Christopher T. Simons and Earl Carstens, "Oral Chemesthesis and Taste," in *The Senses: A Comprehensive Reference,* 2nd ed. (Cambridge, MA: Elsevier, 2020), doi.org/10.1016/B978-0-12-809324-5.24138-2.

23 Mouritsen and Styrbæk, *Mouthfeel*, 8–9; try the chip experiment with a friend!

24 For an in-depth look at this concept, check out *Chemesthesis: Chemical Touch in Food and Eating,* eds. Shane T. McDonald, David A. Bolliet, and John E. Hayes (Hoboken, NJ: Wiley-Blackwell, 2016).

25 Simons, Klein, and Carstens, "Chemogenic Subqualities."

26 Simons, Klein, and Carstens, "Chemogenic Subqualities."

27 E. Carstens, "Overview of Chemesthesis with a Look to the Future," in *Chemesthesis: Chemical Touch in Food and Eating* (Hoboken, NJ: Wiley-Blackwell, 2016).

28 Fernández-Alduenda and Giuliano, *Cupping Handbook*, 49.

29 Carlos Guerreiro, Elsa Brandão, Mónica de Jesus, Leonor Gonçalves, Rosa Pérez-Gregório, Nuno Mateus, Victor de Freitas, and Susana Soares, "New Insights into the Oral Interactions of Different Families of Phenolic Compounds: Deepening the Astringency Mouthfeels," *Food Chemistry* 375 (2022), doi.org/10.1016/j.foodchem.2021.131642.

30 Yue Jiang, Naihua N. Gong, and Hiroaki Matsunami, "Astringency: A More Stringent Definition," *Chemical Senses* 39, no. 6 (2014): 467–469, doi.org/10.1093/chemse/bju021.

31 Mouritsen and Styrbæk, *Mouthfeel*, 21.

32 See sca.coffee/research/protocols-best-practices.

33 "What Is Astringency?" Coffee ad Astra, accessed August 29, 2022, coffeeadastra.com/2019/11/12/what-is-astringency.

34 Fernández-Alduenda and Giuliano, *Cupping Handbook*, 54.

35 "What Is Astringency?"

36 Fernández-Alduenda and Giuliano, *Cupping Handbook*, 53.

37 Alina Surmacka Szczesniak, "Texture Is a Sensory Property," *Food Quality and Preference* 13, no. 4 (2002): 215–225, doi.org/10.1016/S0950-3293(01)00039-8; I have synthesized information from multiple tables from the study into one table, and focused them on the terms I've heard coffee people use.

38 The World Coffee Research *Sensory Lexicon* does include a few entries for mouthfeel, but like I said, it's not exhaustive.

39 Roberto A. Buffo and Claudio Cardelli-Freire, "Coffee Flavour: An Overview," *Flavour and Fragrance Journal* 19, no. 2 (March 2004): 100, doi.org/10.1002/ffj.1325; Fernández-Alduenda and Giuliano, *Cupping Handbook*, 53.

40 Andréa Tarzia, Maria Brígida Dos Santos Scholz, and Carmen Lúcia De Oliveira Petkowicz, "Influence of the Postharvest Processing Method on Polysaccharides and Coffee Beverages," *International Journal of Food Science and Technology* 45, no. 10 (2010): 2167–2175, doi.org/10.1111/j.1365-2621.2010.02388.x; Josef Mott, "Understanding Body in Coffee and How to Roast for It," Perfect Daily Grind, June 17, 2020, perfectdailygrind.com/2020/06/understanding-body-in-coffee-and-how-to-roast-for-it.

41 Mott, "Understanding Body."

42 Shepherd, *Neurogastronomy*, 5.

43 Shepherd, *Neurogastronomy*, 113–114.

44 Shepherd, *Neurogastronomy*, 123; sensory fusion also comes into play with visual stimuli, such as color. We talk about how coffee can taste "red" or "brown" on page 101. These associations are why the flavor wheel is color-coded the way that it is.

45 Mouritsen and Styrbæk, *Mouthfeel*, 20.

46 Shepherd, *Neurogastronomy*, 122; as of this writing, Dr. Fabiana Carvalho is currently researching cross-modal influence as it relates specifically to coffee.

47 Shepherd, *Neurogastronomy*, 155.

48 Shepherd, *Neurogastronomy*, 159; as a reminder, sight and sound also play a role in flavor—they are just not the focus of this book.

49 Shepherd, *Neurogastronomy*, 157.

50 Shepherd, *Neurogastronomy*, 124.

51 Colleen Walsh, "What the Nose Knows," *Harvard Gazette*, February 27, 2020, news.harvard.edu/gazette/story/2020/02/how-scent-emotion-and-memory-are -intertwined-and-exploited.

52 Yasemin Saplakoglu, "Why Do Smells Trigger Strong Memories?" Live Science, December 8, 2019, www.livescience.com/why-smells-trigger-memories.html; if you are interested in learning more about smell and emotion, check out *The Scent of Desire* by Rachel Herz.

53 In case you didn't know: Hay is grown specifically to be fed to animals, and straw is a by-product of harvests, such as grain harvests, that is bundled up and used primarily for animal bedding (and fall holiday decorations). They both smell similar: dry, musty, earthy.

54 Wenny B. Sunarharum, David J. Williams, and Heather E. Smyth, "Complexity of Coffee Flavor: A Compositional and Sensory Perspective," *Food Research International* 62 (2014): 315–325, doi.org/10.1016/j.foodres.2014.02.030.

55 If you are interested in reviewing lists of chemicals and aroma descriptors, check out chapter 33 of *Coffee: Production, Quality and Chemistry*. It summarizes the results of some research that sought to identify aromatic volatile compounds in green and roasted coffee. See: doi.org/10.1039/9781782622437.

56 Marino Petracco, "Our Everyday Cup of Coffee: The Chemistry Behind Its Magic," *Journal of Chemical Education* 82, no. 8 (2005), doi.org/10.1021/ed082p1161.

57 Chahan Yeretzian, Sebastian Opitz, Samo Smrke, and Marco Wellinger, "Coffee Volatile and Aroma Compounds: From the Green Bean to the Cup," in *Coffee: Production, Quality and Chemistry* (London: The Royal Society of Chemistry, 2019); this source informed the basic facts of this section.

58 Sunarharum, Williams, and Smyth, "Complexity of Coffee Flavor."

59 Gilberto V. de Melo Pereira, Dão P. de Carvalho Neto, Antonio I. Magalhães Júnior, Zulma S. Vásquez, Adriane B. P. Medeiros, Luciana P. S. Vandenberghe, Carlos R. Soccol, "Exploring the Impacts of Postharvest Processing on the Aroma Formation of Coffee Beans: A Review," *Food Chemistry* 272 (2019): 441–452, doi.org/10.1016 /j.foodchem.2018.08.061.

60 Pereira et al., "Exploring the Impacts."

61 Thompson Owen, "What Is Dry Processed Coffee?" Sweet Maria's, March 19, 2020, library.sweetmarias.com/what-is-dry-processed-coffee.

62 Angie Katherine Molina Ospina, "Processing 101: What Is Washed Coffee and Why Is It So Popular?" Perfect Daily Grind, December 18, 2018, perfectdailygrind.com /2018/12/processing-101-what-is-washed-coffee-why-is-it-so-popular. The term *clean* is also used by coffee cuppers. In that context, it means "free of defects." Once the coffee gets to us, we hope it's already free of defects!

63 Pereira et al., "Exploring the Impacts."

64 Petracco, "Our Everyday Cup."

65 Petracco, "Our Everyday Cup"; Pereira et al., "Exploring the Impacts."

66 Buffo and Cardelli-Freire, "Coffee Flavour."

67 Petracco, "Our Everyday Cup."

68 Petracco, "Our Everyday Cup."

69 Sunarharum, Williams, and Smyth, "Complexity of Coffee Flavor."

70 This is done through three processes: dissolution, hydrolysis, and diffusion. These are summarized well in "Coffee Brewing: Wetting, Hydrolysis & Extraction Revisited," published by the Specialty Coffee Association. See www.scaa.org/PDF /CoffeeBrewing-WettingHydrolysisExtractionRevisited.pdf.

71 "Coffee Brewing: Wetting, Hydrolysis & Extraction Revisited."

72 Nancy Cordoba, Mario Fernández-Alduenda, Fabian L. Moreno, and Yolanda Ruiz, "Coffee Extraction: A Review of Parameters and Their Influence on the Physico-chemical Characteristics and Flavour of Coffee Brews," *Trends in Food Science and Technology*, 96 (2020): 45–60, doi.org/10.1016/j.tifs.2019.12.004.

73 "Coffee Brewing: Wetting, Hydrolysis & Extraction Revisited," 3–4.

74 "Coffee Brewing: Wetting, Hydrolysis & Extraction Revisited," 5.

75 Sunarharum, Williams, and Smyth, "Complexity of Coffee Flavor"; M. Petracco, "Technology IV: Beverage Preparation: Brewing Trends for the New Millennium," in *Coffee: Recent Developments* (Malden, MA: Blackwell Science, 2008).

76 Sunarharum, Williams, and Smyth, "Complexity of Coffee Flavor"; Petracco, "Technology IV."

77 Sunarharum, Williams, and Smyth, "Complexity of Coffee Flavor"; Petracco, "Technology IV."

78 Karolina Sanchez and Edgar Chambers IV, "How Does Product Preparation Affect Sensory Properties? An Example with Coffee," *Journal of Sensory Studies* 30, no. 6 (2015): 499–511, doi.org/10.1111/joss.12184.

79 Yeretzian, Opitz, Smrke, and Wellinger, "Coffee Volatile and Aroma Compounds."

CHAPTER 4

1 You can download the full lexicon for free at worldcoffeeresearch.org/resources /sensory-lexicon. For more information about how the lexicon was developed, see Edgar Chambers IV, Karolina Sanchez, Uyen X. T. Phan, Rhonda Miller, Gail V. Civille, and Brizio Di Donfrancesco, "Development of a 'Living' Lexicon for Descriptive Sensory Analysis of Brewed Coffee," *Journal of Sensory Studies* 31, no. 6 (2016): 465–480, doi.org/10.1111/joss.12237.

2 The lexicon is considered a "living document." As such, it will be updated as new attributes are identified and codified, and references may be updated or added as needed. Since its publication in 2016, it has been updated once already, in 2017. The lexicon acknowledges that its references sometimes aren't widely available outside of the United States. To combat this, the new edition includes globally available references made in partnership with a flavor company called FlavorActiV. These may be more accessible to professionals; it's not practical for consumers like us to purchase these kits. I've taken this into consideration when selecting attributes for this book.

3 Mario Roberto Fernández-Alduenda and Peter Giuliano, *Coffee Sensory and Cupping Handbook* (Irvine, CA: Specialty Coffee Association, 2021), 65.

4 Fernández-Alduenda and Giuliano, *Cupping Handbook*, 65.

5 See worldcoffeeresearch.org/resources/sensory-lexicon.

6 Wenny B. Sunarharum, Sudarminto S. Yuwono, and Hasna Nadhiroh, "Effect of Different Post-Harvest Processing on the Sensory Profile of Java Arabica Coffee," *Advances in Food Science, Sustainable Agriculture and Agroindustrial Engineering* 1, no. 1 (2018), doi.org/10.21776/ub.afssaae.2018.001.01.2.

7 Fabiana Carvalho (@thecoffeesensorium), "Artificial fruit-like aromas in coffee, part 1/3," Instagram photo, January 6, 2023, www.instagram.com/p/CnEz5q-OxUd; Fabiana Carvalho (@thecoffeesensorium), "Artificial fruit-like aromas in coffee, part 2/3," Instagram photo, January 10, 2023, www.instagram.com/p/CnPPBdkOQU7.

8 "The Chemistry of Organic Acids: Part 2," Coffee Chemistry, May 6, 2015, www.coffeechemistry.com/the-chemistry-of-organic-acids-part-2.

9 "The Chemistry of Organic Acids in Coffee: Part 3," Coffee Chemistry, last modified August 17, 2017, www.coffeechemistry.com/the-chemistry-of-organic-acids-part-3.

10 "Acetic Acid," Coffee Chemistry, last modified November 10, 2019, www.coffeechemistry.com/acetic-acid; "The Chemistry of Organic Acids in Coffee: Part 3."

11 Togo M. Traore, Norbert L. W. Wilson, and Deacue Fields III, "What Explains Specialty Coffee Quality Scores and Prices: A Case Study from the Cup of Excellence Program," *Journal of Agricultural and Applied Economics* 50, no. 3 (2018): 349–368, doi.org/10.1017/aae.2018.5.

12 Natnicha Bhumiratana, Koushik Adhikari, and Edgar Chambers IV, "Evolution of Sensory Aroma Attributes from Coffee Beans to Brewed Coffee," *Food Science and Technology* 44, no. 10 (2011): 2185–2192, doi.org/10.1016/j.lwt.2011.07.001.

13 Chambers et al., "Development of a 'Living' Lexicon."

14 Bhumiratana, Adhikari, and Chambers, "Evolution of Sensory Aroma Attributes."

15 The lexicon calls for ¼ cup, but you'll get the idea if you use just 1 teaspoon. That will make the amount for both the chocolate chips and the Lindt chocolate equal and easier to blind taste.

16 Bhumiratana, Adhikari, and Chambers, "Evolution of Sensory Aroma Attributes."

17 See page 20 of the booklet that comes with Le Nez du Café.

18 Tasmin Grant, "What Is Potato Taste Defect & How Can Coffee Producers Stop It?" Perfect Daily Grind, July 28, 2021, perfectdailygrind.com/2021/07/what-is-potato -taste-defect-how-can-coffee-producers-stop-it.

19 Bhumiratana, Adhikari, and Chambers, "Evolution of Sensory Aroma Attributes."

20 W. Grosch, "Flavour of Coffee: A Review," *Molecular Nutrition* 42, no. 6 (1998), 344– 350, doi.org/10.1002/(SICI)1521-3803(199812)42:06<344::AID-FOOD344>3.0.CO;2-V.

21 Su-Yeon Kim, Jung-A Ko, Bo-Sik Kang, and Hyun-Jin Park, "Prediction of Key Aroma Development in Coffees Roasted to Different Degrees by Colorimetric Sensor Array," *Food Chemistry* 240 (2018): 808–816, doi.org/10.1016/j.foodchem.2017.07.139.

22 Fernández-Alduenda and Giuliano, *Cupping Handbook*, 43.

23 Chambers et al., "Development of a 'Living' Lexicon."

CHAPTER 5

1 See sca.coffee/research/protocols-best-practices.

2 You can download the official cupping form at sca.coffee/research/protocols-best -practices. However, during this writing, the SCA announced it has been reevalu- ating its cupping protocol and form, since it has been twenty years since they were revisited. The original form was designed to distinguish "specialty grade coffee" from "commercial coffee." The SCA wants the new form to "[respect] diverse consumer preferences while simultaneously strengthening producers' understanding of how to communicate and increase the value of the coffees they produce." It is currently conducting research to determine how both resources should evolve. Read more at sca.coffee/sca-news/25/issue-18/valuing-coffee-evolving-the-scas-cupping-protocol -into-a-coffee-value-assessment-system.

3 Mario Roberto Fernández-Alduenda and Peter Giuliano, *Coffee Sensory and Cupping Handbook* (Irvine, CA: Specialty Coffee Association, 2021), 99.

4 The Coffee Lovers TV YouTube channel has a nice demonstration: youtube.com/watch?v=Dw7TrYPOjHY.

5 Fernández-Alduenda and Giuliano, *Cupping Handbook*, 30.

6 Fernández-Alduenda and Giuliano, *Cupping Handbook*, 111.

7 Fernández-Alduenda and Giuliano, *Cupping Handbook*, 4.

8 Ida Steen, *Sensory Foundation* (Denmark: CoffeeMind Press, 2018), 15.

9 Steen, *Sensory Foundation*, 14.

10 Stumptown does not characterize roast on its bags, and I've been told it describes almost all of its coffees as "medium-ish." But, still, I think these options fit this cat- egory. I chose Stumptown coffees for this exercise because of their nationwide availabil- ity in many coffee shops and supermarkets, but you can also order coffee online.

11 Fernández-Alduenda and Giuliano, *Cupping Handbook*, 31.

12 Fernández-Alduenda and Giuliano, *Cupping Handbook*, 74.

13 Fernández-Alduenda and Giuliano, *Cupping Handbook*, 75.

14 Fernández-Alduenda and Giuliano, *Cupping Handbook*, 31.

15 Steen, *Sensory Foundation*, 11.

16 Steen, *Sensory Foundation*, 29.

17 See sca.coffee/research/protocols-best-practices.

18 Fabrice Chéruel, Marta Jarlier, and Hélène Sancho Garnier, "Effect of Cigarette Smoke on Gustatory Sensitivity, Evaluation of the Deficit and of the Recovery Time-Course after Smoking Cessation," *Tobacco Induced Diseases* 15 (2017), doi.org/10.1186/s12971-017-0120-4.

INDEX

Page numbers followed by n indicate notes.

ABOUT THE AUTHOR

Jessica Easto is a writer and editor based in Northwest Indiana. She received a degree in journalism from the University of Tennessee and an MFA in fiction writing from Southern Illinois University. Her first book, *Craft Coffee: A Manual*, was published in 2017 and was named a top food and drink book of the year by *The Food Network*, *Wired*, *Sprudge*, and *Booklist*. When she's not writing about coffee, she edits books and teaches copyediting and proofreading at DePaul University in Chicago. Learn more at jessicaeasto.com and follow her on Instagram @j.easto.